SECRETS
OF THE SAVVY
CONSUMER

SECRETS OF THE SAVVY CONSUMER

COREY SANDLER

PRENTICE HALL

Library of Congress Cataloging-in-Publication Data

Sandler, Corey, 1950–
    Secrets of the savvy consumer / Corey Sandler.
        p.   cm.
    Includes index.
    ISBN 0-13-673526-6 (cloth). — ISBN 0-7352-0031-9 (paper)
    1. Consumer education.   I. Title.
TX335.S193   1998
640'.73—dc21

97-51692
CIP

Acquisitions Editor: *Tom Power*
Production Editor: *Sharon L. Gonzalez*
Formatting/Interior Design: *Robyn Beckerman*

Printed in the United States of America

10 9 8 7 6 5 4

ISBN 0-13-673526-6

PRENTICE HALL
Paramus, NJ 07652

On the World Wide Web at http://www.phdirect.com

To Janice, my savvy partner.
We get so much more out of life together.

Acknowledgments

This book bears a single name on the cover, but could never have reached your hands without the good work of many others. At Prentice Hall, thanks to Tom Power, the dealmaker and editor who both brought this book from concept to ink on paper, and to Eugene Brissie, the matchmaker and old friend. Dan Bial worried the details of the deal with his usual dedication. Thanks, too, to Sharon L. Gonzalez, Marlys Lehmann, and Robyn Beckerman.

Contents

Introduction

There are two types of consumers: those who buy and those who are sold. This book is for the first group, the relatively small group of consumers who keep the power on their side of the table when they negotiate a purchase. That's right—when they *negotiate* a purchase.

One of the keys to being a savvy consumer is to recognize that when you buy a car, a house, a vacuum cleaner, an airline ticket, a visit to the doctor, or most anything else, you are taking part in a deal.

How does he manage that?

A savvy consumer earns the same salary as the guy next door, and their children go to school together. Yet the savvy buyer has a better house, with better appliances, and better maintenance. And he takes more vacations, too.

What does she know that he doesn't?

A savvy shopper and her family are flying down to Acapulco on a new jumbo jet. Their round-trip tickets cost $309 a seat. The businessman across the aisle will suffer through the same mystery meal, watch the same crummy movie, and arrive in sunny Mexico the same millisecond they do—and pay $804 for his ticket.

They wonder how he does it.

A savvy guy in the next block has a lower monthly payment than the others in his office carpool, but he's got a much nicer car.

How did she figure that out?

A savvy friend's health insurance coverage takes care of all her family's needs, but her annual outlay is several thousand dollars lower than her best friend's up the road.

My goal in this book is to show you how to move the power to your side of the table when you are negotiating a purchase. Actually, in most cases it's not as hard as it might seem; after all, you're the one with the money.

In this book I uncover some rewarding strategies for experienced negotiators, and I share the tricks of the trade to new students of the art.

Who Should Read This Book?

Some people happily pay thousands more than they should for a car, buy televisions and VCRs at list price, write checks each month with hundreds of dollars of wasted credit-card and mortgage interest, pay twice as much as the guy in the next seat for an airplane ticket, and throw away a good portion of their income on unnecessary or improper insurance.

These are the same people who don't worry at all about squandering their income with wasteful computer purchases, driving up costs with poorly chosen automobile and travel-insurance policies, and lavishly supporting their neighborhood electric utility.

These people are *not* savvy enough to be reading these words.

The readers of this book are the people who *hate to waste money.* They want to know the secrets of the savvy shoppers and the inside story from the people who sell them insurance, cars, houses, telephone service, vacation and business travel, and even daily expenditures on food, entertainment, household items, and office equipment.

This is *not* a book for cheapskates or penny-pinchers. You won't find those silly tips that advise you to root through other peoples' garbage (Dumpster Diving) for cast-off food and clothing, that offer 100 recipes for cooking weeds, or that tell you how to save money by burying your own dead family members. (These are all actual brilliant ideas from some sensationally useless tip books.)

Instead, this book offers suggestions on how to maximize your lifestyle. Whether your income is $20,000 or $200,000, you can still find ways to get the most bang for your bucks in almost everything you do.

This is an eclectic collection of tips. Just as we're going to stay away from silly suggestions like Dumpster Diving, we're also going to avoid the obvious. You already know that you should try to pay as little as possible for the most you can get. These are the tips from the insiders.

Here are some of the subjects we explore:

- How to put your car-buying business out to competitive bid.
- How to get the best deal and the best coverage on home and auto insurance.
- How to travel first class on an economy budget.
- How to hire a real-estate agent and how to negotiate the commission you pay.
- How to select the best mortgage and keep it up to date with changing rates and conditions.
- How to outfit your house with the latest and greatest appliances that use less electricity and do the job better.
- How to maximize your chances of getting the most financial aid for your children when they head off to college.
- How to do your bank a favor by giving it your business . . . on your terms.
- How to hire a long-distance telephone company and how to keep it on its toes.

About the Author

I've made my career out of explaining the complexities of business, travel, and computers in more than 100 books. Beginning as a Gannett Newspapers and Associated Press newsman and columnist, I also served as the first executive editor of *PC Magazine*, one of the magazine industry's greatest success stories.

I've appeared on NBC's *Today Show*, CNN, ABC, National Public Radio's *Fresh Air*, dozens of local radio and television shows, and been the subject of dozens of newspaper and magazine articles. I write the best-selling *Econoguide* travel-book series, with titles covering Florida; California; Nevada; Washington, DC; London; golf resorts; and ski resorts.

More to the point—I purchased my most recent car after a short but furious round of bidding, by fax, from several dealers anxious for my business. I squeeze every dime out of promotional offers from long-distance telephone companies and credit-card issuers. And I made a profit of $3,200 on my last set of airline tickets to Europe.

You can write to me (please enclose a stamped, self-addressed envelope for a response) at:

Corey Sandler
Word Association, Inc.
P.O. Box 2779
Nantucket, MA 02584

Or send me an E-mail at:

Sandler@pobox.com

Or consult my Web page:

http://www.pobox.com/~econoguide

Ten Questions for the Savvy Consumer

One of the most important skills you need to develop as a savvy consumer is the ability to speak for yourself.

In shopping, as in most other parts of life, sometimes you get slapped and sometimes you get what you ask for. If you follow the rules of society and business, it doesn't hurt to ask for a better deal. After you've read this book, you'll be a savvy consumer who is prepared to ask questions such as these:

1. *Will you give a discount for cash?* We're not talking about cheating the tax man here. Instead, we're appealing to the merchant who doesn't have to pay 3 to 6 percent to a credit-card company to process your charge. Or to the professional who doesn't have to spend time and money filing paperwork with an insurance company or governmental agency.

Ask your doctor for a discount for immediate cash (or check) payment instead of putting a bill through for an insurance claim.

With your credit card in hand, ask a merchant for a few percentage points off a major purchase if you instead pay in cash or by check.

2. *Will you give me a break on published rates?* Almost everything is negotiable in our free-enterprise society. Remember that except for the motor-vehicle bureau and other fine operations of your government, businesses need your patronage.

Ask your bank to give you a checking account without a service fee, or a change in minimum-balance requirements. Remember that there is always another bank in town, and that whichever institution now has your account doesn't want to lose your deposit and the money it has invested in setting up and managing that account. You can make yourself even more appealing to your bank by offering to have your paycheck directly deposited to your account, or by accepting a credit card issued by the bank (assuming that the rates and charges are reasonable), or by telling the bank officer that you are in the market for a mortgage loan and will consider applying at the bank.

Ask a restaurant for a discount for a large group. Offer to pay in cash or check to remove the fee charged by the credit-card company.

Ask your credit-card company to reduce its interest rate on unpaid balances. Tell them you're about to accept an offer from another card company that offers a lower rate. You may find they'd rather keep you at a lower rate than lose your business.

Ask your long-distance telephone carrier to cut you a special deal that is best suited to your operations. If you want a break on calls you regularly make to Germany on Tuesdays at 3:20 P.M., ask for it. And don't hesitate to ask them to match or beat a competitor's offer. The carriers know full well that you can easily change your affiliation; they need you more than you need them.

3. *You've told me your standard rates. Now I want you to do better.* If a banker tells you the "standard" rate for a business or consumer, tell him or her you'd like a better deal. Almost everything in finance, including interest rates, is negotiable. But it's only negotiable if you ask for a better rate.

4. *I'd like more, please.* Ask a college admissions officer for a bit more in scholarship money or guaranteed loans. They usually have some additional funds for contingencies, but you have to ask. The earlier in the admissions schedule, the better your chances.

5. *What is a fair markup for this product?* A well-informed buyer has some idea of the cost that the dealer pays for an item; with this knowledge you can change the direction of any discussion of price in a negotiation. Instead of asking, "What kind of a discount can I receive off the list price?" you can ask the seller, "What is a fair markup from your cost?"

This sort of negotiating strategy is well suited to expensive purchases such as cars, boats, and furniture.

6. *You lowered the price a week after I made my purchase. Please pay me the difference.* Many stores have price guarantees, which spell out policies to protect you from bad timing. Even if the store doesn't spell this out, you can create your own short-term guarantee: Go back

to the store within its returns period and ask for a rebate because of a change in price. If they balk, tell them you are prepared to return the item. You can always repurchase it at the lower price.

7. *What exactly do you mean by this term?* Do you really know what "low fat" or "reduced sodium" on a package of food means? How about the difference between a "full warranty" and a "limited warranty"?
These are distinctions that can make a real difference in the value of an item or service you purchase.

8. *How do I get the best price-performance ratio?* For most products, the pace of innovation works like this: the latest and greatest product is faster/lighter/more durable or otherwise improved and it costs a bit more or a lot more than the previous hot product.
It may be that the newest version is worth the extra money, but it is also usually true that you'll get the most for your money by buying a product that is one step *behind* the latest and greatest. This is especially true for high-tech devices including personal computers, video cameras, and audio equipment.
After you listen to the sales pitch for the newest product, ask about prices on any leftovers and compare them closely to the latest and greatest.

9. *Is there a better way to purchase this product?* Ask yourself and anyone you know who buys the same items if you should be making a deal with a different seller. Consider warehouse stores, builders' supply houses, catalog stores, and Internet vendors.

10. *Is there a better time to buy this product?* Don't expect a great deal on a barbecue grill on July 3, or on skis the morning after the first major snowfall of the season. Ask sellers about closeout sales, returns from leases or rentals, and preseason specials.

SECTION I

Becoming a Savvy Buyer

Basic Training for the Savvy Consumer

Buy. Don't be sold.

That will be our motto as we explore the everyday deals and the not-so-common negotiations of our lives.

Too many people squander their natural advantage when they spend their hard-earned money. They pay too much, buy unnecessary products, or allow themselves to be sold services they don't need.

Now, please don't misunderstand: I'm not accusing every salesperson, agent, or seller of services of attempting to rob you blind. In fact, most people are pretty close to honest in their dealings. It's just that in our economy, sellers will always try to get as much money for their goods and services as possible.

But that doesn't mean you have to pay the full price. It's time to learn how to use your power to negotiate more for your money.

You've got the power . . . because you've got the money.

In most every purchase you make, you have options:

- You can ask for a better deal.
- You can buy something else.
- You can buy from someone else.
- You can choose not to buy at all.

In this chapter, we'll delve into some basic strategies for the savvy consumer.

We'll start with a discussion of how to shop for the right store. Then we'll consider how to find the right salesperson. We'll move on to insider information about the best time of the year to buy particular products and a few quick lessons on markups and markdowns.

You'll learn some valuable information about when it's to your best advantage to use a credit card, or when you might be better off paying cash.

We'll explore the value of a good warranty and then talk about buying strategies where you can cut your costs by accepting items that are already less than perfect.

And then we'll explore a pair of buying situations where you can become directly involved in the economic laws of supply and demand: buyer's cooperatives and auctions.

✓ Shop for the right store.

✓ Shop for the right salesperson.

✓ Find out if the sales force is commissioned or salaried.

✓ Know when to buy: a counterseasonal calendar.

✓ Understand a retailer's markup strategy before you sit down to negotiate a markdown.

✓ Don't let them get away with a markdown after you've left the store.

✓ Know when to use a credit card and when to pay cash.

✓ Study sales tax laws for fun and profit.

✓ Turn back freebies for fun and profit.

✓ Put the scratch next to the wall and the cash in your pocket.

✓ Consider joining a warehouse club.

✓ Join (or create) a buying cooperative.

✓ Know how to raise your hand at an auction house.

✓ Shop at Uncle Sam's tag sales.

Shop for the Right Store

Here's what I want in a store:

- A wide variety of quality merchandise;
- Prices that represent a reasonable profit for the store and a good deal for the buyer, and
- The most customer-friendly return and warranty policies.

Does this sound like an impossible dream? It's not.

Stores such as these are out there. They may be an outpost of a huge national discount operation or a local mom-and-pop retailer; they may be a major mail-order catalog company or an electronic storefront on the information superhighway that exists only in the memory of some computer.

As a savvy consumer, you should be just as careful in shopping for the places where you spend your money as you are about what you buy and how much you pay.

Don't make any assumptions about sales policies based on the size of the operation. Many major discount-store chains advertise "price guarantees" promising they will not be "undersold." A small local store, where the owner or manager is behind the counter or nearby, may be quite willing to match or beat a major competitor even if he or she doesn't advertise that as a policy. Either way, this is a case of a business that is smart enough to realize that it's better to make a small profit than no profit at all.

You're almost certain to need to come up with your own group of stores: the best place to buy hardware, the best place to buy appliances, the best place to buy clothing, and so on.

My favorite way to shop is by mail or telephone order; this is partly because I live in a very remote corner of this country and mostly because I have found it convenient to let my fingers do the walking through catalogs and Internet Web pages in search of the best prices and policies.

Don't concentrate solely on finding the best price, however, unless you're talking about a commodity you will consume immediately. Instead, be on the lookout for a place that will deliver your product on time, in good condition, with proper delivery and setup if necessary, and one that will stand behind its products after the sale.

Ask a lot of questions, and push—gently and politely—for any reasonable concessions on price or service. Remember this important hard-earned lesson: If a store is difficult to deal with before you make a purchase, what makes you think it will be easy to work with once it has deposited your money in the bank?

Shop for the Right Salesperson

Here's what I want in a salesperson:

- Someone who knows the product.
- Someone who knows the competition.
- Someone who knows that I'm a savvy buyer who is willing to pay a fair price, but not the full list price. *The list price is for someone who is sold, not for someone who buys.*

Here's what I usually get: someone who knows less about the product than I do, has no idea of the competitive position of his or her store, and does not understand that in most negotiations the power lies with the person with the money to spend.

Therefore, I have to take control of the buying process. Start by learning as much as you can about a product before you buy it. You add to the power on your side of the table by showing a knowledgeable salesperson that you're not impressed with meaningless sales and marketing ploys; you can also intimidate a know-nothing into becoming an order-taker (on your terms).

Find Out if the Sales Force Is Commissioned or Salaried

Here's a buying tip that may sound counterintuitive: You may get the best deal by buying from a commissioned salesperson instead of from a salaried clerk.

Here's why: A person who earns his or her income on the basis of a commission has a greater personal interest in seeing that you make a purchase, even if he or she has to cut the price to make you loosen your grip on your wallet. A smaller commission is better than no commission at all.

A salaried sales force often doesn't care whether the customer is happy or not, unless a supervisor is watching.

If you know that a particular store uses a commissioned sales force, you might try shopping there at the end of the month in hopes of taking advantage of sales contests and sales quotas that manufacturers and stores use to place pressure on their staff.

And if you find a particularly accommodating commissioned salesperson, ask him or her for advice on upcoming sales and special events. Make the salesperson your partner in being a savvy consumer. And pass along your compliments to the manager.

Know When to Buy: A Counterseasonal Calendar

The basic rule here is to buy when there is more product than shoppers. Don't go looking for a snowblower as the first winter storm arrives, or for a charcoal grill on July 3. You can bet on a good price, though, if you can find a grill in January or a snowblower in July.

Ski Equipment and Clothing

By early spring, most skiers have made their major purchases and are already thinking about summertime pursuits. So, too, are ski retailers: they want to clear out their inventory to make room for bicycles, tennis rackets, kayaks, and next year's hot new skis.

Look for major sales around Easter, but don't hesitate trying to strike a bargain on skis even later in the season.

Some of the best deals can be found at the stores at ski resorts. Many of these locations are far away from major metropolitan areas and operate seasonally only. Most will be very happy to unload their stock around Easter.

And don't overlook rental shops. I have equipped my up-and-coming hotdog daughter with well-maintained skis and boots from a ski resort at a fraction of the cost of new devices; this is an excellent strategy for keeping up with growing children and for beginners of all ages who will want to work their way from basic equipment to more advanced skis and boots as their ability improves.

Charcoal Grills, Swimming Pools, and Lawnmowers

Buy a grill at Labor Day and put it away in the garage until next season. (Or use it all winter . . . a charbroiled steak or chicken tastes just as good at Christmas as it does on the Fourth of July.)

Prefabricated backyard swimming pools are hot items in the stores in the summer and sit around gathering dust from about Labor Day through May. Offer to help out your local dealer with an off-season purchase.

Lawnmowers start to gather dust on the floor by the Fourth of July; go in and make your best offer while you are still blessed with a few months to go in mowing season.

Theater Tickets

Your best chances of good deals on tickets may come during previews and before the opening for a promising show, or at the end of a run. The worst possible time is immediately after opening of a well-reviewed show.

Air Conditioners

Buy one for yourself for Christmas. Actually, the best time may be just after the start of the year when stores place their orders for summer merchandise. Buy this year's new model as soon as it arrives and before the dealer has had to spend any money on storage and interest.

Another good time to buy summer merchandise is just after Labor Day, assuming that there is any inventory left over. Offer to buy a leftover unit from last season (sealed in its box, with full warranty).

Carpeting, Furniture, and Appliances

Most buyers have their minds on less substantial purchases between Thanksgiving and Christmas; that's a good time to offer to buy.

Bicycles

Shop in October and November for the best prices on closeouts from the summer past. Most dealers place orders for next season in September, and they'll be anxious to clear some space in the warehouse and on the floor.

Tools

With apologies to women carpenters, the two biggest sales periods for consumer hand and power tools are the days leading up to Christmas and Father's Day. So, shop for the best deals in January and late June.

Swimwear

Prices start to plunge soon after customers head to the beach, in May and June. The largest discounts are likely late in the summer, if there are any left in the stores.

Automobiles

The best time to buy a car may well be at the end of the day at the end of the month at the end of a selling season. Oh, and throw in a thunderstorm or a snowstorm and you've definitely moved more of the power to your side of the table.

Let's go over those specifications in more detail:

- *The end of the day.* Salespeople have families and softball leagues, and they get tired, too. And they may be feeling the pressure from the sales manager. Come in an hour or so before the store closes with all of your numbers, ready to make a deal.

- *The end of the month.* Carmakers and dealers, like many other sales organizations, are big on sales quotas and competitions, and they usually run by calendar month. Come in during the last few days of the month to put some of that pressure to work for you. The salesperson may be willing to accept less of a commission for a car if another sale will bring him or her a bonus; the dealership may be willing to sell the car for less to qualify for additional money, model allocations, or a free trip to Hawaii for the boss.

- *The end of the selling season.* New car models generally begin to arrive about September of each year, and both the dealership and the manufacturer will want to clear out "old" cars. You will be in an especially good position if the new-model-year cars do not have much of a price increase; the manufacturer will want to place some distance between this year's model and last year's.

  The downside to buying a car at the end of the selling season is that the value of the car for resale purposes is immediately reduced. The difference in model years makes the most difference for vehicles resold within about the first five years of ownership; for older cars the number of miles on the odometer takes on greater importance, and you will regain some of the value you lost by buying an older model year.

- *A rainy or snowy day.* Think of it: you're the only customer to walk through the door all day and you say you're willing to make a deal today. They may pay you to take a car off their hands.

Computers

PC prices have headed south almost without pause in the 15-year history of the business. Over that time, buyers have seen prices decline by several hundred percent for a basic machine, and at the same time have been able to get more for their money—faster processors, more memory, and larger hard drives.

Even so, you can save even more money by watching the newspapers to learn about introductions of new microprocessors and reductions in prices of older ones. The best buys are usually found by buying one generation behind the latest-and-greatest machines; buy the PCs that have suddenly been relegated to yesterday's news.

Understand a Retailer's Markup Strategy Before You Sit Down to Negotiate a Markdown

Another important way to move the power to your side of the table is to understand a retailer's markup. Some products—cars and personal computers among them—have relatively small markups from whole-sale to retail price. Other items, such as furniture and designer cloth-ing, sport very large profit margins.

Think of markups as the percentage of the asking price that goes to the seller. (It's not all profit, though; the store has to pay overhead—rent, utilities, advertising, and salaries.)

As a buyer, having some idea of the wholesale cost of a product gives you an informed starting point in figuring the sort of discount you can ask for. Here are some general ranges of markups:

Appliances

Dealers mark up larger devices such as refrigerators and washing machines about 15 percent; smaller items such as televisions, VCRs, and microwave ovens are usually marked up about 25 percent.

Automobiles

Big-ticket vehicles have small markups, typically in the range of 5 to 12 percent. As you'll find in the chapter about automobiles, though, car dealers have a number of other ways they use to attempt to squeeze more cash out of their customers and have as well a range of hidden kickbacks and incentives from the manufacturer.

Books

The selling price for most books represents a markup of 50 to 100 percent. One inside note: Most booksellers stock their shelves on a con-signment basis, meaning that they can send back unsold copies to the publisher for credit or sell books at deep discounts if they choose.

Clothing

Name-brand fashion is usually marked up about 50 percent, although manufacturers often strike special deals with major retailers to reduce prices over the course of a season.

Furniture

A furniture or department store usually marks up its wares 50 to 100 percent or more; discount operations work closer to the wholesale price.

Personal Computers

The highly competitive **PC** market usually prices hardware about 10 to 25 percent above cost.

Don't Let Them Get Away with a Markdown After You've Left the Store

Have you ever bought a television set on Friday for $400 and then opened the Sunday newspaper to see the same TV on sale at the same store for $299?

Or how about seeing the same set at a different store for half price?

You didn't take it sitting down, did you? Unless you bought something under a "no-returns" or "final-sale" policy, the power is still on your side of the table, whether the store likes it or not.

Here are some tips that will work for a period within the store's return or price-protection period:

- Take good care of all packing materials and paperwork for the first couple of weeks after you make a major purchase. Don't send in warranty cards until you are certain you will keep an item. Be sure you understand a store's return policy.

- Check to see if the store has a "price-protection" or similar guarantee. These pledges are usually aimed at promising that a competitor won't offer the same item at a lower price within a particular time period. However, most also apply if the price is lowered at the store where you made your purchase.

- If there is no price-protection plan, return to the store with your paperwork and ask to speak with a manager. Ask for a cash refund (or if it suits you, a store credit) for the difference in price. If they resist, you have an ace in the hole: You can always return the item for the price you paid for it. If you still feel like shopping at a store that forces you to such extremes, you can then repurchase the same item at the sale price.

- The same principle can also be applied to airline tickets. If you buy a ticket for $500 with a $35 reticketing fee, and before you fly the airline drops the cost of the flight to $300, call and ask to be reticketed at the lower rate. In this case you'll still be ahead by $165.

Know When to Use a Credit Card and When to Pay Cash

A careful consumer with a credit card is well protected in most shopping situations. I use my credit card for almost everything I buy, making sure that I pay off all bills before the bank applies an interest charge. I collect tens of thousands of free miles in a frequent-flyer program, and at least once or twice a year I enlist my credit-card issuer to resolve a dispute over products not received or not found acceptable.

HERE'S WHEN TO USE YOUR CREDIT CARD:

1. *When you buy by mail or by telephone to protect yourself against failure to deliver.* When you buy by mail or by telephone, you are authorizing a charge to your credit card before you receive the product or check out its quality. That's the scary part.

But the good news is this: Though you have authorized a charge to be put on your account, you hold on to your money for the moment. If the seller does not deliver the goods, or if whatever you bought is not what you contracted for, you can withhold payment and enlist the assistance of the bank or company that issues the credit card.

You'll have the federal Fair Credit Billing Act on your side of the table, which allows you to refuse to pay for a purchase and any finance charges while you make good-faith efforts to resolve a dispute. And your credit-card company can apply pressure on the merchant on your behalf, too.

Be sure to follow the rules for disputing a credit-card bill. They're generally listed on the back of your monthly statement; you can also discuss them with the customer-service department of the credit-card company.

2. *When you are traveling abroad and are paying local currency.* Your credit-card company will convert the bill into dollars at the bank rate, which is usually better than the local merchant or money-changing outlets will offer.

It's fun to go "native" when you travel in a foreign land, paying for your meals and souvenirs with francs in France, pounds in England, krone in Denmark, and shekels in Israel. But you may end up losing 10 to 20 percent or more of your purchasing power by cashing in your dollars at a money-changing counter at the airport or a hotel where you may have to pay a service charge and almost certainly will receive less than the best rate. You'll get a better exchange rate at a major bank and an even squarer deal by using your credit card. The issuer of your card will convert your charge to dollars at the commercial-exchange rate.

I'd recommend you change just enough dollars (or U.S.-denomination travelers' checks) to give you walking-around money for snacks, taxis, and small items.

By the way, when you use your card, be sure to check that the credit slip is marked in local currency.

3. *When you want to take advantage of special features of your credit card, such as frequent-flyer mileage.* Here's a valuable benefit for certain but not for all credit-card users. If you use your credit card fairly heavily—several hundred to several thousand dollars per month—you should consider using a card that accrues points in an airline frequent-flyer program. Some are offered with a direct affiliation with an airline, while others allow you to bank points that can be applied to any air ticket of a certain class.

Here's what you need to do to be a savvy consumer of this type of card: First of all, check out the annual fee (usually a bit higher than other cards and certainly more expensive than a free card) and compare it against the value of a ticket. If it costs you $100 per year for the card and it takes you three years to build up enough miles to obtain a ticket worth $300, this is no deal at all.

Next look at the interest rate charged on outstanding balances. These cards often bear a higher rate than other accounts. This is not an issue if you don't maintain a balance, of course.

Finally, compare the frequent-flyer programs of the various air-lines that offer cards. You don't want to accrue miles on an airline that doesn't serve an airport near you or a destination where you want to fly. And, some airlines give away tickets at a much lower-point level, or may have fewer blackout periods for tickets.

4. *When you want to earn a cash rebate on an account.* Rebate cards, including some Discover and some versions of Visa and MasterCard, promise you a rebate of all charges at the end of the year. The amount is relatively small, usually one or two percentage points. A rebate is a good thing, but be sure you are not paying too much for the privilege in the form of a higher-than-average annual fee or interest rate.

5. *When you want to apply a credit card's extended warranty to your purchase.* Some credit cards offer special insurance policies that extend the warranty for certain purchases. These limited warranties have numerous exclusions, including normal wear and tear and abuse, but can be valuable for items such as televisions and other appliances. Read the small print carefully and be sure to keep hold of all sales slips and manufacturer's warranties.

You do, of course, have to make the original purchase with the credit card, and you must maintain the account in good standing in order to make a claim.

6. *When you want to use your credit card's automobile-insurance coverage when you rent a car.* Many credit cards, especially gold cards, offer special automobile-insurance coverage for rentals made using the card. Be sure to read the fine print from the credit-card company, and don't hesitate to call customer service for clarification before you use the card to rent a car. The insurance coverage usually has exceptions that exclude luxury cars and also withhold payment if it is deemed that an accident was due to negligence by the driver. Finally, some credit-card companies do not extend coverage to international rentals.

7. *When you want to obtain free airline accident insurance on tickets purchased with your credit card.* Special insurance coverage for airline flights, purchased from an airport kiosk or machine or directly from an insurance company, is generally not a good deal; you're better off buying and maintaining a good life-insurance policy. But if your

credit card company offers free coverage for tickets purchased with its card, go ahead and take advantage of the offer.

8. *When you want an interest-free loan from your credit-card company from the time you make your purchase until the due date on your statement.* Here's one of the best uses of a credit card, but only for the financially well disciplined: Make as many purchases as you can on your credit card and then be sure to pay off the bill a few days before the bill is due. The finest art here involves making major purchases just after the closing day of one billing period, which can give you 30 days till the next bill and up to 30 more days beyond then until the statement must be paid.

HERE'S WHEN TO PAY BY CHECK:

1. *If the merchant is willing to offer you a lower rate for cash and you are willing to give up the protections of using a credit card.* Merchants must pay a fee to credit-card issuers, typically 2 to 5 percent, to process charges. You may be able to reduce the price of a major purchase or service by offering a check. Be sure to obtain a detailed receipt and statement of warranty if you do business in this way.

2. *When credit cards are not accepted and you are willing to give up some of the protection of a credit card.* If a merchant or service provider will not accept a credit card, consider whether you should take your business elsewhere. The protection provided by the card has a value. Ask the merchant what sort of written reassurance he or she can provide to make you feel better about the deal.

HERE'S WHEN TO PAY BY CASH:

1. *For small purchases, where issues of warranties and taxes are not important.* The Underground Economy is all around us. Sooner or later, some merchant or provider of services is going to offer you a reduced price if you pay with cash. There are few good reasons for them to do this; instead, they may be seeking to avoid reporting a sale as income or may be selling stolen or gray-market products.

As a buyer, the lure of paying a reduced price is strong, but consider this: What protections do you have against faulty product or service? And if the tax man or the sheriff comes calling, the fact that you received a good deal will not protect you from possible penalties or seizure.

Study Sales Tax Laws for Fun and Profit

In my experience, there are three types of buyers when it comes to state sales taxes: those who ignore them, those who curse them, and those who include them in their savvy shopping strategies.

Here are some ways to save money on taxable purchases:

- *Shop where the tax is less*. If you are within a short commute to a neighboring state, take into account differing tax rates when you make major purchases. Obviously, you don't want to spend more money on gasoline and other expenses than you will save on taxes.

    It would certainly seem worthwhile to cross a state line to buy an expensive and easily transportable item such as jewelry, furs, and many appliances.

    In a number of states, Massachusetts and New Jersey among them, sales tax does not apply to clothing; for that reason so many New Yorkers cross the Hudson River to malls in New Jersey that New York State has experimented with occasional tax "holidays" in recent years.

    In some states it may be possible to cross a state line to buy an automobile in a tax-free or low-tax state; check with your department of motor vehicles about any regulations that might force you to pay the tax anyhow when you register the car.

- *Shop by mail order with companies that do not charge sales tax in your state*. In general, this applies to operations that do not have a physical location in your state. You'll also save time and the expense of driving to a store; be sure to pay attention to shipping costs, though.

Turn Back Freebies for Fun and Profit

Everything costs something, and there is no reason to pay for something you don't need. Here are some ways to turn back freebies:

- If an appliance or mattress store promises "free delivery," ask for a discount—$25 or $50 sounds reasonable to me—if you'll be loading your purchase into your own vehicle.

- Refuse the offer of "free rails" at a bedding store if you're replacing an existing mattress and ask for $10 off the price.

- If you're buying a suit or outfit that includes "free alterations" you don't need, ask for $25 off for your perfect body.

- If a computer dealer packs a PC with "free" software, ask for a price without any unneeded programs. You may not be able to buy the machine without an operating system; Microsoft has deals with many computer makers, for example, that requires them to pay for Windows for every machine they sell. And don't be surprised to learn that the real cost of prepackaged software may be only $10 or $25 even though the dealer may be advertising "hundreds of dollars of free software."

- Call a car dealer's bluff if the dealer advertises something like "free undercoating worth $250." Pass on the undercoating and ask for the $250. You may not get it, but you will put the salesperson on notice that you're going to demand a very sharp deal.

Put the Scratch Next to the Wall and the Cash in Your Pocket

You can save money—from a few dollars to hundreds—by buying a dented or scratched but otherwise new product. The trick is to buy an item where the scratch doesn't matter, or where a perfect version would end up scratched very soon in any case. Some examples:

- *Sporting goods*. A fielder's or catcher's mitt with a mark on the leather (not a tear) will look identical to a new mitt after a few innings. And you can improve the look and feel of leather goods with a rub-in oil.

- *Appliances*. A minor dent or scratch in the side of a clothes washer that is headed for the basement sounds like a deal too good to pass up. Be sure the device is fully covered by warranty.

- *Casual furniture*. Is the damage in an area that will face the wall?

- *Luggage*. A mark on a suitcase may disqualify it from sale as a perfect item, but you can be sure that the case will have dozens of stains and scratches after its first trip in the hands of an airline baggage handler. Don't, though, buy a suitcase with damage to a zipper or other closure.

In some towns you'll find dealers specializing in scratched and dented products. (One old name for this type of store: Railroad Salvage.) You may also be able to find these items in the back of the warehouse at a regular dealer; ask the salesperson for a tour.

Consider Joining a Warehouse Club

Well, first, you're reading a book by a guy who has a closet filled with several *dozen* boxes of his family's favorite breakfast cereal, a chest freezer in the basement with several hundred dollars worth of frozen fish, turkey, and vegetables, and kitchen cabinets stocked with enough salad dressing, bread mix, and sauces to open a small supermarket of his own.

Warehouse stores offer discount prices on large-quantity packages, sometimes in sizes or numbers not offered at supermarkets. You'll also find commercial-size or -quality food and supplies at reduced prices.

But that doesn't mean I recommend everyone shop at a warehouse store. You'll still need to be a careful shopper: When a supermarket puts something on sale, the price is often considerably lower than regular prices at a warehouse store. It is also important to note that some warehouse stores don't accept discount coupons. And then there is one other important issue: If you buy something in large quantity you had better hope that you actually like the food and that it doesn't spoil before you finish it. Finally, although warehouse stores often stock some unusual items, they generally offer a much smaller number of food products than does a large supermarket. If you're looking for tomato paste, you'll find one brand—in a huge can—instead of the half dozen or more you might find at a market.

A good reason to join a club is for nonperishable items, from television sets to furniture to hardware to home supplies. Don't expect much in the way of service or advice, though; do your research before you enter the store.

Most warehouse clubs charge an annual fee, typically $25 or $35; some clubs permit "visitors" to shop, adding a 5 percent surcharge on purchases. Before you object to a surcharge, consider this: At 5 percent, you're still ahead of the membership fee for the first $500 or $700 you spend (for a $25 or $35 fee respectively). If you expect to spend less than that amount per year, you're better off paying the surcharge instead of becoming a member of the club.

Join (or Create) a Buying Cooperative

You're so proud of your 150-pound St. Bernard "Tiny" that you've joined a club of large-dog owners; at meetings you sit around and discuss the fact that you go through a 50-pound sack of dry dog food each week. Stop, think: Don't you think a pet store—or even better, a pet-food wholesaler—would be happy to send a truckful of food to one address at a deep discount? Start a dog-food cooperative.

Or, you and three of your friends are avid photographers. Get together and buy film by the "block" (shrink-wrapped containers of 24 rolls) or the case (four blocks). Film can be stored in a refrigerator or freezer to extend its life, but don't buy more than you expect to use in a year.

The concept of a buying cooperative can extend to major purchases, too. Gather four friends together and seek a fleet discount on a group of car purchases or leases; no auto dealer worth his hairpiece is going to balk at giving an extra-special deal to a bulk purchase.

You should also investigate food-buying cooperatives that purchase from restaurant supply houses or wholesale grocers. Ask around at social-service agencies, churches, and alternative merchants such as health-food stores.

And if you have friends or family you are willing to travel with, consider renting a multibedroom house or condo at your destination instead of a group of hotel rooms. You'll save money, get more space, and have the option to eat some of your meals at your home away from home instead of at a restaurant.

Know How to Raise Your Hand at an Auction House

Private and commercial auctions are exciting places to pick up tremendous bargains, obtain one-of-a-kind items for a collection, and an easy way to go to the cleaners without benefit of a laundry tag.

They are also places where the incautious or uninformed can make an expensive mistake with the twitch of a finger. As a consumer you are basically buying an item retail that you may have to dispose of at wholesale prices later on.

The best advice for auctiongoers is this: Bid only on items you know very well, and have a firm and unbreakable maximum price in mind for any item. Here are some more tips:

- *Know the bottom line before you make a bid.* Many auction houses add a commission fee—often as much as 15 percent—on top of the sales price. The fee is paid by the buyer, not the seller. And in many states, the buyer also must pay sales tax. Together, these two charges can add 20 percent or more to the price of an item.

- *Understand the auction prices.* Most auction houses have an agreement with the seller that sets a minimum price for an item. If bids do not reach to that level, the auction house may withdraw the item for sale.

    You should also be aware that in many states it is legal for the auctioneer to fake the bidding process up to the seller's minimum price. For example, the owner of a fabulous collection of plastic-cup coasters may set a minimum acceptable price of $1,000; the auctioneer can start the bidding at $1,000 or can accept bids from confederates or even phantom bids up to $1,000.

    Is this ethical? You might argue that it is not. But in any case, it shouldn't matter. You should still set your own maximum price for an item. If the plastic coasters are worth $1,200 to you, that should be the most you bid; if they are worth $500 to you and the auctioneer starts above that level, stay out of the market.

- *If an item you want to buy does not fall to the gavel,* don't hesitate to approach the auctioneer or the private seller after the day's sale is over with a private offer at the price you are willing to pay. Insiders say the best deals at many auctions can be had in this "after-sale market."

Shop at Uncle Sam's Tag Sales

Your federal government is the biggest consumer of all in this country and also the largest collector of stolen merchandise, illegally imported products, contraband, and ill-gotten goods. Of course, you've got a lot more use for that 40-foot ocean racer than does Uncle Sam, right? Here's your chance to cut yourself in on the deal at auctions and sales.

For an overall view of government sales, you can purchase the U.S. General Services Administration Guide to Federal Government Sales; it is available for a small charge by calling (202) 512-1800.

Be aware that the government sells everything "as is"; repairs and service are entirely your responsibility. In many cases you'll have to remove your purchases on the day you buy them, too.

The U.S. Treasury Department sells seized or abandoned real estate, automobiles, airplanes, boats, jewelry, and more. Sales are held every few months in Los Angeles, California; El Paso, Texas; Nogales, Arizona; Edison, New Jersey; Miami/Fort Lauderdale, Florida, and other locations. Automobiles are sold near San Diego.

The sales include items seized by the Treasury Department, the U.S. Secret Service, and the Bureau of Alcohol, Tobacco, and Firearms.

For information and to pay to be put on a mailing list for sales, call the Public Auction Line at (703) 273-7373. You can also check the Treasury Department's Web site, at

http://www.ustreas.gov/treasury/bureaus/customs/general.html

The General Services Administration clears out the government's attic, disposing of surplus or used vehicles, boats, airplanes, office supplies, and just about everything else. Sales are conducted in every state as warranted. You can call the GSA in your state, or call (703) 305-7814 for information about regional offices. Internet users can connect to http://www.gsa.gov and go to the search page to look for "auctions."

The Federal Deposit Insurance Corporation sells assets from failed banks, including homes, land, and commercial property. For information, contact regional offices in Connecticut at (800) 873-7785, Georgia (800) 765-3342, Texas (800) 568-9161, or California (800) 234-0867. Or go on the Internet to

http://www.fdic.gov/assets/index.html

Did you ever wonder what the U.S. Postal Service does with packages it cannot deliver or return to the sender? Call the USPS in St. Paul, Minnesota, at (612) 293-3335, Atlanta at (404) 344-1625, or San Francisco at (415) 536-6425 for information about auctions and sales. You can also check out a Web page at

http://www.usps.gov/consumer/auctions.htm

2 Your Rights As a Buyer

By now you should recognize this book's mantra: The buyer has the advantage because he or she has the money.

But the power begins to shift as soon as you hand over the cash (or the credit card or the signed contract) to the seller.

The scariest situation is to pay in advance for a product or service and then wait for its delivery. And yet we do it all the time: We purchase airline tickets weeks or months ahead of a flight, we put down a deposit on a special-order item, and we reveal our credit-card information over the phone to a mail-order company.

The good news is that consumers are protected by a web of state and federal laws and regulations. Add to that policies of credit-card companies and the sellers themselves and you have a pretty good consumer safety net. The trick, though, is to know your rights . . . and demand that they be honored.

✓ Send it back.

✓ Know how to cool off a mistake.

✓ Search for a good warranty and understand its terms.

✓ Protect yourself when you shop away from home.

✓ Protect yourself when you make an online purchase.

✓ Know how to return a mail-order purchase properly.

✓ Know the ins and outs of layaway-purchase plans.

✓ Know how to avoid duty-free duress.

✓ Understand the value of Value-Added Tax rebates.

✓ Learn how to freeze out cold calls.

Send It Back

I once sent back a house. My wife and I had made an offer on a fix-me-up summer cottage, and the owner had accepted the deal. But then we got cold feet. There was just too much fixing up to be done, and a second look at the cost of the house and the repairs that needed to be done convinced us we would be better off spending more money on a property in better condition. Although we had, in theory, a binding contract for purchase and sale of the house, there were enough loopholes in the agreement to drive a motor home through. And so we sent back the house.

That was, of course, an extreme situation. But the fact is that in most situations you have the right to cancel a deal and receive your money back because of nonperformance, unacceptable quality, or even a limited right to merely change your mind.

You should include in your purchase decision an appraisal of the returns policy of any store you deal with. If Store A sells a widget for $75 but proclaims that "all sales are final" while Store B offers the same widget for the same price and allows returns for 30 days after the sale, you should bring your business to Store B. In fact, it may be worth paying a bit more for a product if you feel more comfortable with return policies at the higher-priced store.

When you pay for a repair on your car, or a fix to your leaky plumbing you have the right to expect that the problem be fixed. Read the fine print on a service agreement *before* the work is done and be sure you understand it and agree with it. If the repair service makes an oral promise to you ("It'll be as good as new," or "We won't charge you a penny if we can't fix it") have that written into the contract.

When you order a meal at a restaurant, you are making a deal with the management based on the specifications laid out in the menu as well as a general expectation that the food will be of acceptable quality. If you order a steak and are given chicken instead, send it back. If you order a steak cooked rare and receive it one step short of incinerated, send it back.

Some deals are less formal but still valuable to you as a consumer. If you order a meal and receive what you ordered but find it not to your liking, politely inform the waiter or waitress or speak with the manager. I've never heard of a restaurant not making an effort to accommodate a diner; a smart businessperson is well aware of the value of the goodwill of its customers.

Keep your receipts from all purchases and attach them to any published guarantees from mail-order catalogs or store flyers. They'll help you with any warranty claims, and you may even want to take advantage of spectacular policies at some stores: a money-back guarantee with no strings attached. For example, some tools come with a "lifetime" guarantee. And my sometimes indecisive wife once returned a jacket that had hung—unused, with tags still attached—in her closet for more than a year.

Know How to Cool Off a Mistake

We've got a special deal, but you've got to sign up for it right now, right here.

Watch out! These are some of the tactics of high-pressure sales, a situation that has brought many a buyer to grief days later when the bill comes due.

We can thank the Federal Trade Commission for something called the Cooling-Off Rule, intended to protect buyers who sign on the bottom line in situations that are outside the normal business settings. Any time you buy an item in your home or at a location that is not the seller's permanent place of business, you have the right to cancel a deal and obtain a full refund until midnight of the third business day after the sale.

The Cooling-Off Rule applies to sales at the buyer's home, workplace, or dormitory, or at facilities rented by the seller on a temporary or short-term basis, such as hotel or motel rooms, convention centers, fairgrounds, and restaurants.

An important benefit: The rule applies even if you invited the salesperson to make a presentation in your home.

Here's what the FTC requires of salespersons in an environment outside their place of business:

- They must tell you about your cancellation rights at the time of sale.
- They must give you two copies of a cancellation form (one to keep and one to send).
- They must give you a copy of your contract or receipt, and it must be dated, show the name and address of the seller, and explain your right to cancel. The contract or receipt must be in the same language used in the sales presentation.

Alas, there are some exceptions to the Cooling-Off Rule. Sales not covered by the regulation include:

- Items or services sold for less than $25.
- Real estate, insurance, or securities.
- Automobiles, vans, trucks, or other motor vehicles sold at temporary locations, provided the seller has at least one permanent place of business.
- Arts or crafts sold at fairs or locations such as shopping malls, civic centers, and schools.
- Goods or services not primarily intended for personal, family, or household purposes.
- Sales made by mail or telephone.
- Deals that are the result of prior negotiations that were done at the permanent business location where the goods are regularly sold.
- Items purchased for an emergency need such as plumbing or pest control. (You may be asked to waive your rights to a cooling-off period in such a situation.)

Here's how to cancel:

- Sign and date one copy of the cancellation form. Mail it to the address given for cancellation, making sure the envelope is post-marked before midnight of the third business day after the contract date. (Saturday is considered a business day; Sundays and federal holidays are not.)

Because proof of the mailing date and proof of receipt are important, you may want to bring the letter to the post office and obtain a hand cancellation of the letter. To be even more careful, send the cancellation form by certified mail and obtain a return receipt. Or, consider hand delivering the cancellation notice before midnight of the third business day. Keep the other copy of the cancellation form for your records.

- If the seller did not provide a cancellation form or if you cannot find the one given you, write your own. Be specific about what you are calling off and include the date of the contract and the date of the cancellation. You do not have to give a reason for canceling your purchase.

If you cancel your purchase, the seller has 10 days to cancel and return any promissory note or other negotiable instrument you signed, refund all your money, arrange for the pickup of any product you still have, and return any trade-in. Within 20 days, the seller must either pick up the items left with you or reimburse you for mailing expenses if you agree to send back the items.

If you received any goods from the seller, you must make them available to the seller in the same condition as when you received them. If you do not make the items available to the seller, or if you agree to return the items but fail to, you remain obligated under the contract.

Some state laws give you even more rights than does the FTC rule.

Search for a Good Warranty and Understand Its Terms

There is no law that requires a manufacturer to offer a warranty on its products. Instead, it is the pressure of the marketplace that convinces a maker to make promises about the quality or longevity of its offerings.

As a savvy consumer, you should include consideration of the type and length of warranty as part of your buying decision. All things being equal, buy the product with the better warranty. If a product with a better warranty costs more, weigh that cost against possible expenses down the road for the lower-priced product.

If a company does offer a written warranty, though, its provisions must follow several federal laws including elements of the Magnuson-Moss Warranty Act and regulations put forth by the Federal Trade Commission. An important distinction to look for in a written warranty is whether it is "full" or "limited."

A full warranty means that the maker promises to repair or replace malfunctioning parts at no cost for the length of time promised. This sort of broad warranty is relatively rare.

A limited warranty typically promises protection against defects in material and workmanship with certain specified exceptions, and therein lie some major differences from one warranty to another. For example, a limited warranty might say that coverage does not extend to problems caused by abuse or accident, or failure to follow maintenance procedures outlined in the instruction manual; some makers will not honor a warranty if alterations have been made to the system by an unauthorized service provider, and other companies will exclude items that wear out through ordinary use such as tires on a car, blades on a lawnmower, and the like.

A limited warranty may also say that its promises apply only to the original owner, or set restrictions on how warranties are transferred if the product is resold.

A written warranty must include details of how service is to be provided. Read the terms carefully to find out where the repairs are done and whether the owner is responsible for paying any shipping costs in one or both directions. On some products, including major appliances and computers, repairs may be offered in your home or office; if you live in a remote location find out beforehand whether your area is excluded in some way.

What if the manufacturer or seller does not offer a written warranty? You're not completely out of luck, although you're going to have to be your own best advocate.

State laws establish the outlines for "implied warranties" for products. Two common types for these protections are an "implied warranty of merchantability" and an "implied warranty of fitness for a particular purpose." State law may set a time limit or place other limitations on implied warranties.

Merchantability means that a product must perform as it obviously should: A washing machine must wash clothes, a computer must compute, and a tennis ball must bounce. There is no promise that the washing machine must do its job particularly well or quickly, that the computer does the same, or that the tennis ball bounces to a particular height or helps you beat Pete Sampras at Wimbledon. The definition of merchantability, though, can be extended to include any promises made in packaging or advertising.

Fitness for a particular purpose is related to any discussions you have with the seller and any promises made to you in return. For example, if you tell a computer seller that you need a particular piece of software to manage an office of 12 power users and the seller knows you are relying on his or her recommendation, the product is warranted to be fit for that purpose. If you tell an appliance salesperson you need a microwave that can be in almost constant use in a restaurant, this is a similar situation where the product is warranted to be fit for such a situation.

If you want to make a claim based on an implied warranty, you had better be prepared to back up your assertion with anything you received in writing and any notes you made at the time of sale. Consult your state or local consumer-protection agency for assistance.

One possible exception to an implied warranty is an "as is" sale, which is supposed to indicate that the seller is making no representations at all about the product. So long as the buyer understands the full terms of the sale, there would seem to be nothing wrong with this sort of transaction. Some states, though, including Kansas, Maine, Maryland, Massachusetts, Mississippi, Vermont, West Virginia, and the District of Columbia, do not recognize "as is" sales.

Protect Yourself When You Shop Away from Home

Here are some other concerns about buying any product away from your home:

- *Warranties*. Many policies are limited to specific countries and you may have to pay full fare for any repairs.
- *Voltage and other standards*. There are more than a dozen designs of electrical plugs in use around the world and several incompatible video standards.

Not every part of the world uses the same 110-volt AC current offered in the United States. Many modern devices such as laptop computers and video cameras are capable of switching back and forth between 110 and 240 volts, but you'll need adapters to plug into most foreign electrical outlets.

Similarly, low-voltage electrical devices that use transformers, such as Nintendo games and portable computers, may have different positive-negative configurations for DC power in different nations. And there are half a dozen different video standards in use around the world, making it impossible to use the same type of videotape used in the United States (NTSC), in places like the United Kingdom or France (PAL), or other areas. Similarly, television sets manufactured for the U.S. market cannot be used everywhere in the world without adaptation.

Protect Yourself When You Make an Online Purchase

Shop for a magazine subscription, airline tickets, vitamin pills, books, records . . . an automobile . . . from the comfort of your own home with just the click of a mouse. That's the beauty of online shopping from one of the hundreds of retail outlets now available on the Internet.

The advantages of shopping electronically include convenience, the ease of price comparison, and the possibility, but not the guarantee, of lower prices for items and services purchased online.

But beware: Some stretches of the electronic superhighway are just as fraught with danger as are the retail alleyways of the downtown shopping district. The principal problem is this: The Internet is not quite a private den.

There are three points of vulnerability:

- Your PC, where you may have stored passwords, credit-card numbers, and bank information;
- The computer at the other end of the connection, where the merchant records the same sort of data; and
- The Internet itself, where the details of your transaction can travel thousands of miles in a form that can be intercepted by a determined wrongdoer.

Here's how to protect yourself in online commerce:

- Use a secure browser that includes data encryption facilities. The current versions of Microsoft Internet Explorer and Netscape Navigator permit you to go into secure mode; the business you are dealing with must have the same capability at the receiving end.

- To be absolutely safe, don't give out your credit-card number over the Internet. Many companies permit you to place an order electronically and then follow it up with a fax or telephone call to report your credit-card number. This way of doing business is not perfect; someone could still obtain your number at the business you are dealing with, but it reduces the possibilities of fraud.

- Shop with companies you already know. Obtain a printed copy of their refund and return policies before you place an order.

- Be sure you understand shipping and handling costs. Make certain they are appropriate and comparable to any charges you might face from a mail-order operation or a store. Determine how soon the order will be shipped.

- Understand your rights as a credit-card user, and read your statements closely when they arrive to be sure you are being charged properly for your purchases and that there are no unauthorized charges assessed.

- Take care with your Internet passwords. Try to pick one that is not obvious—don't use your name, birth date, phone number, children's names, or other choices that a creative electronic thief might be able to guess. The best kind of password is one that is nonsensical and mixes letters and numbers but you can nevertheless remember. Here are a few: I82MUCH (I ate too much), MY42N (My fortune), or CLBR8 (Celebrate).

- Watch out, too, for Web sites that ask you for information that goes beyond the bounds of an ordinary transaction. Don't give out your social-security number, your bank-account number, or other information that does not seem appropriate. A good rule of thumb: Don't respond to any question electronically if it is one you would not expect to be asked if you were buying an item in a store.

- Check the order form carefully before you send it to the merchant. If you make a mistake on the product name or number, or the quantity, you could end up with 100 pairs of super-extra-large pantyhose instead of one set of Amazon hip waders.

Under federal laws and FTC regulations, companies should ship orders within the time stated in their ads. If no time is promised, the company should ship your order within 30 days after receiving it, or give you an "option notice." This notice gives you the choice of agreeing to a delay or canceling your order and receiving a prompt refund.

Note that if a company does not promise a shipping time and you are applying for credit to pay for your purchase, the company has 50 days to ship after receiving your order.

Know How to Return a Mail-Order Purchase Properly

One of the best things about buying by mail order is the ability to send back your purchases if they don't work or if they don't match your expectations. Reputable mail-order houses are very good about taking back returns for most any reason.

But you've got to know the rules. Before you make any purchase by mail, phone, or by Internet, be sure you carefully read the return policies. Keep a printed copy of the policy until you're certain your order is exactly what you want.

For clothing, books, and other small nonmechanical or nonelectronic items the return process may be as simple as packaging up the item and sending it back with a note that includes your home address and account number.

But more expensive and complex items may require a super-secret magic code, commonly called an RMA, which stands for Return Merchandise Authorization. The way it works is like this: You call customer service and explain your predicament. If there is a problem with the operation of the item, a support person may try to help you fix the problem. But if the decision—yours or theirs—is for you to return the item, a file is opened at the shipper with all of the information and you will be assigned an RMA that you'll need to feature prominently on the outside of the package.

They do this to help track incoming shipments, and it makes sense. Some manufacturers go so far as to instruct their shipping departments to refuse any returned products that don't have the RMA in place.

A combination of the RMA and an insured shipment back to the manufacturer also protect you. If the package is damaged or lost, you have a chain of custody that goes from your hands to the shipper and (perhaps) to the manufacturer.

Know the Ins and Outs of Layaway-Purchase Plans

Layaway plans are ways to reserve merchandise and pay for the item in installments before you take it home. Less common now than in years past, layaways are in some ways like credit-card purchases in reverse: You are paying for an item before you take possession.

Make sure you understand a store's layaway policy before using the service; remember that you are giving your money to someone else without receiving something of substance in return until the end of the contract. If you have any doubts about the store's likelihood of continuing in business you probably should stay away; similarly, you might want to check with the local Better Business Bureau to see if there are any complaints recorded there.

First of all, obtain a written copy of the layaway policy and make sure the same language is present on any receipt you are given for payments made under the plan. The paperwork should identify your merchandise in writing to ensure that you will receive the exact item you are purchasing. Finally, keep a record of your payments.

Here are some questions to ask:

• Are there any service charges added to layaway arrangements? This is money out of your pocket above the price if you were to pay cash. If there is a large service charge—illegal in some states—you should compare the cost to credit-card charges for the same item.

• What are the terms of the layaway? How much time will you be allowed to pay for the item? Is there a minimum payment? When are payments due? Is there a penalty for late payment?

- What happens if you are unable to pay the full amount, or if you decide not to buy the item? If the store does not offer a full refund or at the least a full credit toward another purchase, I'd suggest you stay away from the layaway department.
- Will layaway items be kept apart from merchandise on sale? If you are laying away an item that must be ordered, what assurances can the store give you that the item will be available when you have paid for it?
- What happens if the item you want to purchase goes on sale at a lower price? Can you convert your contract to the new price?

There are no federal laws that specifically govern layaway plans. The Federal Trade Commission Act, however, makes illegal unfair or deceptive sales practices in or affecting commerce. There also may be state or local laws that cover layaway purchases in your area. To find out about appropriate state or local laws, check with your state or local consumer-protection agency and your local Better Business Bureau.

Know How to Avoid Duty-Free Duress

The idea of duty-free shopping is appealing: Here's your chance to purchase foreign and some domestic products without paying state and local sales taxes, excise taxes, duty, and other surcharges.

Duty-free shops in airports operate in a legal netherworld that allows them to act as if the items they have for sale have never entered the country; their warehouse is "bonded" by the customs department, and all sales must be limited to people who will not be immediately reentering the country. At some shops, your order is delivered to you as you board your airplane. Some airlines operate duty-free shops with flight attendants hawking wares on board the plane.

Here's the problem: In today's highly competitive marketplace, the duty-free shops do not always deliver the lowest prices. (One reason may be the large fees assessed by airport authorities.) Discount shops outside the airport may have lower prices, even with taxes and duty. Your best defense is to know the prices of items you may buy, including perfume, liquor, cameras, and jewelry.

And nonresidents can receive a refund of value-added taxes applied to purchases, which reduces the value of duty-free shops.

Understand the Value of Value-Added Tax Rebates

Many countries, including most European nations and Canada, have a somewhat-hidden sales tax on purchases, called a value-added tax (VAT) or a goods-and-services tax (GST).

As a nonresident visitor, you are entitled to a refund of some or all VAT or GST when you take your purchases out of the country.

Obtain information on refunds for taxes at tourist bureaus or major shops. Some countries permit retailers to send you the refund directly, while in other systems you must apply to the government for your money back.

And in some countries, there are businesses that will immediately pay you your refund minus a hefty service charge; you sign over the full amount due to the agency. If you have any questions about the legitimacy of such an offer, contact an area tourist bureau or government agency.

Learn How to Freeze Out Cold Calls

There are few more annoying features of modern life than the telephone call that always seems to come in the middle of dinner, or as you try to put your children to bed, or some other moment of your precious personal time: "Hello, this is a courtesy call for BigBucks Bank. We'd like to offer you a . . ."

That's about as far into the sales pitch as I allow the caller to get. I used to say something rude. Now, though, I say something firm: "I do not want to receive telephone solicitations. I want you to remove my name from your call list. Is that clear? Please give me your name so that I can keep a record of this conversation."

For any legitimate telemarketing operation, this is a very serious response. According to the Federal Trade Commission's Telemarketing Sales Rule, which took effect in 1996, a telemarketer is not supposed to call you again once you've asked to be removed from its call sheet. If the calls persist, the FTC encourages you to call your state attorney general's office or the National Fraud Information Center hot line at (800) 876-7060 with any information about possible illegal activity.

The rule also prohibits unsolicited sales calls between the hours of 9 P.M. and 8 A.M. and also requires telemarketers to identify the company they represent and the sales motive at the beginning of their pitch. If the call promotes a prize, the caller must tell you that no purchase or payment is necessary to enter or win. Telemarketers who violate any of these rules should be reported to the FTC.

If you're really serious about it, keep a notebook by the telephone and record the date, time, company, and name of the caller. You may be able to collect a judgment against an offending company, or at the least cause an annoying telemarketer some grief.

For more information about the Telemarketing Sales Rule, you can check out the FTC's Web site at **http://www.ftc.gov** or call the FTC at (202) 326-3128.

SECTION II

Shopping for Yourself

Chapter

3 A Power Tour of Home Electronics

The pace of technological change in America's homes is faster than at any time in history. According to the Consumer Electronics Manufacturers Association, color televisions are in 98 percent of homes in this country, VCRs in 89 percent, CD players in 49 percent, personal computers in 40 percent, and cellular phones in 34 percent.

That means we're all experts on home electronics, right? Or are you among the 75 percent of that 89 percent whose VCRs are forever blinking 12:00 because you can't figure out how to set the clock?

The fact is that electronic devices are becoming more and more capable . . . and more and more complex.

But the good news is that televisions, VCRs, and compact disc players are all mature products. You are safe in making a purchase on the basis of price, warranty, and things you can hear and see for yourself.

Here are some more tips on some common electronic purchases:

✓ Scan the horizon for new technologies.

✓ Enlighten yourself about dark-screen TVs.

✓ Buy big screens for the best technology.

✓ Watch out for misleading showroom conditions.

✓ Tune into a deal on a compact disc player.

✓ Shop the used CD bins.

✓ Fast-forward to a new VCR.

✓ Go slowly with TV-VCR combinations.

✓ Hear the news about cordless telephones.

✓ Avoid radar-detector speed traps.

Scan the Horizon for New Technologies

Here's a good-news bad-news situation if ever there was one: The longer you wait, the more fabulous the technology you will find in consumer electronic devices and personal computers, and the lower the prices will tumble. But if you wait, you don't get to use the new technologies. And in any case, as soon as you take home your new television set or computer, it is already obsolete.

Here are some examples:

- Digital television and HDTV (high-definition television) are both on the horizon. Depending on government action and industry standards agreements, both may be on the market before the arrival of the year 2000. That's the good news.

   The bad news is that early sets will be very expensive (thousands of dollars per unit), and early users will find relatively few channels broadcast in the new standard. And there are almost certain to be some bugs in the new system in early years.

   But here is some good news: Look for relatively inexpensive converter boxes that will allow today's analog televisions to display digital signals. The picture won't look much better than today's broadcasts, but you won't be frozen out of new sources of programming. And after a few years on the market, digital television sets are sure to come down in price to levels near current analog prices.

- Personal computers seem to improve in speed and capacity by the hour at the same time as actual or relative prices plummet.

   There are two factors to watch to help buying decisions.

First, keep an eye on major new technologies and consider buying one or two steps behind the state of the art. Buy whatever was the previous "must-have" computer and you'll be all but guaranteed an excellent machine at a suddenly reduced price.

Second, keep watch on the regular cycles of price reductions on microprocessors (most chip prices head in one direction only—down—after introduction). Intel Corp., the principal maker of microprocessors for Windows machines, usually adjusts its prices quarterly, and computer makers almost always follow suit with reductions of their own. You can learn about pricing changes on the wholesale and retail levels from industry publications as well as from general-interest business newspapers such as the *Wall Street Journal*.

Enlighten Yourself About Dark-Screen TVs

The latest and greatest technology for many television makers is the "dark" or "tinted" screen, a design that is supposed to produce improved color and better contrast and to reduce glare. You can spot a dark screen most easily when the TV is off; you'll see a black or near-black screen instead of the traditional light-gray color.

Most viewers prefer the quality of the dark screens. But there is a dark side to the dark screens: Some television designs lose picture brightness and detail, while other manufacturers make up for the dark screen by boosting the brightness of the electron tube to a level that can shorten the life of the tube.

You may be able to extend the life of the tube—on any set—by lowering room lighting and the brightness of the set. Some bells-and-whistles TVs have an electric eye that senses ambient lighting and adjusts the brightness accordingly.

You're not likely to have a lot of choice; untinted tubes are becoming increasingly difficult to find, and those that remain may be older designs or older units from the back of the warehouse. What you can do is insist on a good warranty and purchase your set from a dealer that will stand behind the products it sells.

Buy Big Screens for the Best Technology

The latest and greatest bells, whistles, and quality can be found in large-screen televisions: traditional tube sets, rear-projection units, and front-projection systems. The main reason for this is economic: There is more money to be made on larger units because buyers are less price sensitive. (A quick tour of an electronics store will show the great divide between 15- to 25-inch TVs that sell for about $200 to $400 and the big-screen territory of 27-inch to 50-inch units generally priced from about $800 to $2,000.)

Let me put that in a different way: If you want more bang for your bucks, go for a good value on a conventional set up to about 25 inches in diagonal measure. If you want the most bang for the most bucks, go for a large-screen set.

Here's what you can expect to get in a big-screen system: the latest technology in picture tubes, beefed-up power supplies, extra input and output jacks for home-theater setups, special features such as Picture-in-Picture to allow you to monitor two programs at once, and multifunction remote controls.

By the way, when you choose a big-screen TV be sure to take into account its physical size. Will it fit in your rec room or living room? Will it fit through the door? And remember that large sets can weigh several hundred pounds.

You'll also need to pay attention to the recommended viewing distance. Each set has an optimum distance for viewing; one rule of thumb is to plan on watching the set from a distance equal to twice the diagonal measure. For example, you'll want to be at least 100 inches away from a 50-inch screen.

Conventional television sets with a glass tube now max out at about 35 inches diagonal measure. To go larger, you'll have to buy a projection television set; they are available in rear- and front-projection designs.

Rear-projection units are usually self-contained large pieces of furniture. Early models were gargantuan, extending as much as four or five feet back from the screen; newer designs use wide-angle lenses and are shallower than some conventional televisions. These devices are usually very bright and can be seen from almost any angle in the room.

The largest projection systems send the image from the front, like a movie projector and screen. The projector can be suspended from a ceiling mount or placed on a table. Front-projection systems are generally not as bright as rear-projection devices and are subject to focus or distortion problems because of aging of the components, movement of the lenses or tubes, or shifts in the room itself.

Most projectors, of either design, use three super-bright tubes that send the red, green, and blue components of the image through a single lens to the screen; some early models were prone to distortion caused by one or more of the images moving out of perfect register with the others. Some new systems use a single tube or an LCD (liquid crystal display) tube.

You should also pay close attention to warranty and service offerings for projection sets that may require tune-ups or replacement of tubes from time to time.

Watch Out for Misleading Showroom Conditions

Before you buy a television—especially a projection system—view it in the showroom in a lighting setup similar to your home. If you expect to watch TV with lights on, or during the day with unshaded windows, replicate that situation in the store. If you have a media room that can be darkened, ask that the showroom lights be turned off to show off the television to its best advantage.

If you intend to use a videodisc player with your new TV, bring a favorite disc with you and ask to view it on screen; videodiscs offer a higher number of lines of information than does broadcast TV, and this is one way to put a set to the ultimate test.

Sometimes large electronics stores end up doing a poor job of presenting their own wares if they feed a wall full of television sets from a single cable-television or satellite signal. The signal may be much weaker than the one at your home. Then again, this may be a way to see how well a set works with a weakened signal.

Or, a store may boost the performance of its sets by feeding a high-resolution videodisc or satellite signal to its display units. That's a good way to show off sets at their absolute best performance, but it may be misleading when it comes to the signal you receive at home.

Ask the salesperson about the source of the signal and ask for alternative feeds if necessary.

Tune into a Deal on a Compact Disc Player

The quality of CD players has advanced to the point where nearly all consumer-level devices are capable of producing superb sound. Listen to the quality of output to see if there are any differences you can detect and then for units priced from about $100 to $250 make your decision on the basis of the sturdiness of construction, special features such as multidisc changers, and warranties.

For the true audiophile, someone who can claim to hear differences in sound that your pet Weimaraner would miss, there are some spectacular—and spectacularly priced—players. One spec we can all check out is oversampling, which is an electronic circuit that essentially checks and then rechecks digital information before converting it into a sound signal. The higher the oversampling rate the better; at least that's what our family dog tells me.

Here are some more tips on buying a CD player:

- Test out the mechanism, especially with multidisc models. If the floor model jams or chokes, stay away from that model. Look for solid construction, with metal or heavy-duty plastic rails and other moving parts.

  Turn off other music in the test area if you can and listen to the sounds of the changer mechanism and observe how quickly it moves from disc to disc. Some machines are very slow and noisy, drawing attention to themselves with gaps in music and annoying clunks and grinds.

  There are two common designs for machines that can store more than one disc: a fixed platter that rotates within the machine and a removable cartridge or magazine that, depending on the design, can hold from 5 to as many as 100 discs. The removable cartridge allows you to maintain collections of CDs ready to pop in and play, although you'll have to pay extra for additional cartridges. You may also be able to use the same magazine in a CD player in your car.

The platters allow you to make quicker changes—in some designs while the machine is playing another disc—but you'll have to move the discs in and out of their storage cases.

- Don't pay for features you won't be using. Useful features for casual users include a "random" button that lets you shuffle the order of tracks or discs. If you're really into controlling your musical environment, consider the ease of programming, which allows you to be your own disc jockey; for most of us, though, the most important buttons are play, pause, and manual selection from among multiple discs.

Shop the Used CD Bins

The advent of the compact disc has brought better sound and greatly extended life for music in your home. That's why you should consider shopping at stores that sell used CDs, usually for 50 percent of the original price or less.

Examine the CD to look for scratches or other marks and ask to try it out on a player at the store. Check to see if CDs are returnable if they turn out to be damaged when you get home.

And don't overlook selling off some of your less-favorite CDs if you've outgrown them; you may be able to trade several of them for one you prefer without having to lay out any cash.

I'd be a lot more wary of used cassettes or records, both of which are more susceptible to hidden damage and in any case have a more limited life.

Fast-Forward to a New VCR

The best prices on VCRs can often be found in the dead of winter, as dealers prepare for the arrival of new models in the spring. The pace of innovation in VCRs, though, has slowed in recent years as the device has become more of a commodity and less of a novelty. Look for sales at discount stores and national electronics retailers. Consumer-grade machines sell for as little as $150 to nearly $1,000.

Pay less attention to the brand name and remove from your consideration any fancy doodads that you don't need. For most of us the most important feature of a VCR is the quality of its recording and playback, followed by the relative ease of setup and recording. Some expensive models have instruction manuals that look like the technical guides for the space shuttle, while some inexpensive units are so simple that you don't need a 12-year-old to operate them. Guess which VCR will be more satisfying to use?

The most basic machines have just two "heads" for recording and playback. Better quality, especially at slower speeds and with special effects such as freeze frame and high- and slow-speed playback, will come with four-head machines.

Try out any VCR before you buy it. Ask the salesperson for a blank tape and make a short recording at each of the available speeds; then play the tape back using any special functions you're interested in, such as high-speed, half-speed, or still-frame playback. If you have a collection of tapes you've made on your previous machine or on a camcorder, bring one to the store and see how it looks. Does the new machine "track" the old tape properly? Is the sound clear?

VHS is the most commonly used format, although it has been surpassed in quality and convenience by other designs. If you rent movies from a video store or exchange tapes with someone else with a VCR of that design, you'll need a VHS format. An extension of the VHS format is HiFi, which vastly improves the quality of sound. A tape recorded on a standard VHS system will play on a HiFi VHS system, though with lower audio fidelity.

An improved version of VHS is called S-VHS, which delivers noticeably improved video quality; unfortunately, this standard has not been widely accepted and tapes recorded on an S-VHS machine cannot be played on a standard VHS device.

There are three compact cartridge formats that were developed for use in camcorders:

- VHS-C is a small version of the VHS cassette that yields the same quality as its full-size companion. The advantage of VHS-C is that its small cassettes can be taken out of the camcorder and installed in a special carrier that allows them to be played in a standard VHS machine.

- Tiny 8mm cartridges—about the size of a deck of cards—are capable of video and audio equal to that of a HiFi VHS system. You'll need an 8mm VCR or videotape player, or use your camcorder as the playback source to your TV.

- Hi8 is a very high-quality extension to the 8mm standard that uses a specially formulated (and more expensive) type of videotape to yield near-broadcast quality video. You must play a Hi8 cartridge in a Hi8 VCR or videotape player or use a Hi8 camcorder as a playback source; it will not work properly in a standard 8mm device.

   Hi8 camcorders can record and play back 400 lines of resolution, more than even the 330 lines of broadcast television and the 250 lines of VHS and standard 8mm. Hi8 is an especially good match if you own a television or monitor with an S-Video input, which can work with the finer image.

The latest and greatest is DVD, a fully digital recording standard that is being introduced in camcorder and home VCR units. DV camcorders go even further, capable of recording more than 500 lines of horizontal resolution. A digitally recorded tape can also be duplicated over and over without loss of quality. The quality is excellent, the special effects extremely clear, and the price (in its initial release) sky-high. Unless you have a professional need to use DVD, wait a year or two for prices to drop.

By all rights, the future should belong to Hi8 or the high-tech DVD standard, since both are notably improved over VHS. But the sheer size of the installed base of millions of VHS machines will make any changeover to a new standard a slow process, if it comes at all.

Go Slowly with TV-VCR Combinations

Buyer beware: You may be attracted to a new class of combination video devices, the TV with built-in VCR. This type of packaging offers some advantages, including ease of use, a compact "footprint" in your bedroom or den, and a good price.

On the downside, though, is one significant drawback: The life expectancy of a solid-state television is typically several years longer than a mixed electronic and mechanical device such as a VCR. If the VCR fails, you'll have to bring the entire unit in for servicing and you'll lose the use of both for a while.

You also lose flexibility in choosing the best or most appropriate monitor and VCR in separate modules. And the combo unit may lack some valuable features, including the ability to watch one program while taping another.

Hear the News About Cordless Telephones

Cordless telephones, once a luxury item, are now common, and entry-level units are priced not much higher than a decent desktop phone with a cord. But not all cordless phones are worth cutting the cord for. Here are some tips:

- The older, more limited technology uses radio frequencies from 46 to 49 MHz. You'll find the lower-priced models using this range; these devices generally have a shorter range and are more susceptible to static and interference than are newer phones.

- Current cordless models use the 900 MHz radio frequency and can transmit either analog or higher-quality digital signals. The best of these units add something called digital spread-spectrum electronics that improve reception to as much as three times the range of older models.

  All of the 900 MHz units, and especially those with digital-spread technology, are less liable to end up sharing a conversation with a neighbor; this is most important for apartment dwellers and urban residents.

- Look for cordless phones that are comfortable to use. Many of the original units were flat as a brick and about as heavy; they did not lend themselves to long use.

Avoid Radar-Detector Speed Traps

First of all, let's skip over the rather flimsy rationalizations for radar detectors, the claims that they are "safety devices" intended to help you drive carefully. We all know the truth: Their purpose is to help drivers avoid speed traps, and by inference, to drive faster than the speed limit when the police are not on patrol.

Personally, I'd rather see drivers obey the speed limit. It saves lives and it saves fuel.

If you insist on going forward, here are a few considerations:

- Radar detectors are illegal in some states. Some police radar systems are capable of detecting detectors; in response, some detector makers have responded by including circuitry that can warn you if a radar system is trying to detect your detector. In any case, in some states you can be cited if a trooper spots one on your dashboard, turned on or not.

- The latest advances include remote units that place the detector in the front grill or rear of the car and the display electronics on your dashboard; this is supposed to be more sensitive than one-piece units. A drawback is that this type of device cannot be moved to another car easily. You can also find units that claim to be able to detect signals from in front of you (a stationary speed trap) as well as from behind (a police vehicle coming up from your rear).

4 Save on Clothing Purchases

Dressing well does not necessarily mean dressing extravagantly. If you've got unlimited funds and want to spend them on real gold threads in a diamond-encrusted cocktail dress ("What? This old thing?") go right ahead.

But most readers of this book would get more of a thrill out of paying a whole lot less for something that makes you look like a million.

Here are some high-tone haberdashery and haute couture hints:

✓ Learn the secrets of women's clothing.

✓ Keep your head warm at the millinery.

✓ Shop for haute couture hand-me-downs.

✓ Restyle your furs.

✓ Rent a display of elegance.

✓ Start your marriage out well with a discount on the wedding dress.

Learn the Secrets of Women's Clothing

One of the great mysteries of the ages is why a woman's jacket, typically made with flimsy stitching and light lining, can sell for so much more than a man's jacket with more material, better craftsmanship, and an overall higher level of quality. It has something to do with "fashion," but that does not deter many savvy women from shopping in the men's aisle or catalogs.

Here is a conversion chart that equates women's sizes to men's clothing:

Men's size	XS	S	M	L	XL
Women's size		S	M	L	XL
Women's dress size		6–8	10–12	14–16	
Waist size		26–28	29–31	32–34	36–38

Keep Your Head Warm at the Millinery

Once again, for most of us, you're not likely to find men wearing women's hats, but going the other direction many women top off their outfits with a man's fedora or other headgear.

Here is a chart that compares the three measures of hat sizes: size name, head size, and hat size.

Size	S	S	M	M	L	L	XL
Head size	$21 \, ^1/_8$	$21 \, ^1/_2$	$21 \, ^7/_8$	$22 \, ^1/_4$	$22 \, ^5/_8$	23	$23 \, ^1/_2$
Hat size	$6 \, ^3/_4$	$6 \, ^7/_8$	7	$7 \, ^1/_8$	$7 \, ^1/_4$	$7 \, ^3/_8$	$7 \, ^1/_2$

Shop for Haute Couture Hand-Me-Downs

Does anyone really have to know that your gorgeous wedding gown, fur coat, or jewelry was purchased secondhand?

Wedding gowns are expensive clothing that are usually worn just once . . . and carefully. Fur coats are usually very sturdy, and styles tend to change rather infrequently. And, as it has been observed, diamonds are forever.

Look for outposts of a growing market: Retail stores that sell high-quality secondhand clothing. Know your prices before you go into the store. If you're shopping for an expensive fur or jewelry, ask about obtaining an independent appraisal of the item.

One other place to shop: pawnbrokers. Here you need an especially fine eye to pick the wheat from the chaff. And again, don't trust the seller's appraisal; obtain your own for any expensive purchase.

Restyle Your Furs

If you own a fur coat in a style that time has passed by, consult a furrier about having it restyled. You'll be able to reuse the expensive pelts, and the cost of a modernized coat should be less than half the price of a completely new one.

Rent a Display of Elegance

Who says you have to buy a fabulous gown for a formal occasion, or a spectacular dress for your wedding? Look into renting a top-of-the-line outfit. Ask at bridal shops, and check the Yellow Pages in most major cities for more listings. It may be worth a trip for measurements and alterations to save hundreds or thousands on clothing you will wear only once.

If you are concerned about the possibility of the same gown appearing twice at an event, ask the renter. Chances are he or she stocks only one of each outfit; there is nothing you can do about someone choosing the same outfit from another source, but you would run the same risk if you were buying the clothing from a retail store.

Start Your Marriage Out Well with a Discount on the Wedding Dress

If you find the wedding dress of your dreams in a retail store, here are some ways you can bring the price down to earth:

- *Shop around.* Write down the dressmaker, model or name, and any other details such as color, special beading, or accessories. Then call other shops with that information and ask their price.

Don't be afraid to call long distance, either. If you could save $500 by buying from a store a few hours away, it should be worth one trip for a fitting and a second to pick it up.

And let the original store know you are shopping around. The price may magically melt down to a more reasonable level.

- *Buy wholesale.* Consider calling one of several national companies that sell bridal wear by mail order. You'll need to hire your own seamstress for alterations, although the company may be able to refer you to a local seamstress.

  One such company is Discount Bridal Service, at (800) 441-0102.

5 Eating with the Best of Them

We've all got to eat. You might as well do it well.

In this chapter we reveal some of the inside secrets of the supermarket as well as give a guided tour of food labels and nutrition claims.

✓ Make the most of sales.

✓ Watch out for hidden price hikes.

✓ Watch out for bad bargains on big packages.

✓ Collect rain checks for sold-out items.

✓ Read something interesting with dinner: decoding nutrition labels.

✓ Learn the true meaning of food-marketing terms.

✓ Help! Send out an SOS to food experts.

✓ Know how to save on a cuppa.

✓ Be a smart egg at the dairy counter.

Make the Most of Sales

In my family, we can go through four or five boxes of breakfast cereal per week. And in case you hadn't noticed, those boxes of wheat, oats, corn, and sugar have crested $4 in many stores. The kids, alas, also drink a lot of soda, and we like a certain brand of frozen noodle dish.

And so we keep a close eye on supermarket flyers for sales and when we find one we go out and pick up a "few"—as in a few cases of 24 boxes of cereal, a half-dozen flats of 24 soda cans each, and a whole bunch of frozen noodles.

We keep a large chest freezer in the basement to hold turkeys purchased at Thanksgiving and served at Eastertime, fresh-frozen fish, and a basket full of English muffins purchased on sale months ago and frozen rock solid while waiting their reawakening in the microwave oven.

Here are some hints on making the most of sales:

- *Read the fine print carefully*. Find out when the sale begins, and get there early. Most supermarkets run their sales from Sunday to Saturday, or Saturday to Friday.

    See if there are any limits on quantity, and be sure to exercise your rights to the full. Take advantage of any rain checks offered if the store doesn't receive the special item or if someone else has cleaned them out. (Ask if the store expects to be restocked with the item during the course of the sale.)

- *Don't buy more than you can use before it goes bad*.

- *Test out a small quantity of a new product* before filling your closet with it.

- *Properly store nonperishable items* such as paper goods, cleaning supplies, canned goods, bottled goods, and the like. Avoid damp places such as the basement and under the sink or hot spots such as the attic for most items. Make use of the backs of closets throughout the house.

    Canned goods are generally good for one to two years, although you can't know how long they have sat on the grocery shelves or in a warehouse before then; look for expiration dates and buy the youngest cans you can find. The best place to store cans is in a relatively cool, dry place, such as in closets; keep them away from heaters, stoves, and other warm spots.

    With frozen food, consult cookbooks or your local health department if you have any questions about shelf life. Again, it's hard to know how long a frozen product has been on the shelves; the expiration or "use by" date is an important source of information.

    Meat can be expected to keep for 6 to 12 months at zero degrees; ground beef and processed food should be kept for less than 6 months. Fish can be kept for 6 to 9 months. Vegetables can keep for as long as a year without a problem.

- *Experiment with store brands*. Almost always considerably less expensive than name brands, they are often manufactured by the big-name companies. Check ingredients and the FDA nutrition labels for clues on identical products.
- *Buy larger packages*. In most, but not all, cases larger cans or bottles cost less per ounce than smaller portions. Do the math or consult shelf labels that may tell you the unit price. Watch out, though, for sales or special promotions that can sometimes make it cheaper to buy smaller packages.

Watch Out for Hidden Price Hikes

Pay attention at the supermarket to quantities and weights in packaged food. One sneaky way to increase the price of a product is to reduce the quantity or weight; a 24-ounce can of beans selling for 89 cents could become a 23-ounce can with the same price, hiding a 4 percent boost in cost per ounce.

Another way to do the same thing is to reduce the quantity—35 ribbons in a package instead of 36 for the same price.

And some manufacturers have found ways to reduce the quantity or weight of a product without changing the size of the packaging.

The only protection against this particular form of pocket-picking is to pay close attention to prices. Be on the lookout for unusual weights or quantities, and be sure to compare the per-unit price of a product with its competitors.

Watch Out for Bad Bargains on Big Packages

The natural assumption is that a larger package of a commodity costs less per unit of measure than a smaller one. That's not always the case.

Sometimes a product will be introduced in a new size based on a higher price than the same product in an older, smaller-quantity version already on the shelf.

Always compare prices on a per-pound, fluid ounce, or per-unit basis. And don't automatically trust the calculations you may find on the shelf tag: Price changes may not be reflected, and on more occasions than I can remember I have found dumb errors—such as comparing fluid ounces (32 to the quart) to avoirdupois ounces (16 to the pound) for the same item.

Collect Rain Checks for Sold-Out Items

Super-duper Sugar-frosted Oatios with Walnut Clusters, $1.29 for a four-pound megabox. It's an offer to make the shopper's heart race, but, oh, the disappointment when you arrive to find a "sold out" sign on the empty shelf.

Here's the scoop: Under the unavailability rule that is part of the FTC's Retail Food Store Advertising and Marketing Practices Rule, grocers must offer rain checks to consumers if they run out of advertised items. The loophole in the rule, though, is that if the ad clearly states that "quantities are limited" or advises that products are available only at some stores, no rain check is required.

Without the advisory, a store must offer a rain check that allows customers to buy the item later at the lower price, a substitute item of comparable value to the sale item, or some other kind of compensation that is at least equal in value to the advertised item.

Read Something Interesting with Dinner: Decoding Nutrition Labels

In my opinion, one of the best things our Washington bureaucrats have provided for the national defense is the Nutrition Facts label on food. It is also, potentially, one of the most misleading and misunderstood indicators in our consumer society.

Here's an example: I love peanut butter. I also try to manage my cholesterol level and weight by keeping down my fat and caloric intake. The Nutrition Facts for one of the major peanut-butter brands includes the following:

Calories	190
Calories from Fat	140
Total Fat	16g 25% Daily Value
Saturated Fat	3.5g 17% Daily Value

That doesn't sound too bad for one meal . . . but what exactly are they measuring? Perhaps the most important set of numbers on the label—the ones that put all the others in proper context—are the Serving Size and Servings per Container.

In the instance of the peanut butter, the listed serving is two table-spoons. Alas, if I were going to splurge on peanut butter, I'd probably not be willing to stop at just two tablespoons of the stuff. Be sure you examine closely the portion size and see how it relates to your real intake of the product.

Here's another nutty example: M&Ms with peanuts are listed at 220 calories, 17 percent of total fat, and 22 percent of saturated fat for a serving size of a quarter of a cup. I measured it: That's about 14 pieces of candy. I don't know about you, but my hand would still be heading back for the candy dish after that small amount.

That's why I stay away from peanut butter and M&Ms with peanuts, along with bacon, chocolate-covered shredded coconut, and premium ice cream. A small portion of these favorite but fat-filled foods doesn't seem worth the penalty; I'd rather substitute low-fat or fat-free alternatives.

In a nutshell (sorry): Think about the quantity of food you eat and where a particular product fits in that amount. You'll want to reduce the amount of fat you eat as much as is reasonably possible, and in any case keep fat below 30 percent of your total daily caloric intake. And don't forget that even a fat-free food can still be high in calories.

Learn the True Meaning of Food-Marketing Terms

Free! Light! Reduced! Low fat! Suddenly, less is more in food market-ing as most of us try to reduce our weight or maintain our health through careful eating.

The federal Food and Drug Administration, which sets the standards for the Nutrition Facts tag on packaged foods, has assigned a set of quantities to qualitative labels. Here are some of the terms, as they apply to the specified serving size:

CALORIES

Calorie-free	Less than 5 calories per serving
Low-calorie	Less than 40 calories per serving

FAT

Fat-free	Less than 0.5 gram per serving
Saturated fat-free	Less than 0.5 gram per serving
Low-fat	Less than 3 grams per serving
Low saturated fat	Less than 1 gram per serving

CHOLESTEROL

Cholesterol-free	Less than 2 mg per serving
Low cholesterol	Less than 20 mg per serving

SODIUM

Sodium-free	Less than 5 mg per serving
Very-low sodium	Less than 35 mg per serving
Low-sodium	Less than 140 mg per serving

LIGHT/LITE AND REDUCED

To bear a "light" or "lite" label, foods must consist of at least one-third fewer calories or 50 percent or less of the fat of a "regular" version of the same food.

A label of "reduced" means that the product has at least 25 percent less fat, calories, or other component of the regular version of the food.

Help! Send Out an SOS to Food Experts

Butterball Turkey Talk-Line. Free advice on preparing, cooking, and carving your bird for the holidays. The phone is answered in November and December only. Call (800) 323-4848. You can also reach the turkey information line all year-round at their Web page at:

http://www.butterball.com

Land O'Lakes Holiday Bakeline. Advice on baking for the holidays, from November 1 to Christmas Eve. Call (800) 782-9606.

USDA Meat and Poultry Line. Recorded information on safe food handling and labeling. During the Thanksgiving and Christmas holiday season, you can talk with a human being during business hours at (800) 535-4555.

Know How to Save on a Cuppa

They grow an awful lot of coffee in Brazil . . . and Africa and other hot climes. And we drink an awful lot of the stuff over here. That's why a bad growing season in the fields can have a fairly significant effect at Starbuck's or your neighborhood supermarket.

Here are some ways to save on your coffee jag:

- *Buy in quantity.* When you see a good price, or your local store offers a sale, stock up. Unopened cans or vacuum-packed plastic or foil bricks of ground coffee should keep for at least two years, while bags of beans can be stored in a freezer to extend their lives to as much as six months.

- *Buy larger packages.* Spend your money on the coffee and not on the can or sack that holds it.

Be frugal in your use. If you don't like to reheat leftover coffee, use a thermos bottle. You can experiment with reusing coffee grounds by mixing them half and half with fresh grounds.

Be a Smart Egg at the Dairy Counter

What's the difference between large, extra-large, and jumbo eggs? About 10 percent in size from one to the other, according to industry grading practice. Therefore, for example, if extra-large eggs are more than 10 percent higher in price than large eggs, your store is offering you a bad deal.

6 Playing the Hobby and Recreation Game Well

One wag's definition of a boat is this: a hole in the water into which you pour money. It is also true that ski enthusiasts often try to avoid calculating the per-hour cost of their skis, boots, bindings, winter clothing, and travel. And have you thought about the difference between a Pebble Beach pro shop Top-Flite Tour SD and a K-mart Top-Flite Tour SD?

In this chapter, we unveil some hints to save money on sports and hobbies.

- ✓ Owe, owe, owe your boat: the true cost of ownership.
- ✓ Put an umbrella over your marine insurance policy.
- ✓ Understand tennis-ball ratings.
- ✓ Buy skis when the grass is green.
- ✓ Pay less for golf equipment.
- ✓ Save money on greens fees.
- ✓ Get the best service or prices or both on books.
- ✓ Snap up a bargain on film.
- ✓ Replace your lost marbles.
- ✓ Save money on computer and video games.
- ✓ Pay less for magazine subscriptions.
- ✓ Know your rights in "of-the-month" clubs.

Owe, Owe, Owe Your Boat: The True Cost of Ownership

There are many pleasures associated with owning a boat, but you should proceed with caution when making a purchase.

The best advice is to employ a professional marine inspector before you buy a used boat of any substantial cost and seek whatever warranty you can possibly obtain from the seller.

A new boat can be just as problematic: Just as important as picking out a worthy boat is selecting a trustworthy dealer who will stand behind the sale.

As with the purchase of a car, consider the effects of depreciation on the value of a boat. Except for the most pricey custom-built yachts and well-maintained classic boats, the value of a boat is certain to decline over time.

Now you may or may not want to know the answer to this question: How much is it going to cost you to fulfill your dream? Start with the cost of the boat and then obtain an estimate of its resale value after a year. (You may also want to do the same exercise for a three-year period, which will temper—somewhat—the cost of depreciation.) Subtract the resale value from the cost of the boat to yield the depreciation on your investment. Then fill in the blanks in this formula:

Taxes on purchase	_____
Property or excise taxes	_____
Interest on loan for purchase	_____
Loss of income on cash paid	_____
Depreciation	_____
Loss and liability insurance	_____
Dock charges	_____
Winter storage charges	_____
Fuel	_____
Boat and trailer license fees	_____
Estimated maintenance	_____
Total cost of ownership:	_____

Divide the cost of ownership by a realistic estimate of the number of days you expect to be out on the water.

Then sit down until the shock wears off. Depending on how often you use the boat, the cost per use can be astronomic. If you live in a warmer climate, you're likely to get a lot more use out of the boat than those who can count on only a few summer months.

If this makes you want to consider renting a boat on a daily or seasonal basis, go right ahead: That may make a lot more sense than owning that hole in the water.

Put an Umbrella over Your Marine Insurance Policy

Basic marine insurance coverage includes physical damage to your boat, bodily injury and property damage liability, and medical payments. You may also want to consider optional coverage for personal effects, emergency service, and trailers.

Consult your insurance agent for advice on purchasing an umbrella policy to expand your liability coverage at relatively low cost.

Understand Tennis-Ball Ratings

Heavy-duty: made with nylon for longer life on hard-surface courts. Not intended for use on clay courts where they will pick up dirt and slow down.

Regular: a softer surface for use on clay courts or, in a pinch, on hard-surface courts.

Buy Skis When the Grass Is Green

Buy last year's leftovers at the end of the season or at a preseason sale in early fall. The worst possible time to buy is during the Christmas season and in the heart of the ski season.

Pay Less for Golf Equipment

A Titleist golf ball is the same whether you pay full list price at the pro shop or pick a pack off the shelf at Wal-Mart or order a box from a mail-order house. The same goes for golf clothing, accessories, and in some instances even clubs: If you know what you want, these are commodities that you can buy based on price.

The one possible exception is a set of clubs. If you don't know much about equipment, it may be worthwhile to buy from a store where you can receive the expertise of a knowledgeable salesperson. If you are looking to buy an additional iron or a new putter for an existing set, you might as well place an order through a discount seller.

Be sure to investigate the warranty and repair policies of any seller; don't assume that the best service is offered by the source with the highest price.

Another way to save big bucks on equipment, especially for beginners, is to buy used equipment until you are sure of your interest in the sport and know your capabilities. Look for clubs at tag sales or in classified-ad listings. Check with local pro shops and retail stores to see if they have formerly used demo or rental sets available for sale.

In recent years we have also seen the growth of stores that specialize in buying and reselling last year's clubs, outgrown boots and skis, and all of that other stuff that clutters our basements.

And about those golf balls: Have you ever wondered how many perfectly good balls sit at the bottom of the pond off the twelfth fairway? A good many of them are now being harvested, cleaned up, and resold as driving range or practice balls; if they are uncut, go ahead and add them to your bag and spend the difference at the nineteenth hole.

Another way to save on golf balls is to purchase X-outs, which are new balls marked with an X or other symbol through the brand name to indicate a defect. In theory, an X-out ball is sold at a discount because of cosmetic flaws such as misprinted labels, off colors, or mottled covers. These are fine; what you have to worry about, though, are balls that have been rejected because of imperfect construction. Problems could include an off-center weighting or a damaged cover.

Save Money on Greens Fees

The best way to save money (and time) is to go golfing when the other players are doing something else. Check with courses for off-peak times and off-peak seasons. At many courses, the best prices are offered in the early spring and late fall when the less-than-obsessed golfer is finding other things to do.

Get the Best Service or Prices or Both on Books

I love a good book, and I appreciate anyone who helps me find a useful or entertaining or thought-provoking or beautiful addition to my collection. And as the author of this particular book, it should also be obvious that I like to buy fine things at reduced prices.

Books are mostly sold at the list price printed on their covers by the publisher, although some stores are willing or able to discount the price. Other shops try to enhance their appeal by offering special services to shoppers.

That's why I am a fan of two types of bookstores:

- First, I love a shop where the owner or the staff knows every title on the shelves and is willing to help you find a perfect match. You'll probably pay list price, but do so only if the service you receive has some value. You're also able to walk out with your purchase immediately, if it is in stock.

- My other new favorite way to shop is by telephone or over the Internet at one of several discount warehouse operations. The best of these offer you a form of automated handholding, with a computerized database you can search by subject, title, or author, plus descriptions and comments on many titles.

  The originator of these services is Amazon (**http://www.amazon.com**), which typically offers discounts of 20 to 40 percent off list price. Even when you include shipping costs, you'll receive a better price than list.

  A competitor is the online service of the huge Barnes & Noble bookselling chain (**http://www.barnesandnoble.com**) with similar discounts.

Snap Up a Bargain on Film

Photographic film is a fragile, perishable, and expensive commodity that most everyone uses and about which very few of us give much thought. Here are some savvy tips for film buyers:

- Don't buy more film than you need. If you plan on taking 12 pictures at a birthday party and want to have the film processed immediately, don't buy a 24- or 36-exposure roll. On the other hand, if you are heading out on a vacation where you expect to take a lot of pictures, stock up on 36-exposure rolls, which are cheaper per frame than shorter cartridges.

- Don't buy more speed than you need. Film speed, measured in ISO or ASA ratings, is an indication of how much light the film requires for exposure. A "fast" film will work in lower light situations, while a "slow" film will be perfectly fine for pictures at the beach. Faster film costs more than slower film, and speed usually reduces the quality of the image somewhat. A film rated at 400 or higher is considered fast; 100 or less is slow, while 200 is a good compromise for most situations.

- Compare the prices of store-brand film to name brands. The dark secret is that most no-name film is made by a major manufacturer anyway, typically a Japanese or European maker. Be sure to check the expiration date on the film and use your good judgment: If the store looks as if it sells merchandise that fell off the back of a truck, take your business elsewhere. The moments of time captured on a piece of film can never be brought back.

    Here's some inside information: The biggest makers of private-label films are Germany's Agfa, Japan's Konica, and an American maker called Imation Corp., a supplier of imaging products. In 1997, megamanufacturer Eastman Kodak began test-marketing its own private-label film under the Colorburst label. If the box says "Made in Germany" there's a good chance it contains Agfa film; "Made in Japan" often means Konica product.

- Purchase in bulk. Packs of three or four rolls are usually cheaper than single rolls. If you are a heavy user of film, consider buying "blocks" of 20 rolls from a photo supplier. Be sure you have sufficient time before the expiration date.

- Bring your own film with you on vacation trips. Prices at vacation spots and in foreign countries are often much higher than you would pay at home, and you can also avoid film subjected to poor storage conditions, including extreme heat.

- You can extend the life of unused film and protect it from damage by storing it in your refrigerator or (even better) your freezer. Be sure that the rolls are sealed in a moisture-proof bag and allow the film to come to room temperature before using it in a camera.

- Never store film in a hot place, such as the glove compartment or trunk of your car. Heat will damage undeveloped film and can even affect images already recorded on it.

- Some frugal photographers save money by buying recently expired film. The truth is that there is still a fair amount of life left in film that has passed its official peak, but this is one money-saving tip I don't recommend. Most photographs capture once-in-a-lifetime moments, and I'd rather not take chances on film.

  If you're going to take this route, you're safer with outdated black-and-white film; color film loses its fidelity and sensitivity a bit faster and is more susceptible to damage from extremes of temperature.

Replace Your Lost Marbles

Are you missing Mr. Mustard from Clue? Has the cat run off with the top hat from Monopoly? Have you lost all of the "E" tiles from Scrabble?

Don't buy a new set if you don't have to. Most of the major American gamemakers offer replacement parts at reasonable rates; sometimes they'll even rescue your game for free. Check the packages for a customer service number. Here are a few to try:

Hasbro   (800) 242-7276

Mattel   (800) 524-8697

Milton Bradley   (413) 525-6411

Parker Bros.   (508) 927-7600

Save Money on Computer and Video Games

Perhaps the only thing more galling than paying $60 for the latest silly video game from Japan is the fact that it will likely have a useful life of perhaps 10 days. Not that the game itself will stop working; it's just that 10 days is a long time in the life of a kid in the Nintendo age.

Here are a few ways to recover at least some of the money you put into those little plastic boxes or discs:

- Sell or trade used games to other players through an ad at the supermarket bulletin board or at school. A fair price for a current game is about half the retail price. Older games may be worth $10 or less.

- Sell used games to a video-game store or game-rental store. Some stores will pay cash for used games, while others will issue credits to be used to purchase other new or used games at the store. Many stores will deduct a large penalty if you don't supply the instruction manual with the game.

You can also buy used games from the same sources. If you can't locate a store in your area, consult the ads in the back pages of the national magazines devoted to video games.

Video-game cartridges are pretty sturdy devices with no moving parts. They basically work or they don't work. Even more reliable are CD-ROM discs. You should try out any used game at the store, or obtain a money-back guarantee if it doesn't work.

You can also purchase used CD-ROM games for personal computers. Be sure that all discs and supplementary materials are in the box.

Pay Less for Magazine Subscriptions

Are you amazed at the variety of magazines in your dentist's waiting room? Don't be too impressed; he or she may be getting them wholesale. Then again, so can you.

Here are two companies that offer deeply discounted subscriptions to most of the major magazines. You'll have to pay in advance, and some publishers require that subscriptions be sent to a business address; you've got a spare business card, don't you?

Delta Publishing. (800) 736-3547

Below Wholesale Magazines (800) 800-0062

Know Your Rights in "of-the-Month" Clubs

There are dozens of "clubs" that sell books, CDs, videos, and just about anything else you can imagine in automatic monthly shipments; in the trade they're called "negative option plans."

Here's how they work: each month (or more frequently) you'll receive an offering in the mail with an item for sale. That product will be shipped to you if you don't respond within a specified period, usually ten days; you can return the notification form before that deadline to cancel the shipment or order a different product.

Typically, these clubs offer a special come-on for new participants. For example, you may be offered 12 free CDs to join.

First, I'll discuss how to analyze just how good a deal you're being offered. Then we'll explore your rights as a club member.

Here's an example pulled from a current magazine. The headline reads "11 CDs for 1 cent." In small print, it says "See details." A page later the details disclose: "Start off with any 11 CDs for a penny plus $1.49 enrollment charge (shipping and handling additional). All you need to do is buy as few as 6 at regular club prices within the next three years."

Read on in the fine print to learn that regular club prices are currently $12.98 to $16.98 for CDs. The offer does not disclose the shipping and handling fees, but in my experience they are typically about $2.50 per CD.

That offer of 11 for a penny sounds great, but here's what you are actually promising to pay:

11 "free"	$ 0.01
Enrollment fee	$ 1.49
Shipping 11 CDs	$ 27.50
Purchase 6 CDs at $15.98	$ 95.88
Shipping 6 CDs	$ 15.00
TOTAL:	$139.88

Your actual cost per CD under this plan works out to about $8.23, which is not a bad price but not exactly free. To get the best deal, you should look for a deal that offers the most "free" items and the fewest required purchases. And you should pay attention to the regular price for the items you are required to buy.

Be aware that the club can raise rates for purchases after you join and can apply shipping and handling charges that can ruin the value of the deal.

In the worst cases, a negative option club can work out to be more expensive than buying through a discount store.

Here are your rights as a consumer, as defined by FTC regulations.

Once you have satisfied the club's minimum-purchase require-ments, you can cancel your club membership; the seller must cancel your membership promptly after receipt of your written request.

You must have at least ten days to return a negative-option form asking that an item not be sent, and the shipper must guarantee free return postage and full credit for any item sent to you without your permission. Most clubs are liberal in their return policies beyond the ten-day period, although they may require that the item not be used while it is in your possession.

If you have fulfilled your obligations and have canceled your membership, you are required only to return (at the shipper's expense) the first selection that may be sent after the seller receives your written cancellation notice. If the club sends additional selections, you may consider them unordered merchandise and keep them as a gift; if you want to avoid dunning notices, send the seller a copy of your letter can-celing the membership.

No Hangups on Telephone Service, Junk Mail, and Shipping Services

Things used to be so much simpler: There was only one telephone company, and you had the choice of paying its (high) rates for local and long-distance calls and rent its equipment . . . or you could do without a telephone.

Today, hardly anyone does without a telephone and every savvy consumer knows that there are dozens of long-distance carriers vying for their business and that in some cities there is beginning to be competition for local phone service from cable-television companies and other utilities. And that renting a telephone is strictly optional and usually a bad deal.

In this chapter we explore money-saving telephone deals, and then I show you some of your rights as a telephone and postal-service customer.

SHOPPING FOR TELEPHONE SERVICE

✓ Shop around for the best long-distance carrier.

✓ Mix and match to get the best rates.

✓ Pay attention to fractions of a minute on phone bills.

✓ Learn how to compare phone services.

✓ Take full advantage of special offers.

✓ Regard long-term commitments warily.

✓ Ask for a better deal.

✓ Understand your local telephone services.

✓ Install a long-distance safety net for critical business.

✓ Understand the pros and cons of prepaid phone cards.

✓ Cut the rental cord with your phone company.

✓ Control phone-installation costs.

✓ Order telephone equipment by phone.

✓ Make the most of phone-company maintenance plans.

YOUR RIGHTS AS A TELEPHONE AND POSTAL CONSUMER

✓ Slam-proof your phone service.

✓ Hang up on telephone solicitation.

✓ Make the most of overnight delivery services.

✓ And while we're at it, cut down on unsolicited junk mail.

✓ Remove your name from a specific company's list.

✓ Block sexually explicit mail.

Shopping for Telephone Service

Shop Around for the Best Long-Distance Carrier

The first question any telephone customer should ask is, "Who is my long-distance carrier?"

When deregulation came to the phone industry in the 1980s, customers were given the option of signing up with the carrier of their choice. Those who did not select a carrier were often assigned to one through a random lottery.

It's your money: Put your long-distance account out to bid. Even if you save only $10 a month, that will pay a good part of your local bill by itself.

Call the major carriers: AT&T, Sprint, MCI, and others. Tell them where you call most often and the times of day you make the calls. Ask for a recommendation of the best plan from that carrier based on your usage pattern and an estimate of your monthly bill under the plan.

Use the same numbers and times with several carriers so that you can compare plans.

There are several online services that may help you select a carrier. One is called Teleworth, at **http://www.teleworth.com**. Teleworth allows you to enter a typical phone bill into a form and it comes up with a menu of plans from long-distance carriers that should save you money; be sure to check with other carriers independently as well.

Here's what the experts say about telephone service: All of the major long-distance carriers offer comparable discount plans. And, despite all sorts of "pin-dropping" claims, the quality of connections is usually also comparable. The savvy consumer will instead concentrate on special offers: If you make a lot of weekend calls, or call late at night, look for plans with deep discounts at those times. If you dial international points often, seek a plan with good rates to the particular country or countries you call.

Mix and Match to Get the Best Rates

You can align only one long-distance carrier with a particular telephone number for direct-dial service—calls that go through after dialing 1 as a prefix to the area code.

There are, however, many other services that allow you to use their lines by dialing an access code. For example, you can dial 10333 before an area code to reach the Sprint service.

Here's how to use these carriers to your best advantage. Let's say Sprint, your primary carrier, offers 10-cents-a-minute calling nights and weekends but hits you for 22 cents per minute for calls made during business hours of 9 A.M. to 5 P.M. Then, in addition to Sprint, you can also use a discount reseller that offers round-the-clock dialing at 14 cents per minute.

In this situation, use Sprint for nights and weekends and dial the access code to the discount service for weekday service. You can add the access code to the preprogrammed buttons on most telephones to simplify the process.

Pay Attention to Fractions of a Minute on Phone Bills

One important distinction among long-distance phone carriers is whether they use full-minute billing or set their bills on the basis of shorter time increments.

Here's an example: Company A promotes a special deal of 15 cents per minute, any time of the day. But they bill on a full-minute basis.

Company B sells time at 20 cents per minute, with 6-second billing.

If you make a phone call of one minute and ten seconds, Company A will charge you 30 cents (two minutes) while Company B will charge 24 cents (one full minute and two six-second periods).

Those pennies can quickly add up into dollars. Ask your carrier about billing calculations when you sign up for a service or make any changes.

Learn How to Compare Phone Services

Comparing long-distance telephone carriers can be a complicated process. There are dozens of different plans, rates, and combinations of special services. Here are a few points of comparison:

- *Price*. It doesn't much matter what a long-distance telephone carrier's best rates are if they don't match your pattern of use. For example, a 10-cent-per-minute rate at night and on weekends does not work well with a business operation. Similarly, a great rate that is based on an unrealistic monthly average use or that requires payment of a high monthly fee may not be a good deal. Your search for a phone carrier should begin with a careful review of your present usage patterns. Some long-distance carriers may work with you to analyze your phone bills to select the best plan.

- *Quality of service*. The first issue involves the quality of the telephone connection itself; today, most of the major companies provide good connections, and many of the smaller companies are actually reselling time on the facilities of the majors. However, you may find some differences in your local area. Ask friends and other businesses in your area about their experiences. You can also try out most long-distance carriers by dialing their access code; ask the carrier for instructions.

Next, consider the quality of customer and technical support. Were you able to get your questions answered and place your order for service easily, or did you end up at the end of an hour-long line? Remember my basic rule about business: If they don't treat you well before they have your money, why do you think they will be more accommodating once the check is in their hands?

Take Full Advantage of Special Offers

Once you've accepted a long-distance phone company's come-on, do what you can to maximize the value you receive.

If the deal offers a significant break for calls made outside ordinary business hours, take advantage of time zone differences to schedule your calls. For example, if you live on the East Coast, pick up the phone after 5 P.M. to call the West Coast where afternoon is still in full swing; if you live on the West Coast, get up a bit early to call the East Coast.

My telephone carrier offers "Fridays free," something I happily take advantage of: I schedule telephone research for Friday, putting on extra staffers for that day to work the phones.

Regard Long-Term Commitments Warily

Be cautious if a long-distance telephone company tries to get you to sign up for a multiyear commitment at a particular service level.

First, no matter how good the deal appears to be, in today's highly competitive telecommunications market the only direction rates have been going is down.

Second, it is difficult to predict your future telephone usage patterns, and you don't want to become locked into a plan with a service charge or a minimum billing level.

That said, if you find a deal you consider extraordinary and specific to your needs, ignore the aforementioned advice and lock it in. An example: Sprint offered a "Fridays free" promotion in recent years that had special appeal for some businesses that were able to schedule telephone and fax campaigns for that day of the week. I use that feature in my business: I have two part-timers who work all day Fridays doing telephone research. The works needs to be done anyway, and I might as well schedule it to take advantage of Sprint's offer.

Ask for a Better Deal

Sprint became semifamous with its "dime-a-minute" long-distance deal. (Never mind that the offer was somewhat limited, with calls at that rate offered only at night and early morning or on the weekend. It was still a good deal for some callers.)

The dark secret of telephone service, as the *Wall Street Journal* found in a survey, was that long-distance carriers are willing to cut you a deal matching or even beating a competitor's rates. All you have to do is ask.

Why would AT&T, for example, advertise one rate but offer you a better one if you call them? The answer is that in this highly competitive world, most companies would rather have all of your business at cut-rate than none of your business at higher charges.

Call the customer-service department of your carrier if you see a better deal from another company, or even from your own carrier. Be sure to include any monthly service charges in your comparison of one company's rates to another's; better yet, ask the carrier to waive the monthly charge. You may be surprised at the answer you receive.

If your carrier refuses to make a deal, go ahead and change carriers for a better offer. Your local phone company may slap a $5 or $10 charge for administrative work on your records; go ahead and ask your new carrier to give you credit for that charge.

Understand Your Local Telephone Services

The most expensive domestic phone calls most of us make are those from our home or office to another part of the state. It can be especially galling if you live near a town in another area code, or one that the local phone company considers to be outside your LATA (Local Access and Transport Area). In most cases, these are calls that require you to enter 1 + area code, even if the area code is the same as your own.

Typical intra-LATA charges are 25 to 40 cents per minute, while any decent long-distance telephone plan should be in the range of 10 to 20 cents per minute.

Obviously it doesn't make a lot of sense when you compare the cost of calling a few miles or a few dozen miles to a much lower rate for dialing across the country. The local phone companies claim that they need higher charges because they must pay for all the local infrastructure, but you contribute to that as part of your lower long-distance calling, too.

Here are two ways to reduce the expense of calls made within your home state:

- Ask your phone company about unlimited service options or package plans that extend your local calling area to elsewhere in your state. Consult your recent monthly phone bills and be sure you don't buy more coverage than you need.

- Ask your long-distance carrier about using it to make intra-LATA calls. In many cases you will be able to reach your long distance carrier by dialing a special code and then be able to call anywhere in your state as well as the nation at your reduced rate.

A LOCAL TELEPHONE SERVICE GLOSSARY

LATA (Local Access and Transport Area). There are 161 geographical areas (LATAs) in the United States within which a local telephone company may offer telecommunications services.

Intralata. Calls placed within your LATA.

Interlata. Calls placed from one LATA to another LATA.

LEC (Local Exchange Company). This is the company that provides basic local telephone service to the customer.

Install a Long-Distance Safety Net for Critical Business

Several of the major long-distance telephone companies have had embarrassing system failures in recent years, with service outages of as much as a full day.

Such problems are extremely rare and all but impossible to predict. But if your business has a mission-critical network or telemarketing operation you should consider splitting off at least part of your phone service to a different carrier. In this way, if one carrier experiences a problem you should be able to switch your outgoing calls to the other; most incoming calls will likely be unaffected in any case.

You're probably better off having accounts with two or more of the major carriers with their own cables and satellite networks—companies such as AT&T, LDDS, MCI, or Sprint. Many smaller long-distance carriers merely lease space on the facilities of the majors. This strategy will not protect against a problem with your local phone company.

For a true "belt-and-suspenders" solution, add a cellular phone account and make arrangements with your local or long-distance carrier to switch incoming calls to that wireless service in an emergency.

Understand the Pros and Cons of Prepaid Phone Cards

One of the hottest trends in telephone marketing in recent years has been the "phone card." You can buy them at grocery stores, at post offices, and from vending machines; you can even pay a little extra for an especially pretty picture on the front.

The idea behind the phone card is elegant: You can make calls from any phone at any time without having to fuss with coins. You make a call by dialing into a central computer and entering your card number and the number you want to dial; the computer keeps track of the time you are on line and subtracts the cost for the time from the amount of money in your account. Some cards offer advanced features including speed dialing for frequently called numbers, information services, and a monthly activity report.

Some phone cards are sold in specific values, while others can be refreshed by credit-card payments.

It's important to differentiate these phone cards from the telephone credit cards issued by local and long-distance telephone companies. The credit cards are charge accounts that are usually tied to your main phone number.

I'll cut right to the chase here: Prepaid phone cards are, in general, a bad deal for the consumer. The biggest problem is the per-minute charge. Typical rates run from 30 to 50 cents per minute, which is two to three times as much as the rate on a telephone credit card. Many of the cards also charge in full-minute blocks, which means that if you talk for 2 minutes and 5 seconds you will be billed for 3 minutes. Some cards add a service charge to the first minute of use, or place a monthly service charge on your account.

A hidden cost of prepaid phone cards: If you lose the card, you may well lose your investment. Some issuers will cancel a lost card if you provide the code numbers.

Watch out, too, for expiration dates on some cards.

It is also important to understand the way prepaid phone-card issuers work: most purchase blocks of time from major long-distance carriers such as AT&T, Sprint, and MCI. They operate little more than a marketing office, sometimes even contracting out the computer tracking of the use of the phone cards. In recent years, a number of small prepaid phone-card issuers have gone out of business or otherwise been unable to deliver service. You may be unable to recover money you have paid in advance.

Because the card issuers do not operate the phone lines, they have no control over the quality of the connection; you may or may not be able to obtain credit for bad connections. And retail stores are not likely to accept returns of cards when they cannot check on the remaining value.

According to the Federal Trade Commission, the most common consumer complaints about prepaid phone cards are:

- Access numbers or PINs that don't work.
- Card issuers that go out of business, leaving card-holders with a useless card.
- Toll-free access numbers that are constantly busy, preventing use of the card.
- Customer service numbers that are busy or don't work.
- Rates that are higher than advertised.
- Hidden connection charges, taxes, and surcharges.
- Cards that debit minutes or units even when you don't connect with the party you're calling.
- Poor quality connections.

Should you use a prepaid phone card? I'd recommend that you instead obtain a telephone credit card from your long-distance carrier. This is a safer, generally less-expensive, pay-as-you go alternative. If you are unable to obtain a telephone credit card because you don't have a home or business phone number, the prepaid card route may be your only option.

Here are some hints on ways to check out the quality of a phone-card service:

- Call their customer service number before you purchase a card. If you are unable to get through before you buy the card, why should you believe you'll have better luck after they have your money?

- Purchase a small-denomination card and use it as a test before investing more money in a service.

- Find out if the retail store where you may buy the card is willing to stand behind the quality of the service.

Cut the Rental Cord with Your Phone Company

Until about 15 years ago, residential subscribers were required to lease their phone equipment from the telephone company. You could choose from a few models and a handful of colors, and you got to pay the price set by the phone company and state utility boards every month again and again.

Today, very few consumers still lease their phones; for most of us, it makes no economic sense. You can buy your own phones for as little as $10 for a cheap basic unit or buy a top-of-the-line electronic unit for under $100. Either way, the purchase price will quickly pay for itself when you compare it to monthly leasing charges.

If you have an old phone-company device in your house, check your bill or call the company to see if you are still being charged for it.

The only good reason to establish a leasing arrangement with the phone company or a third party is if you require an expensive specialized piece of equipment such as a TDD device for the hard-of-hearing.

Control Phone-Installation Costs

Part of the general deregulation of the telephone industry resulted in a major change in the way homeowners should look at the wires in the walls.

It used to be that when you wanted to install a new phone in the bedroom, you'd call the phone company and they would send over a technician to snake a wire up from the basement and install an outlet; if the phone ever developed a problem, you'd call the company and they'd send a technician to fix the problem.

Today, in most cases, the telephone company's jurisdiction stops at the outside wall of your house. All of the wiring within a residence is the homeowner's or renter's responsibility. Think of the situation as much like your relationship with the electric company: The wiring is put in and maintained by an electrician, while the utility's responsibility ends at the electric meter.

Here's what the new phone arrangement means for you:

- You can do your own wiring, installing outlets anywhere in the house. Telephone circuits are relatively simple, consisting of just two copper wires for each phone. There are books and pamphlets on how to wire your own home available through phone companies and "how-to" advice from home-supply or electronics stores.

- You can hire an electrician to install phone wiring as part of construction or renovation of a house.

- The telephone company is bound to make free repairs to the cable that comes from the phone pole or an underground vault to your house. But if the problem lies within the house wiring, the company is likely to charge you—a lot—for fixing the problem.

When something goes wrong, the telephone company should be the *last* number you dial. The first step should be to determine if the problem lies in your phones, the wiring within the house, or the telephone company's cable from the street or pole. Here's a step-by-step to diagnosing phone problems:

1. If you suspect the problem is with a particular phone, unplug it from the outlet box and attach another phone to the same outlet. If the problem goes away, the cause was within the first telephone.

2. Try disconnecting all of the phones in the house from the inside wiring and then trying a known-good phone at several outlets. In some cases, a failure of one telephone or telephone cord can short out the system within the home. If the problem goes away, experiment with all the phones until you find the one that causes the problem to return.

3. If you still have problems, locate the telephone company's Network Interface, which may be on the outside of the house or in your basement. This small box, usually labeled with the name of the phone company, is the end of the utility's cable and where your house wiring meets it. Bring a known-good telephone to the Network Interface and plug it directly into the socket there; you'll usually find a socket marked "customer equipment" for this purpose.

    If the phone works, your problem lies between the Network Interface and the phones in your house, and you'll have to make repairs yourself or call an electrician (or the phone company) and pay them to make repairs.

    If the phone does not work, the problem lies in the phone company's wiring or at its central office. Contact them and tell them of your troubleshooting process; they may be able to remotely test the Network Interface from the central office.

4. If your home does not have a Network Interface—likely only in older homes—check with the phone company to see if they are obligated to install one. State regulators may require them to make free repairs until the interface is installed.

Order Telephone Equipment by Phone

Over the years, I've equipped my office with some pretty sophisticated telephone equipment—automatic line switches, speakerphones, headsets, handset amplifiers, and much more—without setting foot in an electronics store. The fact is that most electronics salespeople understand very little about modern telephone devices anyway.

Here are two sources for just about anything that plugs into a phone line:

- *Hello Direct.* A catalog of telephone productivity tools for the non-technical user in an office or home (800) 444-3556.
- *Telecom Products.* A Chicago company's catalog of some amazing devices, including many of the tools used by phone-company repair crews, as well as phone devices (630) 980-7710.

Make the Most of Phone-Company Maintenance Plans

Homeowners are now responsible for the maintenance of their own telephone wiring. Phone companies can—and generally do—charge high rates to fix any problems that lie beyond the Network Interface where their cable meets your inside wiring.

My unfriendly local phone company in New England has a minimum charge of $62.50 for half an hour's poking around, plus the cost of any materials.

You might want to consider subscribing to a Wire Maintenance Plan offered by many phone companies; for the price of a monthly charge to your phone bill, the phone company will make repairs inside or outside your home at no charge and will even provide a loaner telephone set if the problem is found to be within your equipment.

In New England, the NYNEX TeleSure Plus Service was priced at $1.95 per month as this book went to press. That works out to $23.40 per year, which is fairly reasonable if you expect to need a repair visit at least once every three years or so. The bad news is that you'll have to pay separately for each line if you have more than one phone number in your house.

Check with the phone company to see its policy on how long you must subscribe to a maintenance plan before you can call for free service. If you are experiencing an intermittent problem, it might make sense to sign up for the plan and wait a few days or a week before calling in for a service call.

Your Rights As a Telephone and Postal Consumer

Slam-Proof Your Phone Service

"Slamming" is an illegal, unscrupulous, but not all that uncommon practice among some telephone-service marketing companies. It boils down to this: A consumer is switched to a new long-distance carrier without permission. The slam may come after a telephone pitch, or you may not even know that a marketing company has set you in its sights until you see a different notation on your telephone bill. (You do read the fine print on your monthly bill, right?)

If your account is changed, you have the right to demand that it be changed back to your original carrier. And you should work with your local phone company to report the "slam" to the FTC.

One way to protect against a slam is to request a "PIC freeze" on your account. This requires that the local telephone company receive a written notification form signed by the customer of record before any change in the Primary Interexchange Carrier (the long-distance provider) is made.

Hang Up on Telephone Solicitation

Is there anything in our modern society more annoying than receiving a call from a telemarketer? How about receiving a call from a telemarketer just as you sit down to dinner?

We've already discussed how you can demand that a caller put you on a list of numbers not to be called again; that should take care of that particular operation.

Here's a way to further reduce the chances of unsolicited phone calls. The Direct Marketing Association maintains a central database of phone numbers whose owners have asked not to be called; the list is made available to the members of that association, and they have agreed to not call. DMA includes most of the major telemarketing companies, but not all.

To get on the list, send a letter to:

Telephone Preference Service
Direct Marketing Association
P.O. Box 9014
Farmingdale, NY 11735-9014

Include your name and address and the telephone number, including area code. Ask that the number or numbers be included on the Direct Marketing Association's Telephone Preference Service list of consumers and that you not be called by telemarketers. Be sure to date and sign the letter.

You must register with TPS directly; you cannot file on behalf of someone else. When you register with TPS, your name, address, and telephone number are placed on a do-not-call file. This "delete file" is updated four times a year, in January, April, July, and October, and is made available to telemarketing companies who choose to use it. Expect a few months' lag before the number of calls starts to drop off. Your name remains on the file for five years.

This is not a cure-all; local merchants, religious and charitable organizations, political candidates, and other groups not participating in the DMA program may continue to call. And TPS does not block calls placed to business telephones. Finally, the system may not work against one of the crudest of telemarketing tools, the computerized sequential dialer, which just goes through every possible telephone number in a particular area; the sequential dialer, by the way, also gets through to unlisted phone numbers although the caller may not know your name unless it has obtained that information in another way.

Make the Most of Overnight Delivery Services

Overnight delivery services are a marvel of our age, part of our demand for near-instant service in almost everything we do; it is sometimes hard to remember how we got along without FedEx and fax machines.

FedEx, of course, now has significant competition from other carriers, including Airborne Express, DHL, and premium services of United Parcel Service and the U.S. Postal Service. They're all good and highly reliable.

For occasional users in small businesses and from home, one of the best deals is the Postal Service's Priority Mail. If you can squeeze it into one of their free cardboard carriers, you can ship as much as a two pounds of material anywhere in the country with delivery promised (but not guaranteed) within two to three days for a charge of $3 as this book goes to press. This is a basic service, without tracking, insurance, or anything more than best of intentions on delivery. On the plus side, Priority Mail will be delivered on Saturdays for no extra charge, and pickups by your regular postal carrier are free.

The Postal Service's Express Mail one-day overnight service is priced at a level comparable to other carriers, but it is the only carrier that will deliver on Saturdays, Sundays, and holidays without extra charge.

If you need faster delivery, or special services, here are some ways to save:

- First, ask yourself if you really need overnight service. Most carriers offer discounted second-day delivery; in some instances, packages shipped in this way will actually arrive the next day anyway, although that is not assured.

- If you must get something to someone the next day, you can save money by specifying next-afternoon (sometimes called next business day) rather than premium service of next-morning delivery. The most expensive courier option is next-day by 8 or 8:30 A.M., offered by some carriers.

- You can save a few dollars with some carriers, including FedEx and United Parcel Service, by bringing packages to their offices or to a drop box rather than calling for a pickup.

- If you regularly ship a package to a particular client, you can save money by calling various services and finding the one with the lowest price to that address; it may make sense to have different accounts with several services for shipments to different places. (The prolonged strike against UPS in 1997, though, convinced many shippers of the value of spreading their accounts across several services as a precaution.)

- If you send several packages a week, put your business out to bid. Most services will offer discounts to regular shippers.

And While We're at It, Cut Down on Unsolicited Junk Mail

You can also cut down on some of the printed advertising materials you receive in the mail through another service of the Direct Marketing Association.

The Mail Preference Service is provided to national nonprofit and commercial direct-mail companies that are affiliated with the DMA.

To register, send a letter with your name and home address to:

Mail Preference Service
Direct Marketing Association
P.O. Box 9008
Farmingdale, NY 11735-9008

Be sure to include as many versions of your name as you can think of; look at a stack of incoming mail. For example, Janice Sandler may find mail sent to that name, to J. Sandler, to Mrs. Corey Sandler, and to her maiden name, which she uses in her professional life.

The mail service works in the same way as the phone service, with four updated lists issued each year. Your name will remain on the list for five years.

Remove Your Name from a Specific Company's List

You can request your name be deleted from a specific company's mailing list by writing to the firm's customer-service department and asking to be put on the "suppress" list.

Block Sexually Explicit Mail

The U.S. Postal Service maintains a list of people who have requested that sexually oriented advertisements not be sent to their homes; the list is provided to mailing companies. To get on the list, contact your local post office to obtain Form 2150 to stop mail from a particular company or Form 2201 to stop sexually oriented mail in general.

You can cut down on the number of mail-order solicitations you receive asking the companies you deal with not to rent your name to other companies or organizations.

SECTION III

At Home

8 Savvy Home Improvements

Your home is your castle; the savvy consumer is a tight-fisted Chancellor of the Exchequer when it comes to maintenance, repairs, and improvements.

In this chapter, we look at some ways to choose a contractor, how to save money on energy use, air conditioning, and heating. I also help you keep from getting hosed when a water-treatment company tries to sell you equipment or service.

✓ Don't be penny-wise and home foolish: Know how to choose a contractor or repairperson.

✓ Give your home an energy checkup.

✓ Keep your energy dollars from flying out the window: understanding energy ratings.

✓ Buy your air conditioning by the ton.

✓ Cool down your air-conditioning bills.

✓ Save money with low-tech air conditioning.

✓ Get a warm feeling for your heating bills.

✓ Paint the town house without going into the red.

✓ Dry off water-testing scams.

✓ Know the inside story of home water treatment.

Don't Be Penny-Wise and Home Foolish: Know How to Choose a Contractor or Repairperson

Few things cost more money than a job done poorly. You are always better off hiring a licensed contractor for any structural job or major home system (carpentry, roofing, plumbing, and electrical work among them). You should expect a state or municipal license, worker's compensation coverage, and proper insurance for any worker who will enter your home.

If it is a simple job, such as replacing a faucet or fixing a faulty electrical outlet, you can make a deal based on a fixed price. Anything more complicated should be based on a written contract that spells out the work to be done and the price for the job.

It is acceptable for a contractor to ask for a down payment, usually a portion of any supplies that must be purchased for the job. Do not sign any contract that requires full payment before satisfactory completion of the work.

For major work, check out the quality of work by calling former customers. If you've ever had good work done by one tradesperson, call and ask for a reference. For example, call the carpenter who worked on your deck to ask about good plumbers or electricians he or she may have worked with.

Give Your Home an Energy Checkup

To get the most bang for your bucks and time in energy conservation, find out the most fruitful areas for improvement with an energy audit.

Contact your local utility to see if they offer a free or subsidized inspection of your home. You can also hire a professional home inspector on your own; your utility may be able to make recommendations here.

Here is the big three of energy conservation and use:

- Weatherizing, including weatherstripping, insulation, and windows that keep the outside heat or cold away from tempered indoor air.

- Heating and hot water systems.
- Major appliances including refrigerators, dryers, and other devices.

Keep Your Energy Dollars from Flying Out the Window: Understanding Energy Ratings

One of the biggest holes in the heat shield that surrounds your home is the window system. That doesn't mean that you can't select a window design that minimizes the escape of heat or air conditioning.

Window manufacturers use a rating called the U-value that measures how much heat is conducted through a window or skylight. Here's the key: the lower the U-value, the more energy-efficient the window is.

An official U-rating is accompanied by an NFRC (National Fenestration Rating Council) label.

Buy Your Air Conditioning by the Ton

Most air conditioners are measured in BTU (British Thermal Units). To figure the necessary BTU, calculate the square footage of the room to be cooled (multiply the length by the width). For a basic room with an 8-foot ceiling, figure 24 BTUs per square foot; a 16 x 22 rec room is 352 square feet and would require an air conditioner of about 8,400 BTU. If the room has a cathedral ceiling, or is a kitchen or other room with heat-producing appliances, you'll want to increase the BTU capacity of the air conditioner.

Other factors that influence the size of the machine you'll need: the number of windows in the room (especially southern exposure), the amount of insulation in the house, and the ambient temperatures common in your area.

Larger systems, including central air conditioners, are measured in tons; this is an old equation based on the cooling effect of melting a ton of ice. In air-conditioning terms, one ton is equivalent to 12,000 BTUs.

Machines that are too small will have to run more often and may cost more to operate; machines that are too large can also waste energy and are not as effective at controlling humidity.

Look for the federally mandated Energy-Efficiency Rating (EER); compare units of the same BTU rating to find the one with the highest EER.

Cool Down Your Air-Conditioning Bills

Here are some ways to reduce the load on your air conditioner and reduce the pain when you pay the electricity bill:

- Reduce the heat gain inside the house. Among the things you can do are lowering the shades on the sunny side and cutting down on use of ovens.
- Be cool to your air conditioner by shading it from the direct sun with shrubbery or an awning. You should also clean filters according to the manufacturer's recommendations to allow a free flow of air; this will also help reduce pollen and dust.
- Adjust the settings on the air conditioner so that it does not run at its highest settings when the house is unoccupied or during the night hours when it may not be necessary. For a central air conditioner, purchase a programmable thermostat that allows you to set different temperatures for specific days and hours.

Save Money with Low-Tech Air Conditioning

If you live in a temperate zone, you might want to consider some low-tech and low-price ways to cool your house before buying an energy-hungry air conditioner.

- Start by considering your windows. Pull the shades on the southern side of the house to reduce heat gain. Open windows on upper floors to allow rising heat a place to escape.

- Make sure your attic is properly ventilated with louvers to permit the exit of the hot air up there.

- Use window fans to exhaust hot air and bring in cooler air. Windows on the south side of the house should blow out; windows on the north side should bring in air.

- Consider installing a powered attic fan in the highest point of a multistory house; these large fans can create a cooling breeze throughout the house, exhausting heat to the outside where it belongs and drawing in cooler air from open north-facing windows. A large attic fan can cool for about one tenth the cost of air conditioning.

    Attic fans are rated by the cubic feet per minute (CFM) of air they can move; in most installations the air goes into an attic and out a vent. To calculate the proper size you'll need to figure the square footage of the house and multiply it by the ceiling height. (You can subtract any rooms that will be closed off, such as basements and closets.)

    For the best cooling effect, purchase a fan with a CFM equal to the cubic feet of the house. Some experts say you can get away with a ventilating fan that gives a changeover of house air every three minutes, in which case you can divide the cubic feet by three to reach an acceptable CFM.

- Minimize use of ovens, stoves, television sets, halogen lamps, and other sources of heat, especially during the middle of the day. Microwave ovens give off very little heat, and outdoor gas grills or barbecues keep cooking heat away from living quarters.

Get a Warm Feeling for Your Heating Bills

- For every degree you turn down the thermostat, you'll reduce your energy consumption by 2 to 3 percent. Reduce the thermostat setting to 68 degrees or slightly less during the day, and 60 degrees at night or when no one is at home.

    Elderly and infirm people should not reduce the temperature below 65 degrees at any time and should consult with doctors before making any changes in their environment.

To avoid frozen pipes and other wintertime damage, do not turn down your thermostat below 50 degrees.

- Upgrade the insulation in an older house. Ask your utility company or state energy department for advice on the needs of your home and the most efficient use of your money.

- Use caulk and weatherstripping to seal leaks in the gaskets around windows and doors.

- Use foam gaskets, available at hardware stores, to block air leaks through electrical outlets and switches on outside walls of the house.

- Fireplaces can suck much of the heated air from your house up the chimney. Install glass fireplace doors to close off the chimney when the fireplace is not in use. Be sure to properly close the fireplace damper when the fire is safely out.

- Make use of solar energy to help heat your house. Open curtains during the day to let the warming rays into the house, and then close them at night and on cloudy days to help insulate against heat loss.

- Be careful not to overuse kitchen and bathroom fans during the heating season. Experts say that a fan left running for an hour can exhaust all of the heated air from the house.

- Clean or replace filters according to the manufacturer's recommendations. A dirty filter can reduce airflow and affect the overall efficiency of the system.

- Vacuum air vents, baseboard heaters, and radiators to keep them clean and to help transfer heat efficiently.

- Keep furniture and draperies away from heater vents or radiators.

- Consider installing a reversible ceiling fan to move air, bringing heated air down toward the floor in winter and up to the ceiling in summer.

- Close vents in the foundation in the winter to insulate pipes and air ducts; the same vents should be opened in the summer to help remove moisture and help with cooling.

Paint the Town House Without Going into the Red

What kind of paint should you use inside or outside your house? Water versus oil-based paint.

Oil is old technology and not much used except if you are repainting a surface that already has oil paint in place; oil or alkyd paints will bond properly with older oil-paint surfaces. This is especially so in exterior jobs.

Otherwise, the trend is clearly in the direction of water-based paint, including latex and acrylic formulations. The many advantages of water-based paints include the ease of cleanup, the speed of drying, and its reduced odor. Latex and acrylic paints are also much more forgiving of the amateur painter, forming a rubberlike coating that hides brush or roller marks. And because they dry so quickly, painters can often put on two coats in one day, saving time and inconvenience.

You should also look into the new power-feed roller-painting systems that can apply paint two or three times as fast as a standard roller and pan and with a bit less strain on your back and shoulders.

Dry Off Water-Testing Scams

Be wary of a "free" test from a company that sells an item dependent on the results of that test. Some examples: asking an orthodontist whether your kids need braces; asking a transmission-repair shop whether you car needs a new transmission; and asking a company that sells water filters or treatment devices whether your water needs attention. (In each of these cases, and many others, you are much better off paying for the services of an independent specialist who draws his or her income from the test or exam and not from the sale of services.)

Do you really know what is in your water? That's a pretty frightening question to most of us and a very powerful sales pitch for some honest and not-so-honest sales organizations.

First, instant tests done in your home are not likely to be accurate or informative. Second, the results reported to you may misrepresent safe levels of minerals and other substances. Or, there may be out-and-out fraud about the results, including contamination of the sample or introduction of meaningless but dramatic color changes or instrument readouts.

Ask your local water superintendent for the latest test results of the public water supply and then compare them to state and federal standards available from your state government and the EPA. If you use well water, ask your local or state health department if it offers free water testing for bacterial contaminants.

Under the federal Safe Drinking Water Act, all public water supplies must meet the drinking-water standards set by the EPA. If you draw water from a private well, though, your only protection is state and local law, which may be more or less stringent than federal standards and which may not take into account conditions on or near your property.

To test your water, use a lab certified by your state's health department or environmental agency. You can also obtain a list of state-certified labs from the EPA's Safe Water Drinking Hotline at (800) 426-4791.

Tests for bacteria range from $15 to $45, while tests for chemical contamination can cost hundreds, even thousands of dollars, depending on the depth of the analysis.

Know the Inside Story of Home Water Treatment

Home water treatment is a burgeoning industry, and many of the products can improve specific problems.

There are several types of water-treatment units, and no single device can solve all water problems.

- *Physical filters.* These units use fabric, fiber, ceramic, or other types of screens to remove particles, grit, sediment, dirt, and rust from the water. Some ultrafine filters can also remove some bacteria from the water, although they should not be used to treat microbiologically unsafe water.

- *Activated carbon filters.* This special class of filter can remove some organic chemical contaminants from the water, improving smell, taste, and appearance of your drinking water. Activated carbon filters are available in several forms: granular; powdered; powdered coated paper; and pressed carbon block.

This class of filter is not effective against most inorganic chemicals including salts or metals. Some special carbon filters are appropriate for taking lead out of the water.

Activated carbon filters can become saturated with the impurities they remove from the water and must be replaced from time to time—consult the manufacturer or installer for details. Be sure to factor in the cost of replacement filters in your buying decision.

- *Bacteriostatic carbon filters.* A certain class of carbon filters contains silver as a pesticide. According to the EPA, though, these claims of bacterial growth control have not been proven. These filters are not recommended for water that is microbiologically unsafe, such as water contaminated with fecal matter.

- *Reverse osmosis (RO) units.* These systems pass water through a membrane to a storage tank; most designs waste much of the tap water put into them—as much as 75 percent in some units. Membranes must be replaced from time to time.

  Reverse osmosis units remove substantial amounts of most inorganic chemicals, such as salts, metals (including lead), asbestos, minerals, nitrates, and some organic chemicals.

- *Distillation units.* These units, which are available in many different shapes and sizes, vaporize water and then condense it. This process removes most dissolved solids, such as salts, metals, minerals, asbestos fibers, particles, and some organic chemicals. Distillation units, however, may not remove all chemical pollutants, and some bacteria may pass through in some instances. Although distillation may be an effective water treatment, the water heating will add to your energy use.

- *Ultraviolet (UV) disinfection.* These units use a light to destroy bacteria and inactivate viruses, without leaving a taste or odor in the water. UV units do not remove most chemical pollutants and may not be effective against spores and cysts.

  UV systems must be cleaned regularly; consult the manufacturer's instructions.

For background on federal regulation of drinking water contact the U.S. Environmental Protection Agency, Office of Drinking Water, Washington, DC 20460. Or call the Safe Drinking Water Hotline at (800) 426-4791.

For more information on specific water-treatment devices contact The National Sanitation Foundation, P.O. Box 130140, Ann Arbor, MI 48113-0140, or call (313) 769-8010.

For information about bottled water contact the Food and Drug Administration, U.S. Department of Health and Human Services, 5600 Fishers Lane, Rockville, MD 20857, or call (301) 443-4166. Or, International Bottled Water Association, 113 N. Henry St., Alexandria, VA 22314, or call (703) 683-5213.

9 Saving on Home Supplies

Here's a bright idea: Read the small print on light bulbs to get the most illumination for the best price. I also show you how to buy batteries and how to set your table with discount china and silverware.

✓ Shine some light on bulb ratings.

✓ Shop smart for alternate types of light bulbs.

✓ Don't let them charge too much for batteries.

✓ Use a high-tech aid for calculating wallpaper needs.

✓ Set your table with discount china.

✓ Replace the missing lemon fork from your silverware set.

Shine Some Light on Bulb Ratings

Light bulbs have three standardized numbers plus a price: the voltage (almost always 110 to 120 volts), the wattage (the amount of power the bulb draws), and the often-overlooked "light-output" rating.

Light output, measured in lumens, is an indication of the amount of light a bulb produces. Not every 100-watt bulb gives off the same amount of light.

Shop for bulbs by light output and you will save energy costs; a 60-watt bulb that yields the same lumens as a 75-watt bulb can save 20 percent on electricity bills.

A fourth number on light-bulb packages claims to represent "bulb life in hours." These numbers are estimates of the durability of the filament of the bulb; consider them as broad benchmarks. One time it does make sense to seek out a claim of a very long life is an installation where changing the bulb is a major hassle such as the light at the top of a cathedral ceiling, or one buried within a lamp that has to be disassembled to make a change.

Shop Smart for Alternate Types of Light Bulbs

Standard light bulbs are incandescent devices that generate light through heat.

Fluorescent lamps, which work by exciting a gas, can last as much as ten times longer than incandescents, use less power to generate the same amount of light output, and rarely cost more than a few times as much.

Fluorescent bulbs are now available in compact designs that can be screwed directly into a standard socket, replacing an incandescent bulb. On the downside, fluorescents cannot be used with dimmers, and they give off a light that is generally whiter than an incandescent; they may not be appropriate for mood lighting in a living room, but are well suited as a task light in a study or office.

Many electric utility companies offer discounted prices on fluorescent bulbs as a way to reduce power demands.

Here's an example of electrical light economics: The lamp in your bedroom is used for about 1,000 hours a year (about three hours per night). Your local electric utility charges eight cents per kilowatt-hour.

You can purchase a 23-watt compact energy-saving fluorescent bulb with a light output of 1,500 lumens for about $15. It has a rated life of about 10,000 hours, which in the case of the bedroom lamp is ten years. Your cost to operate the lamp is a mere $1.84 per year. Split the cost of purchase across 10 years, to make a total annual cost of about $3.34.

Or you could install a 90-watt general-service incandescent bulb, which yields about the same light output, for about $1. It has a rated life of 1,000 hours, or about one year. The electrical cost to operate the bulb will be about $7.20 per year, plus the cost of purchase, for an annual cost of about $8.20.

At the end of ten years, you would have spent about $30.34 for the single fluorescent bulb versus about $82 for ten incandescent bulbs.

Don't Let Them Charge Too Much for Batteries

The number of battery-operated devices in the typical home has run away like the Energizer bunny: portable CD and tape players, smoke detectors, "smart" thermostats, television/VCR/stereo remote controls, clocks, cameras, and much more.

As a user of these devices, you have many choices of battery types, from relatively inexpensive standard batteries to high-capacity alkalines and exotic long-life designs such as lithium hydroxide; you can also purchase rechargeable batteries to extend their lives. Here's a guide to household batteries:

- Alkaline batteries generally offer the best ratio of price to performance. They have a good capacity, which make them appropriate for most devices including those you want to depend on, such as smoke detectors, and those you use a great deal, such as portable stereos and remote-control units.

  Alkalines also have a long storage life of several years, which means you can stock up on them when you find them on sale. Look for any major brand including private-label brands you find in major discount stores. Pay attention to expiration dates you'll find on most packages; some makers now include a small battery tester in their packaging. Be wary of no-name brands from uncommon sources such as Malaysia or Mexico; these batteries may already be elderly by the time they make it to your store's shelves.

- Heavy-duty and standard batteries are lower in cost and lower in value, best reserved for short-term use in flashlights and other low-draw devices. They should not be counted on for important uses such as smoke detectors.

- Rechargeable nickel-cadmium batteries can save money in uses such as portable stereo systems, flashguns for cameras, and toys. These batteries typically cost about five to ten times as much as a disposable battery, but can be recharged hundreds of times; even when you factor in the cost of a recharging station, they are still a good value. The cost of electricity to recharge a battery is very low.

    Rechargeables are not appropriate, though, for long-term uses such as smoke detectors or remote controls because they hold their charge for only a few weeks or months at best.

    Another plus of rechargeables is that they reduce the number of disposable batteries with toxic metals and chemicals reaching landfills; you should dispose of rechargeables (and all other batteries) properly when they reach the end of their useful life.

    Be wary of battery rechargers that claim to bring alkaline or standard batteries back to life; experience has shown that batteries not specifically formulated to be recharged cannot be reused more than a few times, with reduced capacities in reuse.

- Lithium batteries have a high capacity but come at a high premium. They are useful in cameras and flashes or in some camcorders or computers capable of accepting disposable batteries.

Use a High-Tech Aid for Calculating Wallpaper Needs

Not I, but perhaps you would like to attempt installing your own wallpaper. Before you even get down to the nitty-gritty of pasting the stuff on the wall, you'll need to do the difficult work of calculating how much paper you need.

Here's a computer-assist for the job, located on MetLife's Life Advisor page on the World Wide Web. Connect to

http://www.metlife.com/lifeadvi/brochures/tools/tools.html

You'll also find a calculator on the same page to figure out how much paint you need for a particular job.

For either job, be sure you buy your supplies from a store that will give you a refund for any unused rolls or packages of paste.

Set Your Table with Discount China

You won't find the most delicate, eggshell-like designs, but you can find some attractive and sturdy china sets at a restaurant-supply store.

You'll probably have to buy a case of 10 or 20 sets, but the price is almost certain to be good, and you may find that the dishes will last for many more years than consumer lines. While you're shopping, look for pots, pans, and cooking implements.

Look for Restaurant Equipment listings in your Yellow Pages. If you live in a big city with a Chinatown or other gathering of restaurants, you may find supply stores nearby the eateries.

Another source of china is a factory outlet for a china maker. There you may find "seconds" with minor flaws in the glazing or decoration.

Replace the Missing Lemon Fork from Your Silverware Set

You suspect that Cousin Lenny walked off with the butter server from your prized sterling silver, but your husband suspects the family dog. In any case, the silver service hasn't been manufactured in ten years and the store where you purchased the set went out of business after a closeout sale last Christmas. How can you fill out the set?

The answer lies with one of several companies that specialize in filling holes in silverware sets. If the service is still in production or relatively recent, you can expect discounts from the list price; older sets may be offered at a premium over earlier prices. Prices may also fluctuate with major changes in the price of silver.

Some companies also offered preowned sets and pieces gathered from estate sales and jewelers' stocks.

Try the following companies: The Silver Queen (800) 262-3134, and Replacements, Ltd. (800) 737-5223.

10 Give Your Home a Security Blanket

Chance favors the prepared mind, said scientist Louis Pasteur.

What does this have to do with home security and health issues? I operate on the related theory that luck is the residue of planning. A homeowner who spends the time and effort to make it difficult for a burglar to enter a home undetected, or who equips a house with smoke, carbon monoxide, and radon detectors is manufacturing his or her own good luck.

Here are some tips on home security and peace of mind:

✓ Buy something to watch over you.

✓ Protect your loved ones with a set of smoke detectors.

✓ Buy the best fire extinguisher.

✓ Keep the air clear with a carbon monoxide detector.

✓ Keep watch over a silent menace.

✓ Keep it down out there: dealing with noisy neighbors.

✓ Hear the bad news about halogen lamps.

Buy Something to Watch Over You

The best advice before you set out to burglarproof your home: Think like a burglar.

"Case" your home. Walk around the outside and look for ways to enter. Could a burglar easily force a window or door? Are there places shielded by shrubs or fences for someone to hide while they break in?

Your neighbor may not like this, but your goal should be to make your house less appealing as a target than the one next door. If your house is better lit, better locked, and just a bit more difficult to get in to than another house on the block, most burglars will move on to easier pickings. Here are some things you can do to make a burglar feel less comfortable:

- Install exterior lights on timers or connected to motion-detection sensors to illuminate hiding places.

- Cut back on shrubs that block the view of doors and windows.

- Try to avoid ostentatious displays of wealth. Don't, for example, place paintings or large-screen televisions in plain view of the front windows.

- Don't make it too easy. If you have some valuable jewelry, install a heavy safe that can be bolted to the floor or into a wall.

- There are no foolproof locks, grates, or bars, but anything that slows down a burglar or makes noise will work in your favor.

  Deadbolt locks that require a key to open from the inside and the outside are the best hardware, especially if the lock is on a door with a glass panel; deadbolts that use a thumb knob on the inside are easy for a burglar to reach through a broken window. One downside to deadbolt locks with keys on both sides: You are making it difficult to get out of the house in case of a fire or other emergency. The best compromise is to keep an exit key a few feet away from the door and make sure that everyone in the family knows it is there and does not use that emergency key on a regular basis.

- Safeguard your keys. Do not put your home address on your key ring. If you lose your keys, you are better off paying a few dollars to have new keys made than to have to worry about a criminal paying you an uninvited visit with keys in hand.

  Don't leave house keys hidden under the mat, over the doorway, inside the mailbox, or any of the other usual places: A clever burglar has a pretty good eye for hiding spots. You might consider leaving an extra key with a neighbor, but be sure your name and address is not attached to those keys either, or a burglar of that house could end up with a two-for-one deal.

- Make your house seem occupied. Install timers for lights in several parts of the house, set to go on and off in a realistic pattern. Stop delivery of newspapers and mail, or have a neighbor pick up anything left on your lawn. Arrange for the lawn to be mowed or the snow to be cleared. Ask a neighbor to park his or her car in the driveway at night.

- Consider a burglar alarm; consult your neighbors and your local police department about their experience with various burglar-alarm designs, installers, and monitoring services.

Protect Your Loved Ones with a Set of Smoke Detectors

The most important tips about smoke detectors are very basic ones: If you don't have one, get one. If you have one, get a second or third or fourth.

There are few better investments in security than this: Industry experts say that having a detector in your home reduces your chance of dying in a fire by half.

You should have at least one smoke detector on each level of your home or apartment, and experts recommend you have a mix of photo-electric and ionization models.

Photoelectric models, which work by detecting a reduction in light passing between an emitter and detector, are quickest in detecting smoldering, smoky fires.

Ionization smoke detectors use a tiny radioactive element that electrically charges a compartment inside the detector; when smoke enters the device it changes the electrical current and sets off the alarm. Ionization detectors are quickest in sounding the alarm to flaming fire with little smoke.

You should also consider any smoke detector more than ten years old to be suspect and worth replacing. And if you can't remember the last time you replaced batteries in a detector, replace them now. (Batteries should be swapped at least once a year, or sooner if a detector's low-power warning goes off. Use fresh alkaline batteries; rechargeable batteries are not appropriate for detectors because they do not hold a charge for a long period of time.)

If you are constructing a new home or undertaking a major renovation project, consider installing an interconnected AC-power system; many building codes now require these devices. In an interconnected system, if any of the detectors in the house detect a fire, all of the alarms work. This is especially valuable if you place detectors in the basement or attic, two remote areas that are common sources of fire. A top-of-the-line interconnected system can also be extended to include a carbon monoxide detector.

Follow the instructions of the manufacturer in locating detectors. In general, they should not be placed near a window or exterior door because air drafts might direct smoke away from them; similarly, avoid dead-end corners where air may not circulate properly.

Buy the Best Fire Extinguisher

You are your own first line of defense against a fire in your home, apartment, or office; there should be at least one fire extinguisher, of an appropriate type.

The most important lesson to learn is that not all fires are the same. Here's a lesson in the ABCs of buying an extinguisher:

- Fires are classified based on the type of material or fuel that is burning.

    An "A" fire includes burning paper, wood, and cloth; these are blazes that can be safely extinguished with water.

    A "B" fire involves flammable liquids including grease fires in a kitchen or garage, gasoline, oil, and paints. These are fires that can usually be extinguished by smothering or otherwise removing a source of oxygen; pouring water on such a fire tends to spread it rather than put it out. Type B extinguishers often use dry chemicals such as alkaline sodium bicarbonate powder that smothers a fire and reacts chemically with fat to make it less likely to burn.

    Type "C" fires include electrical devices, wiring, and appliances.

- For a home or nonindustrial workplace, you can use a multipurpose (ABC) extinguisher. These units often use chemicals such as ammonium phosphate. But an ABC extinguisher is not very effective against a grease fire. For your kitchen, garage, or hobby room, a BC device would be more appropriate.

  Look for the Underwriters Laboratories ratings of extinguishers for a quick appraisal of the relative capacity and strength of a device. The UL system places a number in front of the A and B ratings. A typical unit might read 2A 5B C; compare that to another unit with a rating of 1A 10B C. The second extinguisher is half as effective on type A fires and twice as effective on type B blazes.

- Another important consideration is the weight and size of an extinguisher. Don't buy a safety device that is too heavy or large for all adults and responsible children to handle.

- Read the instructions on proper use of all extinguishers in your home or office, and conduct informal fire drills.

  Fire experts advise that in case of a significant fire you do the following: (1) Alert everyone in the house or office and advise them to leave, (2) call the fire department, and (3) attempt to put out the fire with the proper extinguisher if possible.

  Check the pressure gauges on extinguishers regularly and throw away or have recharged any unit that falls below the usable level. Most consumer-grade units have a shelf life of about 10 years.

Keep the Air Clear with a Carbon Monoxide Detector

Another inexpensive, precious form of protection that should be in most homes is a carbon monoxide (CO) detector.

Carbon monoxide is a colorless, odorless gas given off as part of the combustion process. If you have a fuel-burning furnace, stove, or oven, or a fireplace, you should install at least one of the devices in your home.

The best location: within each sleeping area, starting on the floor closest to the furnace or appliances. To be even safer, put an additional detector in the basement or furnace room.

Ironically, the risks from CO have gone up in recent years with new construction techniques that seal up homes from air infiltration.

Most carbon monoxide detectors plug into house current, which is acceptable because a power outage will also turn off gas and oil furnaces and hot-water heaters. A battery-backed system, though, is safer if you have a fireplace or a wood-fired heating system.

Keep Watch Over a Silent Menace

Radon is a colorless, odorless gas that seeps up through the soil; it decays into radioactive particles that can be inhaled and have been linked to as many as 20,000 lung-cancer deaths each year in this country.

That's pretty frightening stuff, but the good news is that radon is relatively easily and inexpensively detected. And eliminating radon gas in most cases is similarly simple.

Radon gas, which has been found in every state in almost every type of geology, tends to accumulate in basements and lower floors of a home, entering through holes or cracks in the foundation or through well water. You should be especially vigilant if you have a finished basement.

According to the Environmental Protection Agency, about 6 percent of American homes have radon levels above the danger level. A lifelong exposure to radon in this concentration raises the risk of lung cancer to about 1 in 500 for nonsmokers, and about 15 in 500 for smokers.

Radon levels can vary due to temperature, precipitation, and other factors. The best way to test is to perform both a quick short-term test that takes a weeklong snapshot of current conditions and a longer-term test that is more likely to report on varying conditions. The testers consist of a tube of activated charcoal or a specially treated film that are exposed to the air for a specified period of time and then closed up and mailed to a reporting lab. They typically sell for about $20 to $50 and are available at most hardware and home-supply stores.

If the testers report significant levels of radon, you should contact a specialist in removing the gas; the testing company or your local health department should be able to direct you to the proper service. In most cases the repair consists of a power ventilation system that removes basement air to the outside.

Keep It Down Out There: Dealing with Noisy Neighbors

One man's ceiling is another man's floor, which also applies to walls and doors . . . and is something that apartment dwellers know all about. What do you do if your neighbor thinks it is perfectly acceptable to crank up her stereo with heavy-metal noise at 3 A.M.? Or how about a homeowner who turns on the floodlights to mow his lawn at 4:30 A.M. on a Sunday? And that dog that barks all night. . . .

You might want to start with a polite but firm request for reasonable quiet. But if that doesn't work, explore your legal rights:

- If you are a renter, check your lease for a clause called "Quiet Enjoyment." This is a common element of rentals that gives you the right to live in peace and demands that you afford that same right to your neighbors. Your landlord, by making that promise, is supposed to enforce the clause and could evict your neighbor if he or she doesn't deliver you that quiet enjoyment of your space.

- Homeowners should consult their local government to find the terms of a noise ordinance. A typical law limits certain activities such as lawn mowing, snowblowing, construction work, and outdoor parties for certain hours of the night and early morning. The code may also set decibel noise limits.

  You can request that police enforce the law. In most cases you can also file a civil suit seeking a court order or even monetary damages.

- Many governments have ordinances requiring dog owners to keep their animals leashed or fenced and reasonably quiet. If not, a general antinoise statute may apply. Consult your police department for advice.

Hear the Bad News About Halogen Lamps

Tungsten-halogen filament incandescent bulbs, or "halogen" bulbs, contain a small capsule filled with halogen gas, which emits a bright white light. Halogen bulbs are designed to produce more light, use less energy, and last longer than standard incandescent bulbs of the same wattage, but they cost more than standard incandescent bulbs. They last about 3,000 hours—about three years.

That's the good news. The bad news is that halogen lamps generate a great deal of heat.

In recent years, consumer and fire-prevention agencies have issued warnings about widely available halogen "torchiere" lamps with an open top. They advise that you take special care to be certain that draperies, pieces of paper, or other flammable objects not come into contact with the bulbs of the lamp. And they suggest that you turn off any halogen lamp any time you leave a room.

11 At Home with Your Appliances

In most houses appliances, including a refrigerator, dishwasher, washer, dryer, stove, and ovens, are second in cost and importance after the house and its heating and cooling systems. And yet we tend to pay relatively little attention to cost and ease-of-use issues with our appliances.

In this chapter, we explore how to use energy ratings for savvy shopping and how to get the most out of the devices already in place in our house.

✓ Use EnergyGuide ratings for smart appliance shopping.

✓ Keep your refrigerator cool.

✓ Treat yourself to a new refrigerator every decade or so.

✓ Clean the dishes in style.

✓ Keep the dishes clean and your bills spotless.

✓ Cook up a deal on a microwave oven.

✓ Try do-it-yourself appliance repair.

✓ Use these hot tips for oven efficiency.

✓ Clean up your clothes washer's act.

✓ Dry out energy use by clothes dryers.

✓ Warm up with hot news on water heaters.

✓ Know the dirt on vacuum cleaners.

Use EnergyGuide Ratings for Smart Appliance Shopping

The yellow and black EnergyGuide tags on major appliances help you compare the efficiency and operating costs of various models. They are one way to decide whether a more expensive model will pay for itself after a few years of use, or conversely, whether a "cheap" model may actually end up costing you more money over its lifetime.

The EnergyGuide ratings are based on standard tests developed by the U.S. Department of Energy. They measure efforts by manufacturers to improve insulation, motors, compressors, pumps, and computer controllers. Some appliances—clothes dryers and microwave ovens among them—are exempt from the requirement for display of EnergyGuide ratings because there is little difference between energy use from model to model.

Keep Your Refrigerator Cool

Does your ice cream look like soup, your lettuce like ice cubes, and the floor beneath your refrigerator like a soupy swamp?

Here are some tips to bring a still-functioning refrigerator back to life:

- Read the instruction manual, the one you stuck in a drawer five years ago without a glance; check that all of the settings are correct for your type of use and environment.

- Check to see that air vents inside the refrigerator and freezer sections are not blocked by large items and that they are not obstructed by chunks of ice.

- Vacuum the condenser coils at the back or bottom of most units, a job that should be done every six months or so to remove dust that interferes with the machine's ability to get rid of heat. Do the job more often if you have pets or live in a particularly dusty area. (Some newer models of refrigerators do not have exterior coils.)

- Locate the refrigerator away from heating vents or radiators, stoves, or dishwashers.

- Remove frost more than a quarter-inch thick in the freezer.
- Check the door gaskets for air leaks and make repairs or replacements if necessary.
- Consult your operating manual for proper cooling and energy-saving settings.
- Give a call to the refrigerator maker's consumer telephone line and ask for further suggestions. Make a note of your machine's model and serial number and ask if there have been any product recalls or repair programs you may not be aware of.

Treat Yourself to a New Refrigerator Every Decade or So

If you are convinced that your trusty old cold box can no longer be trusted, go ahead and treat yourself to a new refrigerator. The fact is that a good new refrigerator can save $50 to $100 per year in electricity over a typical ten-year-old model of the same size. In other words, it can come close to paying for itself over the course of its average ten-year life.

Be sure to dispose of your old refrigerator properly; it should not be dumped without its ozone-depleting chlorofluorocarbon refrigerants being professionally drained and disposed of. New machines use chemicals that are less dangerous to the environment.

Here are some tips on purchasing a new refrigerator:

- Top-mounted freezer designs are less expensive, more energy efficient, better able to handle large items, have more overall usable space, and are more common.
- Despite all of their disadvantages, side-by-side models have some appeal in very tight kitchens where their narrow doors require less clearance.
- Bottom-mounted freezers have all the advantages of top-mounted models, may be even more energy efficient (cold air sinks to the bottom), and place refrigerated food at eye-level (you'll have to stoop for ice cream, though). In any case, this design is generally hard to find, although most dealers can order a unit for you.

- Measure the available space—width, depth, and height—for a refrigerator before you go shopping. Pay attention to any nearby furniture that might interfere with the swing of a wide door. This is especially a problem with an L-shaped kitchen where a counter or other appliance may be kitty-corner to the refrigerator. Most top- or bottom-freezer units require about 28 to 30 inches clearance for their doors; side-by-side units require less.

  Consider drawing a diagram, with measurements, to bring to the appliance dealer. Your goal is not to have to ask the delivery guys to carry your huge new refrigerator back down the stairs and into the truck because it won't fit.

  Most refrigerator doors can be reversed to open from the right if that is necessary in your kitchen. I'd recommend you have the appliance dealer do the job for you; a slight misalignment in the door can warp the hardware and create air leaks.

- Choose a refrigerator of the proper capacity; buying too large a box will waste electricity.

- An ice or chilled-water dispenser is a convenience and can save a small amount of energy because the freezer door may not have to be opened as often; the ice-making equipment will take up a portion of the freezer unit.

- Pay attention to the shelving arrangement in the refrigerator. The unit should be able to be adapted to your style of life, not the other way around.

Clean the Dishes in Style

Looking for an excuse to buy a dishwasher? A modern machine uses considerably less hot water—perhaps six to eight gallons—than does handwashing. Given enough dishes and enough time, a dishwasher can start to pay for itself. (A lot of dishes, and a lot of time, but you were looking for an excuse to buy a dishwasher, right?)

To maximize those savings, consider water consumption and energy-saving settings on machines as part of your purchase decision.

Tests by consumer groups show that nearly every dishwasher does a decent job at cleaning basic messes. Heavy-duty messes benefit from extra washing cycles and extra washing wands and sprayers.

Examine the loading basket of the dishwasher, bearing in mind the type of dishes and pots you expect to use with the machine; some models may be more suited to your particular kitchen than are others.

Machines that boast of quietness use extra insulation in their cabinets and may use specially designed mechanical parts; near-silence comes at a price.

Before you buy a dishwasher, consider the kinds and the sizes of items you wash frequently. If the dishes you use are unusual (larger than normal, say) you may want to take at least two plates with you when shopping for a dishwasher to check their fit. Some features also make loading certain items easier.

Keep the Dishes Clean and Your Bills Spotless

Use your dishwasher smartly to clean up on your water, power, and fuel bills.

- If your dishwasher has a prerinse or rinse/hold cycle you should not prerinse your dishes by hand in the sink. Instead, merely scrape food off dishes.

- Use energy-saving settings on dishwashers to reduce water and heating energy.

Cook Up a Deal on a Microwave Oven

Microwave ovens have moved beyond novelty to a commodity in most kitchens. As with most consumer appliances, the trick to buying a microwave oven is to buy one that is the proper size and wattage and comes with the best warranty provisions.

If, like most microwave owners, you will be using the oven mostly to reheat frozen food and for cooking simple prepared dishes, don't pay extra for doodads you won't use. These may include temperature probes and multifunction-control panels intended for complex recipes.

Think about the largest plate or dish you expect to put into the oven; you might want to bring it with you to the store to try it out. On models with a revolving turntable (a good feature to help ensure even heating) make certain the large dish can turn completely.

The larger the oven, the more watts it should draw for cooking. Even in smaller units, increased wattage will speed cooking. Manufacturers use a six-ounce cup of water as a standard for cooking; a 600-watt oven should take about 2 minutes and 20 seconds to bring the water to boil, while a 1,000-watt oven will require a full minute less.

Try Do-It-Yourself Appliance Repair

Sears offers an unusual service for do-it-yourselfers: You can call one of their technicians who will help you diagnose a problem with many major appliances, order repair parts, and offer assistance in making the repair yourself. You can call back as often as you want within a month of your first call for assistance.

As we go to press, the cost of the service is $11.99; if you are unable to fix the problem yourself, the cost of the phone call can be applied to the hire of a service technician who will come to your house. Call Sears at (800) 927-7957.

Use These Hot Tips for Oven Efficiency

An oven and a range, especially an electric unit, can be one of the most energy-intensive units in your home. There are, though, some things you can do to lessen the load on your power bill.

- Don't preheat an oven unless the recipe demands it.
- Turn off the oven five or ten minutes before a recipe is due to be done but keep the door closed; the heat in the oven will finish the cooking.
- Match the diameter of your pot to the size of the stove burner to avoid wasting power.

- If your recipe allows, use a lid on the pot to use less energy and allow cooking at lower temperatures.

Clean Up Your Clothes Washer's Act

Make the most of your modern washing machine by using the bells and whistles; spend the time to learn the controls and refresh your memory with the instruction manual from time to time.

- Match water-level settings to the size of the load in the tub; unnecessarily high water levels waste the energy needed to heat it and require more power for the washer to work.
- Follow the manufacturer's recommendations on temperature settings to most efficiently clean your clothes.

Dry Out Energy Use by Clothes Dryers

The harder your dryer has to work, the more it's going to cost you . . . in energy dollars and time.

- Make sure your clothes washer has fully spun out excess water from items before they are placed in the dryer.
- Follow the manufacturer's recommendations for temperature and time settings.
- Clean lint filters regularly to maintain the most efficient airflow.

Warm Up with Hot News on Water Heaters

Consult the manufacturer's recommendations for temperature settings. Many thermostats are delivered from the factory with a setting of 140 degrees, which is warmer than necessary for most households. Reducing the setting to 120 degrees will reduce energy consumption by about 15 percent and may also reduce the chances of an accidental scalding of young children or other people in your home.

Know the Dirt on Vacuum Cleaners

There aren't too many appliances with the price range of vacuum cleaners, which can run from less than $50 to more than $500, a ratio of 10:1. At heart, they are all the same: a motor spins a fan that pushes air away from the machine, creating a vacuum on the other side of the fan.

Here are some things to look for:

- Most vacuum cleaners use an upright design, which is generally more effective with thick or plush carpeting than a canister. Uprights usually have a rotating agitator brush that helps lift dirt from carpeting, and they are usually easier to move around the room because of their wheeled design.

- Canisters are well suited for hardwood or other uncarpeted floors and work well with accessory tools for cleaning furniture, upholstery, draperies, and stairs.

- Consider the weight and construction of the unit. A sturdy unit that uses metal may be too heavy for some people to carry up stairs or even from room to room; on the other hand, a very light-weight unit may make too many compromises on the quality of its components.

- One measure of the power of a vacuum cleaner is the number of amps of electrical current it draws. All things being equal, a 12-amp motor is more powerful than a 5-amp motor. However, some machines are better than others at applying that power-to-vacuum force.

- Some users may want to choose a model that is quieter than others of similar power. There is usually a small premium for this feature.

- Some buyers will want to look for a vacuum cleaner that includes multilevel filtering of the airstream to remove dust and allergens from the exhaust.

SECTION IV

Wheels

Chapter

12 Buying a New Car

For most people, buying a new car is one of life's major shopping events, second only to buying a house.

Today's shopper will find a dizzying range of automobiles in dozens of configurations, from major American, Japanese, Korean, and European makers. Typical vehicle prices for family sedans and popular sports utility vehicles have crossed $20,000 at the same time as car dealers have expanded their reach into their customers' pockets: car sales, add-ons, leasing, financing, service, and more.

Is it any wonder that most car buyers look forward to the process about as much as a visit to the dentist for root canal without anesthesia?

But there is hope for the savvy consumer. Car buyers who know how the game works and who are willing to assert themselves in the car showroom (or on the phone or over the Internet) can save thousands of dollars off the list price of vehicles.

The number-one tip for car buyers is this: Go to school before you go to the dealership.

Your goal should be to know as much about the car you want to buy as the salesperson does. Know the car, available options, and the actual cost that the dealer pays the manufacturer. And then remember on which side of the table the power resides: You are the one with the money and the one who knows just how much you are willing to spend.

Here are some of the keys to success in the new-car showroom:

✓ Know the product better than the salesperson.

✓ Pay no attention to the MSRP (Manufacturer's Suggested Retail Price).

✓ Apply the Savvy Consumer's new-car pricing formula.

✓ Learn how to read a car ad.

✓ Watch out for a bait-and-switch deal.

✓ Trade up . . . at the dealer's expense.

✓ Pick the best day to shop.

✓ Research the value of a trade-in and understand how it is in your best interest to keep new-car and trade-in negotiations separate.

✓ Don't weaken your bargaining hand by revealing information that moves power back to the dealer's side of the table.

✓ Recognize the beauty of a broken record.

✓ Don't get sucked into the "us versus them" game.

✓ Know the answer to the question every salesperson asks.

✓ Turn the tables on the sales team.

✓ Don't discuss financing until the price is set.

✓ Walk away from dealer packs, extended warranties, and other unscrupulous offers.

✓ Drive away from auto-service contracts.

✓ Do the math yourself.

✓ Consider alternative ways to buy a car: over the Internet, by telephone, and by fax.

✓ Consider ordering a car from the factory.

✓ Negotiate a better deal at a "no-negotiation" dealership.

Know the Product Better Than the Salesperson

The best way to conduct a negotiation for any item, including a car, is to know the product line better than the salesperson who hopes to get your name on a contract.

Study the brochures and sales material, especially the pages at the back that list optional and standard equipment. Ask for any supplemental listings of option packages. (Sometimes the option packages are listed only in third-party pricing guides such as Edmund's.)

Spend some time cruising the lots and taking notes on what you find there. I like to make my tours on Sunday mornings, a time when most car dealerships are closed. I'm looking to get some idea of what types of cars the dealer has in stock, and the option packages ordered. I consider it good news if I find more than a few cars of the type I want to buy, since it increases my bargaining power a bit when there are more vehicles than bidders.

If you care about camber angles and horsepower ratings, read one of the enthusiast magazines such as *Automobile, Car and Driver*, or *Road and Track*. Writers here are a lot less concerned about things such as purchase price, resale value, and maintenance and repair. And bear in mind that the publishers of these magazines make their profits based on advertising placed by automobile makers; a "do not buy" recommendation is rare in these publications.

The savvy consumer will want to read the reviews in *Consumer Reports*, the publication of an independent testing organization that accepts no advertising and pulls no punches. Here you'll find independent determinations of miles per gallon, quality of construction, and reliability ratings based on tests and surveys of owners. Car reviews are published in most monthly editions, with an annual automobile roundup in the April issue. If you don't have a subscription, you can hope to find *Consumer Reports* at most libraries.

For MSRP and dealer cost, buy a copy of the current edition of *Edmund's New Car Prices* book, available at most magazine stands and bookstores; the same information is available through several online services including Edmund's online service at **http://www.edmunds.com** and CarPoint at **http://www.msn.com** or **http://www.carpoint.com**

Here's how to use that information:

- It can help you be on guard against attempted ripoffs by the dealer: a charge for a radio that is already included, an extra fee for floor mats if those are standard or part of an option package you are already paying for, or a claim that a particular charge represents a "required option," which is by definition a contradiction in terms.

- If you're faced by any of these shady practices, I'd recommend you take your business elsewhere . . . and consider letting the automobile maker's customer service department know about the business practices of their local representative.

You may be able to find a less expensive option package that brings together items for which you are willing to pay extra, but at a better price.

You don't even have to set foot in a car dealership to do your preliminary research. Here is a list of mostly toll-free phone numbers and Internet Web pages where you can request brochures, specifications, and other information from carmakers:

DOMESTIC MANUFACTURERS

AM General. (800) 3-HUMVEE. Brochures, dealers, financing.
http://www.hummer.com

Buick. (800) 4A-BUICK. Brochures, dealers, financing.
http://www.buick.com

Cadillac. (800) 333-4CAD. Brochures, dealers.
http://www.cadillac.com

Chevrolet. (800) 950-2438. Brochures, dealers.
http://www.chevrolet.com

Chevrolet truck. (800) 950-2438. Brochures, dealers.

Chrysler. (800) 4A-CHRYSLER. Brochures.
http://www.chryslercars.com

Dodge. (800) 4-ADODGE. Brochures, rebate hotline.
http://www.4adodge.com

Eagle. (800) JEEP-EAGLE. Brochures, dealers.
http://www.eaglescars.com

Ford. (800) 392-FORD. Brochures, dealers, financing.
http://www.ford.com

Geo. (800) 327-6278. Brochures, dealers.
http://www.chevrolet.com/geo

GMC. (800) 462-8782. Brochures, dealers.

GMC Truck. (800) GMC-TRUCK. Brochures, dealers.

Jeep. (800) JEEP-EAGLE. Brochures, dealers.
   http://www.jeepunpaved.com

Lincoln. (800) 446-8888. Brochures, dealers.
   http://www.lincolnvehicles.com

Mercury. (800) 446-8888. Brochures, dealers.

Oldsmobile. (800) 442-6537. Brochures.
   http://www.oldsmobile.com

Plymouth. (800) PLYMOUTH. Brochures, dealers.
   http://www.plymouthcars.com

Pontiac. (800) 762-4900. Brochures, dealers.
   http://www.pontiac.com

Saturn. (800) 522-5000. Brochures, dealers.
   http://www.saturncars.com

JAPANESE AND KOREAN MANUFACTURERS

Acura. (800) TO-ACURA. Brochures, dealers.
   http://www.acura.com

Honda. http://www.honda.com

Hyundai. (800) 826-CARS. Brochures, dealers.
   http://www.hmc.co.kr

Infiniti. (800) 826-6500. Brochures, dealers.
   (800) 627-4437. Financing.
   http://www.infinitimotors.com

Isuzu. (800) 792-3800. Brochures.
   http://www.isuzu.com

Kia. (800) 333-4KIA. Brochures, dealers.
   http://www.kia.co.kr/kia

Lexus. (800) 872-5398. Brochures, dealers.
   http://www.lexususa.com

Mazda. (800) 639-1000. Brochures, dealers.
http://www.mazdausa.com

Mitsubishi. (800) 447-4700. Brochures, dealers.
http://www.mitsucars.com

Nissan. (800) NISSAN-6. Brochures.
http://www.nissanmotors.com

Subaru. (800) SUBARU-3. Brochures.
http://www.subaru.com

Suzuki. (800) 447-4700. Brochures, dealers.

Toyota. (800) GO-TOYOTA. Brochures, dealers.
http://www.toyota.com

EUROPEAN MANUFACTURERS

Audi. (800) FOR-AUDI. Brochures, dealers.
http://www.audi.com

BMW. (800) 334-4BMW. Brochures, dealers.
http://www.bmwusa.com

Ferrari. (201) 816-2651. Dealers.
http://www.ferrari.it/ferrari.com

Jaguar. (800) 4JAGUAR. Brochures, dealers.
http://www.jaguarvehicles.com

Land Rover. (800) FINE-4WD. Brochures, dealers.
http://www.landrover.com

Lotus. (800) 24-LOTUS. Brochures, dealers.
http://www.lotuscars.com

Mercedes Benz. (800) FOR-MERCEDES.
Brochures, dealers, technical information.
http://www.usa.mercedes-benz.com

Porsche. (800) 252-4444. Brochures, dealers.
http://www.porsche.com

Rolls Royce. (810) 350-0500. Brochures, dealers, leasing.

Saab. (800) 582-SAAB. Brochures, dealers.
  http://www.saabusa.com

Volkswagen. (800) 444-8987. Brochures, dealers.
  http://www.vw.com

Volvo. (800) 458-1552. Brochures.
  http://www.volvocars.com

Pay No Attention to the MSRP (Manufacturer's Suggested Retail Price)

How can a car dealer afford the fancy showroom, the splashy television ads, and that lovely free coffee and still sell you a car for "$49 over factory invoice"?

The fact is that the dealer cannot afford such a deal, at least if the factory invoice price was really the full wholesale price.

In truth, car manufacturers regularly offer dealers discounts from the "official" factory invoice price. Instead of lowering the invoice price, the manufacturers allow dealers to either (1) lower prices to buyers or (2) keep the extra money themselves.

We, of course, prefer to pay less for our cars.

There are three important terms to define here:

- *Manufacturer-to-buyer-rebate.* Here, the maker of the car offers money back to buyers for the purchase of a particular model of car. The money can be paid directly to you after you take title of the car, or it can be used as part of a down payment against the price of the car. In some situations, the dealer may require customers to sign over their rebate in order to receive a special price; this seems to me to be a purposely confusing arrangement. I'd rather negotiate my own deal on my own terms.

- *Dealer holdback.* If I weren't trying to be polite here, I might call this a hidden kickback from the manufacturer to the dealer. That's exactly what it is, of course. Manufacturers pay dealers a bonus or credit for every vehicle sold, an amount that is not reflected on the invoice price or advertised to the buyer as a rebate. Typical hold-backs are 3 percent on a domestic vehicle and 2 or 3 percent on imports. This is not insignificant: 3 percent of a $25,000 MSRP is $750, which pays for the showroom, TV ads, bad coffee, and the owner's diamond pinky ring at a large dealership.

- *Sales-incentive or dealer rebate.* This is money offered by the man-ufacturer to spur the sales of a particular model or line of cars; it is usually a prod to clear the lots of vehicles that are not selling well or is an attempt to clear a glut of cars. The money goes to the dealer and may or may not result in a reduced price to the con-sumer.

If the manufacturer is offering a customer rebate on a vehicle, you should think of this as a side deal between you and the maker. You still want to negotiate as sharply as you can with the dealer; once you have driven down the price to a fair level, you can factor in the rebate as a bonus.

The dealer holdback and the dealer rebate, on the other hand, should become part of your negotiations with the salesperson.

Here's a hypothetical example of how auto pricing works:

1998 BoxOnWheels

Manufacturer's Suggested Retail Price	$25,000
Dealer Invoice	22,500
Dealer Holdback 3% of MSRP	− 750
Dealer Net Cost	$21,750

If you insist on throwing away your hard-earned cash, you could pay the MSRP, giving the dealer a profit of $3,250, or 13 percent.

Or, you might accept what seems to be a magnanimous offer by the salesperson of $1,000 off the "list price." Though the sales manager may make a big show of moaning about how close to the bone he or she is cutting, in truth this still amounts to a profit of $2,250, or 9 percent.

Now let's get serious. It's the end of the model year and the dealer is running one of those specials that seems too good to be true: $1 over invoice! Your price would be $22,501. Don't let the salesperson cry about all the money the dealership is losing: The profit in our hypothetical example is $751, which is 3 percent—still a decent profit for a quick deal. (It is also not really your concern about how the dealer divides up the proceeds from a car deal; the salesperson's commission should be between him or her and the owner of the place. Your concern is to keep more money in your pocket.)

Let's back up and remember my basic advice on negotiating a price for a car: Don't think in terms of reducing the MSRP. Instead, ask yourself (and the salesperson) the following question: What is a reasonable profit for the dealer? I think the proper answer is something in the range of 3 to 5 percent. If that sounds low, consider that the dealer typically holds a car on the lot for only a few weeks or at most a few months. A 5 percent profit on a vehicle in stock for two months is roughly equivalent to 30 percent profit on an annual basis. And add in the fact that most dealers proceed to make money off their customers for years to come through the maintenance-and-repair shop.

And so, here is a way to come up with the price on our hypothetical BoxOnWheels:

Manufacturer's Suggested Retail Price	$25,000
Invoice Price	22,500
Manufacturer's Holdback 3% of MSRP	− 750
Dealer Net Cost	$21,750
Profit 5% on Net Cost	+$1,087
Our fair offer price to dealer	$22,837

Some buyers take a shortcut to arrive at nearly the same place: They add a few hundred dollars to the invoice price to come up with their offering amount.

In the preceding example, let's include a $1,000 manufacturer-to-buyer rebate: Your fair-offer price to the dealer should still be $22,837, with $1,000 of that money coming in the form of the rebate, or with $1,000 coming directly to you as a check after the title has been passed.

You will, in any case, have to add back into the deal destination charges (the cost of shipping the vehicle from the factory to the dealer; imported cars may have a higher destination charge than domestics), advertising charges set by the manufacturer or regional dealer associations, taxes, and registration and license fees.

You should not have to pay unreasonable "paperwork" and "processing" fees. I have paid the dealer $50 or $75 for the cost of sending a clerk over to the state motor vehicle office to register a vehicle, and I have refused to pay charges of $250 for the same service. Put a price on an hour or so of your time, and remember that almost everything is negotiable when you sit down to buy a car. (And in one memorable car purchase, my insurance agent offered to take care of all of the paperwork of the purchase and licensing as part of his service to me; I happily accepted that offer and struck out the paperwork charge on the sales agreement.)

And unless you insist on buying a car for which there are more buyers than cars, run—don't walk—away from a deal that includes something like "Additional Dealer Profit" or "Additional Dealer Markup." This is nothing less than price gouging.

How do you determine the amount of the dealer holdback? The formula does not change very often; check specialty automobile magazines and Internet Web pages for changes since this book went to press.

In recent years, the Big Three domestic carmakers have been consistent in kicking back 3 percent of the total MSRP of a car. This includes the base price of the car plus all options supplied by the manufacturer. (Not included in the calculation are destination charges, taxes, advertising charges, licensing fees, and any options put into the car by the dealer or a third party.)

Foreign manufacturers, including those makers that assemble some or all of their automobile lines in the United States, sometimes base their dealer holdback on the total MSRP, the base MSRP without options, or on the base invoice (wholesale) price.

Here are the dealer holdback formulas for major carmakers as they were in effect in mid-1997:

DOMESTIC CARMAKERS

Buick (GM)	3% of total MSRP
Cadillac (GM)	3% of total MSRP
Chevrolet (GM)	3% of total MSRP
Chrysler (Chrysler)	3% of total MSRP
Dodge (Chrysler)	3% of total MSRP
Eagle (Chrysler)	3% of total MSRP
Ford	3% of total MSRP

Geo (GM)	3% of total MSRP
GMC (GM)	3% of total MSRP
Jeep (Chrysler)	3% of total MSRP
Lincoln (Ford)	3% of total MSRP
Mercury (Ford)	3% of total MSRP
Oldsmobile (GM)	3% of total MSRP
Plymouth (Chrysler)	3% of total MSRP
Pontiac (GM)	3% of total MSRP
Saturn (GM)	No Dealer Holdback

FOREIGN CARMAKERS

Acura	2% of base MSRP
Audi	No Dealer Holdback
BMW	2% of total MSRP
Honda	2% of base MSRP
Hyundai	2% of base invoice
Infiniti	3% of total MSRP
Isuzu	3% of total MSRP
Jaguar	2% of total MSRP
Land Rover	2% of total MSRP
Lexus	2% of base MSRP
Mazda	3% of total MSRP
Mercedes-Benz	2% of total MSRP
Mitsubishi	2% of base MSRP
Nissan	3% of total MSRP
Porsche	2% of total MSRP
Saab	3% of total MSRP
Subaru	2% of base MSRP
Toyota	2% of base MSRP
Volkswagen	2% of total MSRP
Volvo	Varies by model

Apply the Savvy Consumer's New-Car Pricing Formula

Forget about asking for a discount from the MSRP (Manufacturer's Suggested Retail Price). Instead ask yourself—and the salesperson—what is a reasonable markup from the cost of this car?

THE SAVVY CONSUMER NEW-CAR FORMULA

1. Determine the dealer invoice for the car.
2. Add the dealer invoice for factory-installed options.
3. Ignore any dealer packs such as undercoating, rustproofing, pin-striping, and other unnecessary items.
4. Subtract the dealer-holdback amount.
5. Subtract any rebates to the dealer or customer.
6. Add a profit of 3 to 5 percent.
7. Add the destination charge posted on the official sticker.
8. Add advertising fees as posted on the official sticker.
9. Add state and local tax.

Learn How to Read a Car Ad

It's not your eyes or ears: You don't really think that dealers want you to read the tiny print at the bottom of the car ads or understand the rapid-fire audio mumble at the end of a radio commercial, do you? Here you'll find some of the most entertaining (and potentially misleading) fiction published today.

Before you sign on the bottom line for automobile financing, though, you had better know the terms of the loan—the terms that are laid out in writing in the loan agreement, and not the advertisement or the commercial.

Here are some questions to ask about special offers:

- Will you have to pay an inflated price for the car in order to receive the reduced-rate loan? One tip-off that this may be the case is language such as this in the ad: "Dealer Participation Required." This means that the dealer is cooperating with the manufacturer to create the special offer; something has to give, don't you think?

- Put another way, is the dealer willing to accept a lower price for the car if you pay cash, provide your own financing, or accept a higher interest rate?

- Does the advertised low price require a larger-than-usual down payment? One way to artificially reduce the monthly payments is to require that buyers put down half the cost of the car in advance. That's not necessarily a bad thing, since most experts recommend paying by cash if you can afford to do so. The point here, though, is to be sure to compare apples with apples as you look at various deals.

- Is the low price based on a minimum value for a trade-in applied against the purchase of the new car? Be careful here: Be sure you know the real value of your old car. On the other hand, if you are trading in a junker from the backyard, check to be sure that the dealer's promised trade-in value does not include exceptions for damage, rust, or high mileage.

- Is the loan term unusually short? Some dealers have offered unusually low interest rates, or low lease rates for arrangements that last only 12 or 24 months.

- Is the special rate available on all cars, on certain models only, or only to ones already in stock? Some deals may apply only to cars that are ordered from the manufacturer.

- Are you required to purchase extra options or services such as rustproofing, an extended warranty, or a service contract in order to qualify for a low interest loan? This is nothing less than an increase in the price of the car, and you should consider it in that way.

- Is the special interest rate offered in lieu of a manufacturer's rebate? If so, compare the value of the rebate to the special interest rate.

Watch Out for a Bait-and-Switch Deal

If you find that the salesman is trying hard to talk you out of buying the car on sale in an ad, or if a saleswoman denigrates the quality of her own product offerings you may be the target of a bait-and-switch.

You, of course, are responding to a car ad because you have researched the current models and believe that the vehicle on sale is a good deal for your needs and is well reviewed by independent testers. You're not really interested in the salesperson's opinions, because that person's self-interest is obvious.

If it's a good deal, go for it . . . after you've tried to improve on it, of course. If the salesman tells you it's a bad deal, I'd listen very carefully and apply his own arguments against any other car he would try to sell you.

Finally, if you believe the car dealer was advertising something they did not have available for sale, contact your state attorney general or consumer affairs office and lodge a complaint.

Trade Up . . . at the Dealer's Expense

If the salesperson asks you for a little concession on your offer so that he or she can have something new to bring in to the sales manager, don't do so without asking for a little concession in return. Say something like: "I'll give you $300 more for the car if you throw in for the same price that better set of tires we discussed earlier."

Pick the Best Day to Shop

There are two important concepts to keep in mind here: You want to shop on a day when there are more salespeople and cars than customers, and you might as well take advantage of the pressure that car makers and dealers put on their own salespeople.

Therefore, one of the best days of the year to shop is December 31, especially if it is snowing. First of all, this is an especially quiet time because of the holiday period. The snowstorm helps cut down on visitors, too. Finally, dealerships routinely create sales contests and quotas, and they are almost always tied to the end of the week, the end of the month, or the end of the year.

It's also a bit of leverage in your favor to come in near the end of the day. The sales force is tired, worn down by a day that may not have been a terrific one, and anxious to go home. You come in fresh, full of energy, and ready to buy a car.

Remember as you walk in the door that the salesperson needs you and your money. You're doing him a favor by not going to the other dealer down the block, and you can let him know that you're willing to do him another favor by buying a car on this terribly slow day . . . if he's willing to cut you a fine deal on your terms.

The worst possible time to try to bargain hard is in the middle of a heavily promoted sale when the dealership is packed with customers.

Research the Value of a Trade-in and Understand How It Is in Your Best Interest to Keep New-Car and Trade-in Negotiations Separate

Here's where many car buyers get taken to the car wash. Don't be taken: Your most important goal should be to prevent the dealer from mixing together your trade-in and new-car bargaining.

Do one of the following:

1. Sell your car yourself. Consult guides such as the *Blue Book* or *Edmund's Used Car Prices* (both available at bookstores; you may also find copies at the desk of the bank where you may be seeking financing) to find the wholesale price for your vehicle. Adjust the price up or down if you have any special options and have unusually low or high mileage. Finally, the price has to be adjusted based on the overall condition of the vehicle.

   You can try to sell the car through want ads, pricing it somewhere between the wholesale and retail prices you have found in your research.

   Or, you can bring the car to a used-car lot that is not connected to the dealership where you intend to buy a new car. Here you can expect to be offered a price close to the wholesale value. A visit to a used-car dealership is a good way to obtain a realistic appraisal of the wholesale value of your car; you can take that number with you into your negotiations with a new-car dealer to see if they are trying to lowball you on the value of your trade-in.

2. Offer your car to the new-car dealership. Tell the salesperson early—and often—that you are determined to receive the best possible offer for your used car. Show your research—the wholesale price, or an offer from an independent used-car lot. Concentrate on getting a price you're happy with.

   Then, shift gears. Now you should tell the salesperson that your priority is to get the lowest possible price on the new car.

   Here's what you're trying to avoid: a situation where the dealer underpays you for your trade-in and then let's you think you're getting a "steal" on the new car. Or you could end up with the dealer overpaying you for your trade-in and then taking an unacceptable position on the new-car purchase, pointing to the trade-in as justification.

   You, the one with the power, want to have it both ways: the highest possible price for a trade-in and the lowest possible price for a purchase. Therefore you want to split up the negotiations to your advantage.

Don't accept a lowball price from the dealer for your trade-in. Many people think that the price they are being given is written in stone; remember that everything is negotiable. The dealer will hope you will not protest a low offer, or will try to negotiate only a small increase. If you are offered $5,000 on a car that the *Blue Book* lists at $10,000, demand an explanation.

Be prepared to walk out the door. You can always come back if you are unable to sell the vehicle on your own at a better price, or can't get another dealer to offer you more.

Don't Weaken Your Bargaining Hand by Revealing Information That Moves the Power Back to the Dealer's Side of the Table

One of the first questions you'll be asked when you meet a car salesperson is this: "Do you want to lease or finance the car?" The second question: "Do you have a trade-in?"

Duck! Never begin a car negotiation by telling the salesperson how you plan to pay for the car. If you leave those details for later, you'll have a better chance of keeping the power on your side of the table. I'd suggest you either try to change the subject, or commit a little white lie by saying: "I'll probably pay cash." (Probably doesn't mean certainly, so maybe this is not technically a lie; you can always change your mind.)

Your single-minded goal should be to drive down the purchase price of the vehicle. If you later move on to negotiate financing or a lease you can avoid many of the tricks of the trade that can inflate the purchase price in less-than-obvious ways.

My recommendation: Come to the table with two prices already in mind: a realistic price you would be happy to pay and a slightly higher price that you would be willing to accept. Start with the first number and stick to it for as long as possible. Explain how you came up with the number, demonstrating your understanding of dealer cost, holdbacks, and rebates.

It's even more impressive if you come to the table with some of your research in hand, including information on dealer cost.

If you make any movement on your offer, go to the second number and make it clear to the salesperson that you are willing to walk out the door if you are pushed to go above that level.

Speaking of which, some salespeople will try to push you over the line by declaring that their latest price is a "take-it-or-leave-it" deal. If the price is not acceptable to you, go ahead and call their bluff: leave it.

Walk out the door and see if the salesperson or the general manager chases after you. If one or both is hot on your heels, you're in the catbird seat. If they let you stroll, they either don't want your business or your offer was way out of line.

Always remember that there are other dealers and other cars . . . and other days, for that matter. And you can always come back and take the "take-it-or-leave-it" price if that turns out to be the best offer in town.

Recognize the Beauty of a Broken Record

The sales force is going to do everything possible to wear you down, through a well-rehearsed sales pitch, double-teaming, and other techniques. Why shouldn't you do the same to them?

I call it the "broken-record" method, and it's something any parent with young children will immediately understand. Your kids will just keep asking for what they want, in the same way and in the same terms, over and over again. I don't know about you, but I usually end up caving in to my kids just to get them to leave me alone.

So, try it yourself with an auto salesperson.

Q: What do I have to do to get you to buy this car today?

A: Sell it to me for $18,000 in metallic blue with the roof rack, giving me $9,200 as a trade-in for my old car.

Q: Listen, my boss says he'll let me sell you the car for below the invoice price if you'll give us a little bit of breathing room on the trade-in.

A: That's nice. Here's what I want: Sell me the car for $18,000 in metallic blue with the roof rack, giving me $9,200 as a trade-in for my old car.

Q: What if we threw in a free set of fuzzy dice for the rear-view mirror?

A: Lovely. I'll take them. $18,000 in metallic blue with the roof rack and the fuzzy dice, giving me $9,200 as a trade-in for my old car.

You get the idea.

Don't Get Sucked into the "Us versus Them" Game

One time-honored sales tactic at the dealership is "double-teaming." If the salesperson you're working with senses you have reached a brick wall in the negotiating process, he or she might call in an "associate" or one of the managers of the dealership in a form of tag team. The idea is to bring in an experienced "closer" to get your signature on the bottom line.

In the worst situation, the new person at the table may try to begin the negotiation at square one, or may take a much harder line than the original negotiator; the idea here may be to get you to jump at the chance to get back to a deal with the original salesperson. Or, the new negotiator may be such a nice guy that you'll want to strike a deal to avoid having to see your original companion.

First of all, exercise your right to walk out the door if you don't like the way you are being treated. You don't have to talk to a "closer" or a manager if you don't want to.

And then you might want to turn the tables: Consider taking along a well-prepared buddy when you go in for a negotiating session for a car. (It's called having a "third baseman" by salespeople.) It'll take some of the pressure off you, especially if the dealership tries to double-team you with a salesperson and a manager. And your friend can help you stay on your game plan if you start to waver.

You can also play your own version of the "good-cop, bad-cop" game. Have your buddy take a hard line on price while you pull back a bit from the negotiations; the salesperson may cave in a bit easier in the face of your own double team.

There's one more annoying but common tactic among car-sales forces: I call it the "us against them" whine.

It works like this: After a decent period of back-and-forth haggling, the salesperson suddenly seems to be taking your side, agreeing that your offer is a reasonable one. "Let's write it up and I'll take it in to the general manager to see if she'll accept it," you'll be told. All of a sudden you're being informed that the salesperson actually doesn't have the authority to strike a deal.

What has actually happened is that you have come close enough to a selling price where the salesperson thinks you can be worn down by the general manager. After a few minutes (probably devoted to a cup of coffee and a few hands of bridge with the guys in the back room), the salesperson will come out with a hangdog look. "She turned us down," you'll be told. "I thought we had a good offer, but she says that the car you want is just too hot to let go for that price. In fact, she tells me that there's another customer coming in tonight who wants to buy the car at full price."

It is, of course, all a game intended to get you to cave in and pay a few hundred dollars more. I recommend you keep a polite but businesslike relationship with the salesperson; he's not your friend or else he wouldn't be trying to take more out of your pocket than you want to spend. If things get to be a bit too much for you, call them on it: "Knock off the good-cop, bad-cop game, will you?"

(In the most odious of variations, the salesperson will ask you to give a deposit to show the sincerity of your offer. The effect of this is to make it more difficult for you to stand up and walk out the door when your offer is refused. I would flat-out refuse a request for a deposit until my offer is accepted by the dealership; I want to keep the power on my side of the table.)

Know the Answer to the Question Every Salesperson Asks

Many salespeople are taught to ask the question: "What do I have to do to get you to buy this car today?" What they're trying to do is to get you to simplify your objections to making a purchase and allow them to make you feel as if you are getting your way.

If you answer, "I want to pay less," they may drop the price by a few hundred dollars (while still making an undeservedly large profit) and make you feel guilty for asking for more. If you say, "I want to get more for my trade-in," they may boost the money paid for your old clunker and then point to that when you start to talk about the new-car purchase price.

The proper answer to the question is to state your whole deal in great specificity: "I want you to give me $11,500 for my old car and sell me the new car for $21,500, and I don't want the service contract and the pinstriping you keep asking me about. Is that clear?"

Turn the Tables on the Sales Team

Take control of the negotiating. Stop letting the salesperson tell you, "You'll have to give me something better to bring to the sales manager." Instead, start saying: "You'll have to do better than that on the price or I'll have to go somewhere else."

When you get tired of hearing the salesperson say, "What do I have to do to get you to buy a car today?" turn the question around. Ask: "Why won't you let me buy a car today? I'm ready to take a deal on these terms . . ."

Don't Discuss Financing Until the Price Is Set

A tried-and-true tactic at the dealership is to ask the buyer: "How much do you want to pay per month?"

Stop! Don't fall into that trap. What the salesperson is trying to do is get you to focus on something other than the bottom line. With a few clicks of the desktop calculator, the salesperson can change a three-year loan into a five-year loan, reducing the monthly payment but significantly increasing the real cost to you.

Don't discuss financing with the dealership until you have decided on the car and its price.

Walk Away from Dealer Packs, Extended Warranties, and Other Unscrupulous Offers

Shoppers quickly learn to recognize the federally mandated official sticker price for a car. These labels, produced by the manufacturer and attached to new cars, are not supposed to be altered in any way or removed by the dealer.

Any increases or decreases to the price and addition or removal of options should be considered as part of the negotiation between you and the dealer.

Here are some more warning signs:

- Be wary of any "supplemental" stickers that some dealers may paste to a car window. These are almost always dealer "packs" that do nothing more than add profit. Sometimes charges are levied for unnecessary services such as extra rustproofing or high-cost, low-value pinstriping, while other charges we have seen are things such as "Dealer Markup" or other thinly veiled labels for price gouging.

  I would recommend that you tell a salesperson that you have no interest in discussing anything beyond the manufacturer's invoice and that you intend to ignore any such supplemental sticker and services or items listed on them. Walk away from any dealer who doesn't recognize and respect a savvy buyer.

- Question any entry on the dealer sticker you don't recognize, especially strange sets of unexplained initials.

Drive Away from Auto-Service Contracts

Auto dealers may try to slip this one by you at the last moment, after the price for a new or used car has been negotiated but before you sign on the bottom line. No wonder, either, since these "extended-warranty" contracts are often a great deal—for the dealer.

Most consumer groups and auto experts recommend against buying such coverage. You'd do better researching the repair and breakdown history of the car you want to buy and checking the reputation of the maker and the dealer. If the dealer tries hard to convince you to purchase an extended warranty, ask yourself (or the dealer) if that is because the car is unreliable, or because this is a profit area for the dealer.

Here are the danger areas:

- Don't pay for coverage you already have. Be sure you read and understand the manufacturer's warranty on the car before you consider paying extra for coverage that may duplicate it. How many miles, and which systems are covered by the manufacturer? What systems and what time or mileage limitations are in the extended warranty? You're not going to be able to collect twice.

- Be sure you understand the terms of the extended warranty. Are there large deductibles that must be satisfied before you are repaid? Is the contract valid only at the dealer who sold it to you? What happens if you have a problem on the road? How are reimbursements made? Must you lay out money and then submit a claim, or is the dealer obligated to perform the service and deal with the administrator on your behalf?

- Do not accept any verbal representations about the coverage. If a system is not specifically included in writing, assume that it is not covered by the warranty.

- If you are purchasing a used car, a "demonstrator" car that has been used by salesmen but has never been registered, or a fleet lease vehicle, check to see if the extended warranty has any exclusions. Does its coverage start when you take possession of the car, or is it back-dated to when the vehicle was registered by its original owner?

- Who is behind the contract? The manufacturer? The dealer? An independent company? Of the three, the manufacturer is the one most likely to still be in business at the end of the contract term, followed by the dealer (in most cases). What happens if the provider shuts down?

  Many service contracts sold by dealers are actually products offered by independent companies, called administrators. The administrators act as claims adjusters, authorizing—or denying—payment of claims to dealers. Read the contract carefully to see what happens if the administrator goes out of business; the dealership should be obligated to perform under the contract. If the dealer goes out of business, the administrator should be required to fulfill the terms of the contract.

- What do you know about the reputation of the dealer and the administrator? Check with the local Better Business Bureau, your state consumer-protection office, and other appropriate agencies. If the contract is backed by an insurance company, contact your State Insurance Commission to ask about the solvency of the company and whether any complaints have been filed against it.

- What happens if you sell the car or it is stolen or destroyed in an accident? Is the contract transferable for free or for a reasonable fee? Can you cancel the coverage and receive a full or partial refund?

  If you do purchase a transferable extended warranty, make it part of your marketing pitch when you resell the car.

Do the Math Yourself

You've just spent four hours haggling over every nickel and dime on the purchase price of your new car, the trade-in value of your old vehicle, and the financing plan. You've wisely passed on unnecessary dealer packs such as rustproofing, undercoating, pinstriping, and you've avoided wasteful extended warranties.

Now the salesperson disappears into the business office to prepare the paperwork. There's one critical assignment still to be done: You've got to check the math.

There are dozens of figures to be put in place on the sales agreement and loan or lease application if you are financing the car through the dealer. This means there are dozens of places where an innocent mistake—or a purposeful fraud—can end up costing you hundreds or thousands of dollars.

I'll try to be charitable here. Mistakes happen. But why do they always seem to be in the favor of the dealership? Here are some suggestions:

- Keep a notepad at your side as you do your negotiations and write down all of the numbers as agreed. Keep track of any special options or accommodations. You can show the notes to the salesperson before he or she goes to the business office.

- When you are presented with the paperwork, start by making sure that the car you plan to buy is properly described. If you are buying one off the lot, the Vehicle Identification Number will be listed, and in doing so that model is specified. If you are ordering a car from the factory, make sure the model is listed properly and that all option packages are specified.

- Next, check that the numbers are entered correctly. Watch for transposed numbers and for errors on critical areas such as interest rates and number of months for a loan.

- Finally, whip out a calculator (or borrow the salesperson's) and check the math.

What do you do if you find a whopper of a mistake on the paperwork? If you think it might be the result of an innocent error by the salesperson or the dealership, you can firmly insist that it be corrected. If you believe there has been one last effort to rob you with a fountain pen, walk out the door . . . preferably with a copy of the contract that you can share with your state or local consumer-protection agency and the manufacturer who has granted the dealer the right to sell its cars.

Consider Alternative Ways to Buy a Car: Over the Internet, by Telephone, and by Fax

Here's how I bought a car a few years ago. I did my research in magazines and books to choose the car I wanted and then made a few trips to dealerships for test drives. Then I prepared my offer based on the dealer invoice, subtracting rebates, and adding in a reasonable profit. Finally, I placed phone calls to five auto dealerships within an hour of my home and asked them the name of the sales manager and his fax phone number.

I then prepared a letter that went something like this: "I am ready to purchase a current model GMC Suburban equipped as indicated below. The dealer cost for that car, minus rebate but not including manufacturer's holdback, is approximately $23,100. I would welcome a bid from your dealership for that car at no more than dealer cost plus $300."

I had laid out the fact that I was ready to buy, that I knew more than a little about the car-sales business, and that I would be interested in a bid only on my terms. One of the dealers never responded, a second came back with an unacceptable offer of a discount off the MSRP, but three sales managers called or faxed bids for my business. After a short telephone round of negotiation, I came to an agreement with a dealer. I dropped by the sales manager's office later that day to sign the contract and a little while later drove out with a heck of a deal that came with as little pain as possible.

In recent years, some new methods of car sales have arrived on the scene. There are now several Internet-based services that promise to distribute your request for a bid to area dealers; they claim that the dealers in their network work from dealer invoice up and not from MSRP down.

Here are some high-tech car-dealer links and information services. Remember to apply the same criteria to any price offered by one of these services: Determine the dealer's true cost and add a reasonable markup.

Auto-By-Tel. **http://www.autobytel.com**

Auto Mall USA. **http://www.automallusa.com**

Auto Network. http://www.autonetwork.com

Auto Price Network. http://www.apndeal.com

Auto Web. http://www.autoweb.com

CarPoint. Microsoft's car information and sales service
with dealer cost and other valuable data.
http://www.carpoint.com or http://www.msn.com

DealerNet. http://www.dealernet.com

Edmund's Automotive Buyer's Guides. The best-known and most
complete guide to dealer cost for new cars.
http://www.edmunds.com

Executive Car Buying Services. http://www.execar.com/index.html

Intellichoice. Includes an interesting, but complicated, process to
create your own version of a new car window sticker with all
the options you choose. Note, though, that not all combinations of options are available, and some dealers—especially
those selling foreign makes—are able to order a car for a
buyer in a reasonable time frame.
http://www.intellichoice.com

Kelley Blue Book.
http://www.kbb.com

National Association of Buyer's Agents. Members include
Car$ource, American CarBuying Service, Consumer
Automobile Research Service Inc., Auto Buyers Service of
Rochester, Auto Advisor, Inc., Auto Shoppers' Guardian Angel.
http://www.naba.com

Consider Ordering a Car from the Factory

Should you consider ordering a car to be factory-built to your specifications? This is one way to obtain a car with just the options you are
interested in purchasing, and you may be able to save some money on
the price of the car, although in certain circumstances a dealer may be

more willing to cut a sharp deal on a car already on the lot. Note, too, that it is difficult to factory-order a foreign-built car for delivery in the United States.

The reason a dealer may be willing to cut an even better deal for a car ordered from the factory is that the dealer does not have to pay finance charges (called a "floor plan") for cars received from the manufacturer but not yet sold. But a dealer may also be anxious to unload a car that has been sitting on the lot for several months and has drawn no offers.

The only way to find out the best deal is to push the salesperson hard.

You may also be able to get a dealer to locate a car equipped or painted to your desire on the lot of another dealer and make a wholesale transfer. You shouldn't have to pay extra for this service, and all of the other elements of striking a good deal still apply.

Negotiate a Better Deal at a "No-Negotiation" Dealership

One uncertain trend in auto sales is the "no-negotiation" dealership, sometimes renamed as a "car store." Here, in theory, prices of cars are set at a realistic selling price, discounted from the MSRP. There is no sales staff, only a group of noncommissioned order takers.

General Motors went to the lead of this particular wagon train with its Saturn division. All of the dealerships for that line of cars sell from a fixed-price menu.

In theory, I guess I should like this idea since it removes a great deal of the unacceptable padding that sits between a dealer's true cost and the selling price. But as you might guess, I am skeptical: Most of the no-negotiation dealers position their prices somewhere about midway between dealer cost and list price. That is still a good deal for most buyers, those who are unwilling or unable to negotiate better. But for the rest of us, we can do better.

There are, though, some ways to negotiate a better deal, even at a no-negotiation car store. The trick is to negotiate everything else.

Start with the basic rule of buying: Know as much or more than the salesperson about the product. If you know that a dealer, even a Saturn car store, paid $18,000 for a vehicle, you are in a position to set your own reasonable purchase price (in this case, let's give them a 5 percent markup, for a selling price of $18,900). If the sales price is listed at $19,900, figure that the dealership has to find a way to make you $1,000 happier than you are now.

If you are trading in a car at a car store, ask for a higher price for your old vehicle to make up for any overpayment.

If you are financing the new-car purchase, ask for a reduced interest rate or a subsidized loan.

If you want to add a dealer-installed option or accessory, ask that it be included free or at a substantial discount.

Remember that the power still resides on your side of the table. Most any dealer or car store would rather make a bit less profit on a deal than no profit at all; make it clear that you are willing to go down the road to another dealership where they still haggle over the selling price and see if they'll really let you walk out the door.

Chapter

13 Buying a Used Car

Buying a used car is at the same time simpler and more complex than making a deal at the new-car dealership.

It is most simple if you are making an offer directly to the owner; you'll make a bid based on what you are willing to pay and the seller will accept or reject the offer based on what he or she feels is a fair price. The original purchase price is no longer relevant. The owner will factor in the value received for the use of the car and then make an estimate of resale value in setting a price. And if the seller has to drop the price to make a sale, it represents only a paper loss.

Things become a bit more complicated if you are offering to buy a used car from a dealer. The dealer may have bought the car at auction or accepted it as a trade-in from another buyer; either way, the seller knows its cost and will want to make a profit above the price paid.

Either way, the greatest level of uncertainty in a used-car negotiation is the condition of the vehicle. Here is where you should spend the time and money to conduct an investigation of your own. If you are buying from a dealer, you include in your decision the value of any warranty or money-back guarantee offered.

You should also consider—carefully—other sources of used vehicles, including fleet sales and rental-car lots.

There is one basic reason to buy a used car: In most cases, the moment you drive a new car off the dealer's lot its resale value drops by thousands of dollars. After then, depreciation slows considerably.

If you can find a clean, well-maintained used car that is just a few years old you can let someone else pay for that rapid depreciation. Modern cars are pretty well made, and you can expect them to last 100,000 miles or more before they reach the point where they are not worth maintaining and repairing.

Of course, there is one basic trick here, too: You've got to guard against buying someone else's problem secondhand. Before you worry too much about buying a used car with a troubled background, remember that even a new car can be a lemon.

In recent years, the used-car market has been strong, at least in part because of the high prices of new cars. A second reason is the burgeoning growth of the leasing industry, which returns to the market large numbers of relatively new, low-mileage vehicles each year.

In some cases, a one- or two-year-old vehicle may actually be selling at a price pretty close to its cost when new. The reason: They are being compared to current models that may have risen sharply in price in recent years.

Of course you, as the buyer, can—and should—walk away from an inflated price for a used car. There are still good values to be had; there is no reason to pay new-car prices for a used car.

In this section, I show you some tricks on how to check out used cars, how to consider used-car warranties, and how to negotiate the best price for previously owned vehicles. Here are some important tips that will help you move the power to your side of the table when you negotiate for a used car:

- ✓ Learn how to buy a used car.
- ✓ Know where to buy a used car: the advantages and disadvantages of new- or used-car dealerships and private sales.
- ✓ Should you try harder? The ins and outs of buying a car from a rental fleet.
- ✓ Do you know the difference between a new and used car? When is a used car still new?
- ✓ Never mind what the salesman says: Find your car's true life story.
- ✓ Learn how to conduct a smell test on a used car.
- ✓ Call in the Feds for safety.

✓ Learn how to tell a car's model year.

✓ Understand used-car warranties.

Learn How to Buy a Used Car

The main difference between buying a new car and a used car is the number of variables that enter into the negotiation process.

When you buy a new car, you can have a reasonable assumption that the car has been driven only a few dozen miles in testing and that it has not suffered any accident damage. Beyond that you have a reasonable expectation of service under the manufacturer's warranty from the dealership. And you can make some assumptions about the car's life expectancy and future resale value based on the history of other vehicles from that manufacturer that were sold as new.

When you buy a used car, the number of miles can vary from very low to unreasonably high.

Mileage is an important consideration in car buying. If you figure a car has a useful life of 120,000 miles, buying a car with 60,000 miles on the odometer means you are buying a car with half the expected life of a new vehicle. In addition, the cost of repairs of an older car and especially one with a great many miles on the odometer is higher than a new one: parts wear out, and the vehicle is no longer under warranty.

Here are the three most important steps in buying any used car:

1. Consider purchasing a used car from an individual you know and trust. He or she is more likely than other sellers to charge a lower price and point out any problems with the car.

2. Compare the seller's asking price with the average retail price in a "bluebook" or other guide to car prices found at many libraries, banks, and credit unions.

3. Never buy a used car without having a mechanic you trust give the car a full checkup. In some states an automobile club such as the AAA may offer this service. Ask the mechanic to spend as much as an hour on the job: the $50 to $100 you will pay here can end up saving you thousands on a lemon.

Know Where to Buy a Used Car:
The Advantages and Disadvantages of New- or Used-Car
Dealerships and Private Sales

The largest source of used cars are resales by individuals. About 40 percent of used cars are sold in this way, and this is also where you will find the best prices. About one third of previously owned cars are sold off the used car lots of new-car dealers. The remainder are sold by independent used-car lots and from rental and fleet auctions.

There are pluses and minuses to buying a used car from each source. We'll start with dealers and then move on to individuals.

New Car Dealers

ADVANTAGES

+ Dealers may have the largest selection of recent-model cars, especially those made by the manufacturer they offer in the new-car showroom. New-car dealers want to showcase the best used cars for the models they sell since it helps bolster their claims about resale value and the quality of their product.

+ Dealers should be well equipped to service used cars made by the cars they sell new. This should also increase the value of a warranty offered by the dealer.

+ A well-run dealership understands that its good name in the community is an essential element of its business; although they may sell at a higher price than other sources, they are more likely to stand behind a vehicle they sell. They are also governed by federal and state regulations covering elements of the contract as well as fulfilling all laws about safety and emission standards.

+ Under FTC regulations, all new-car dealers must display a Buyer's Guide sticker on the vehicle; the most important element of this sticker is a written statement of any warranties.

+ You have a good reason to believe that cars resold by a dealership have a clean title. You should request to see a copy of the Carfax report or other history of the ownership of the vehicle, though.

DISADVANTAGES

–   A new-car dealership is usually the most expensive place to buy a used car. Dealers have high overheads and also seek to balance profit margins between increasingly expensive new cars and proportionally more valuable used vehicles.

–   Think twice before buying from a manufacturer a used car that is not a specialty of the new-car showroom at the lot; the dealer's service department may know everything there is to know about Fords, but Volvos are a foreign species in more ways than one.

–   You will be dealing with trained, experienced negotiators. That doesn't mean, however, you shouldn't stand your ground and insist on a fair price.

Used Car Lots

ADVANTAGES

+   Prices are usually lower at a used-car dealer than at a new-car dealer's used lot. Used-car operations have lower overheads and usually do not have service departments.

+   Used-car lots will offer a wider range of manufacturers and may have a good share of questionable vehicles that would not pass muster at a new-car dealer's used-car lot.

+   Under FTC regulations, all used-car dealers must display a Buyer's Guide sticker on the vehicle; the most important element of this sticker is a written statement of any warranties.

DISADVANTAGES

–   The warranty offered by a used-car lot should be considered suspect unless the dealer can convince you otherwise. If the lot does not have its own service facility, who does repairs? If it does have a garage, are the mechanics capable of repairing a 1970 Alfa Romeo, a 1985 Chevrolet Caprice, and a 1995 Hyundai?

–   Used-car dealers, because they do not have a service department and because they are less likely to have a long list of old customers who have an ongoing relationship with the business, are often somewhat transitory operations. They may open and close after a relatively short time in business, they may move to a new piece of land across town, and they may change ownership more often than would a new-car dealership.

That doesn't mean every used-car lot is so shaky. Ask around; check with the Better Business Bureau and from friends and neighbors who may have bought vehicles from them in the past.

Private Car Sales

If you've got the time, and go about it properly, you may find a good deal in buying directly from an owner. Look for ads in the classified sections of your local newspaper, on bulletin boards, and on new online services.

A properly priced used car sold by an individual will come in about midway between the wholesale price (the price a car dealer could expect to receive if it had to dispose of a used car at auction to other dealers) and the retail price (the marked-up price a car dealer might ask for resale).

ADVANTAGES

+ A realistic private seller will price a used car at a level that is better than you will find at a new- or used-car dealer.

+ In most cases you won't be negotiating with a professional salesperson and you can hope for better success in making a deal that is satisfactory to both parties.

DISADVANTAGES

− You can expect no warranty. Your only recourse may be to sue in the case of outright fraud, such as misrepresenting the model year, an odometer rollback, or other violations. Be sure to obtain any representations about the car, including VIN, mileage, and price, in writing.

− Some private car sellers are inexperienced at negotiating prices. They may set their prices unrealistically high and be unwilling to negotiate to a fair level; some sellers may also be emotionally attached to a car or a price for that car, making them less than optimum as negotiators.

On the other hand, a private seller may be desperate to unload a vehicle to raise cash, or to fund the purchase of a new car. He or she may be willing to accept less to end the hassle of meeting with tirekickers.

Should You Try Harder? The Ins and Outs of Buying a Car from a Rental Fleet

Many automobile experts recommend you consider buying a used car from a rental company. Their logic: These are mostly low-mileage vehicles that have received regular maintenance and inspection.

That is all true, and sometimes the price of a car from a rental fleet is quite good. If you choose to go this route, though, be sure you understand any warranty terms and have the car inspected by a competent independent mechanic before you buy it.

Many people are quite happy with this way of buying a used car. Speaking for myself, though, I would be leery of such a deal.

Here's why I would stay away from a rental car: Have you ever rented a car? Then you know how these vehicles have been driven. Drivers are much harder on rental cars than on their own vehicles, especially during the critical first 3,000 miles during which new cars are supposed to be babied. In addition, though the mileage may be low, the wear may be high: Lots of short trips are much tougher on a car than long-distance commutes.

Do You Know the Difference Between a New and Used Car? When Is a Used Car Still New?

A new-car dealer can sell you a used car and legally call it new. A car crosses the line from new to used once it has been "titled" at a state registration bureau. Manufacturers and new-car dealers are permitted to operate cars using temporary paperwork and dealer plates. These cars are sometimes used by the manufacturer in testing, by salespeople at the dealership as personal cars, or may just accrue mileage in test drives by would-be drivers.

The tip-off, of course, should be the odometer, which cannot legally be disconnected or rolled back.

If the car you are considering purchasing has more than a few dozen miles on it, you should ask for a full explanation . . . and a discount off the price you would expect to pay for a new car, perhaps in the range of 15 to 20 cents per mile.

If you buy a new-used car, you should expect to receive a full new-car warranty; make sure that is part of the deal you sign. If there is any uncertainty about the warranty, ask for a declaration in writing by the dealer to that effect. If a manufacturer's warranty is not included in the deal you should be suspicious about the quality of the car, and in any case there should be a reduction of several thousand dollars off the new-car price.

Never Mind What the Salesman Says: Find Your Car's True Life Story

The used-car salesman says this is a real honey, a five-year-old car that has traveled only 50,000 miles, has had only one owner, and was never in an accident. And he seems like such a nice, honest guy.

Do you believe him? More important, how can you verify his claims?

The same is true of claims by a private seller of a car. You can ask why she is wanting to sell the car, and you can ask about its history. But then you have to decide if you believe what you've been told.

There are several ways to check on the true life story of a car, including research at your state's motor-vehicle bureau. One high-tech way to do the search is hire a service like Carfax, available by telephone or over the Internet. This is the same service used by many used-car dealers to check on vehicles offered to them for purchase.

Carfax has a database of millions of vehicles that have been abandoned, junked, or salvaged as well as information about transfers of title from owner to owner over the years. If you are buying from a dealer, ask to see a copy of the Carfax report. Or you can call Carfax at (702) 934-2664.

If you have access to the Internet, you can also run a search for yourself. You'll need the VIN from the car. In 1997 it cost $12.50 for a report, which takes about 10 minutes to receive on your computer. You can reach the service at: **http://www.carfaxreport.com**

Learn How to Conduct a Smell Test on a Used Car

A "clean" used car is usually considered to mean a vehicle that has never been in a serious accident, caught fire, or otherwise sustained damage to its structure. If a car has been junked or salvaged that information should appear on its title. But if repairs have been conducted by the owner, or by a dealer while in its possession, that information may not be readily available. You should ask about the history of the car, but you should also conduct your own smell test on a used car in search of signs of major repair.

- All wisecracks aside about the quality of car manufacturing, a buyer can reasonably expect that the car looks as if it was properly assembled.

- Pay close attention to the doors. Do they open and close properly and line up evenly?

- Examine the finish. Are there bumps or dimples? These are possible signs of body filling. Is the paint color the same across the entire car? Look under the hood for signs of overspray in a different color or of an older age.

- Look under the hood. Does the engine seem newer than the rest of the car? This is an indication of an engine swap. (This is not necessarily a bad thing, but you should demand a reasonable explanation—in writing—for the changeover.)

  Is there evidence of repair to the engine mountings or the firewall? Both are indications of a possible accident in the vehicle's past.

- Does the car seem older than its miles or its age? Are the springs in the seat and its upholstery shot? Are the accelerator and brake pedals worn smooth? These may be signs that the car has been poorly maintained, or an indication that the vehicle has gone through more miles than the odometer might indicate.

- Examine the carpeting, especially under seats, beneath floor mats, and under the dashboard for signs of water damage.

Call In the Feds for Safety

Whom do you trust when it comes to safety: the salesperson or the crash test dummies?

Call the Auto Safety Hotline of the National Highway Traffic Safety Administration for an update on crash tests, recalls, general safety advisories, plus information on important components of cars such as tires and child seats. You can also learn about federal laws regarding odometers and the latest safety information about air bags.

Some of the reports are available by audio recording, while a full set can be sent to a fax machine automatically. Call (800) 424-9393.

Finally, you can also access much of the same material over the Internet at: **http://www.nhtsa.dot.gov**

Learn How to Tell a Car's Model Year

Your car carries around with it a unique identifying code that helps buyers, sellers, and state and federal government agencies track its life. It's called a Vehicle Identification Number (VIN), and it is a federal crime to tamper with or remove it.

You'll find the VIN in several locations, usually on the dashboard near the lower left corner of the windshield on most cars, on the firewall under the hood, on the driver's-side doorjam, and in a less-obvious location on the frame of the vehicle.

The VIN includes a code for the manufacturer and a unique serial number for the vehicle. For our purposes, the most interesting part of the VIN is the tenth letter of the code that tells the model year for the vehicle.

Here is a VIN for an Isuzu Trooper:

JACDH58W2P7892755

The tenth position in the code is the letter "P." The decoding chart is:

B	1981	L	1990
C	1982	M	1991
D	1983	N	1992
E	1984	P	1993
F	1985	Q	1994
G	1986	S	1995
H	1987	T	1996
J	1988	U	1997
K	1989	V	1998

Understand Used-Car Warranties

The Federal Trade Commission requires dealers to post a Buyer's Guide sticker on the side window of used cars; dealers must inform you whether the vehicle is sold with a warranty, with implied warranties, or "as is."

Here's what to look for, and questions to ask:

1. Is the original manufacturer's warranty still in effect? Can it be transferred to you? Is there a fee to do so? What is covered and under what limitations of time, mileage, and systems?

2. If a manufacturer's warranty is not available, you should be able to rely on implied warranties. There are two business terms to understand here: Under a "warranty of merchantability," the buyer has a reasonable reason to assume that a product will do what it is supposed to do. A stove should heat water, and a car should be able to drive (and pass state inspection). If the car does not run, the dealer must fix it or refund the purchase price.

The way around this is to sell the car "as is." If you accept that sort of deal, the car is yours to fix, even if it won't move off the car lot. Some states prohibit "as-is" sales by dealers, or place limitations on them.

A "warranty of fitness for a particular purpose" applies when you buy a vehicle based on a dealer's representation that it is suitable for a particular use, for example, hauling a trailer. You are a lot safer to obtain a dealer's written statement of suitability for a particular use rather than relying on an oral statement.

3. The dealer may offer a service contract on the used vehicle. Be sure to study the written terms of that contract, and do not accept any oral representations about its coverage.

14 Financing an Auto Purchase

How do you pay for your new car?

The simplest (and often the least expensive) way is to walk into the dealership with a check drawn from your own savings. If you don't have the scratch, or if you prefer to leave your savings intact, then you have a choice of financing the purchase with a loan or entering into a leasing arrangement for the car.

It's a very easy trap, one that is encouraged by car dealers and leasing companies, to compare leasing to financing a car on the basis only of the monthly payment.

The ads in the Sunday newspapers are appealing: lease a 1999 Super-Dupermobile for only $198 per month for 36 months instead of paying $298 per month to buy the car. That's an extra $100 in your pocket each month, or $3,600 over the course of the deal. And, you get to pick out a brand-spanking-new car after three years.

Leaving aside all issues of down payments, lease or loan origination fees, and lease disposition fees, there is a major fallacy here: At the end of a loan you own the car, while at the end of a lease you own only memories. A properly cared-for car at the end of three years can be worth 25 to 50 percent of its original purchase price, which is almost certain to be much more than the total difference between loan and lease payments.

It is also true that a loan agreement is much less restrictive than a lease. You are free to sell the car at any point and can close out the loan without penalty. You can make major alterations to the car, from installing a moon roof to a new paint job. And, you are not limited to a specific number of miles over the period of the loan.

All that said, some people like the fact that under a lease arrangement they can always be driving a new or nearly new vehicle, and they don't have to worry about disposing of a vehicle in the sometimes treacherous waters of the used-car market.

Here are some ways to move the power to your side of the table when it comes to negotiating financing for a vehicle:

✓ Consider, very carefully, the leasing option.

✓ Know how to negotiate an automobile lease.

✓ Estimate the mileage you will put on a leased car and make it a part of your deal.

✓ Learn how to negotiate automobile financing.

✓ Consider a home-equity loan as an alternate source of financing.

✓ Compare the true cost of a lease to the cost of a purchase before you sign on the bottom line.

✓ Avoid pressure tactics, misleading statements, and outright fraud at the finance manager's desk.

✓ Consider an advantage of leasing from a dealer.

✓ Put residual value to work for you: obtaining low lease prices on high-priced luxury cars.

✓ Know where borrowers in trouble can obtain help.

✓ What to do when the Repo Man cometh.

Consider, Very Carefully, the Leasing Option

Don't be blinded by the low monthly payments, though; remember that a lease is essentially a rental and not a purchase.

Leasing, once almost used only by big business, has become a common option for consumers. Leases now account for nearly a third of all new-car deliveries, up from single digits ten years ago.

When you lease a car you are essentially renting the vehicle on a monthly basis. The leasing company buys the car from the dealer, figures out its interest costs for the term of the lease, and then makes a carefully calculated estimate of the resale or residual value at the end of the lease term. If the lessor can expect to receive a high percentage of the purchase price when it disposes of the car at the end of the lease, then it can make its monthly charges lower.

If the bottom falls out of the market for the car you have leased and the car is worth less than the residual value, that's not your problem; the lessor will have to bear that loss. On the other hand, if your leased car is in much greater demand than expected at the end of the lease, you can choose to buy the car at its undervalued residual price, sell it to an individual or the dealer, and keep the difference.

The most important hint about leasing is this: Do not concentrate solely on the monthly payment. That is, of course, exactly what the car dealers and leasing companies flash in front of you. If you do that, you are ignoring a much more important number: the total cost of ownership.

As I write these words, I have just returned from a trip where I saw a huge billboard promoting a low leasing rate of about $200 per month for a sporty foreign model. Down at the bottom of the billboard was a block of small type that included, I assume, things like down payment, origination fees, deposit, disposition fee, and other expensive details. I say that I assume that's what it said because it was totally unreadable as I sped by at 65 miles per hour.

That is, of course, exactly how dealers want it to be: They sink the hook with the monthly payments and hope you're in too much of a hurry to read the fine print.

Instead, here are the questions to ask:

1. How many months does the lease term run?

2. How much is the vehicle purchase price for the car? And no, thank you, you do not intend to pay full MSRP for a vehicle.

3. What is the annual percentage rate (APR) on the lease? What is the lease rate?

4. How much of a capital reduction (down payment) is expected for the lease?

5. What is the residual value of the vehicle at the end of the lease term? What are my options for purchasing the vehicle at the end of the lease if I choose to do so? What will be the total cost to me to purchase the car at the end of the lease, if I choose to do so?

6. Is there an origination fee at the start of the lease or a disposition fee for the vehicle at the end? Is a deposit or prepayment required?

7. How many miles are you allowed to drive under the lease term? What is the excess mileage fee?

Know How to Negotiate an Automobile Lease

Remember that nearly every number on a lease contract can be negotiated. All you've got to do is try.

Leasing can seem attractive, and for some buyers it may be the best (or only) way to get any car, or more of a car than they would otherwise be able to afford. But the most important thing is to not just concentrate on the monthly payment.

Before you even begin discussion of a leasing arrangement, you should negotiate the price of the car. Keep your cards close to your chest during the negotiation process: "We'll talk about financing later."

A common mistake for lease buyers is to assume that somehow the lease price is written in stone. In the worst of all cases (and not that uncommonly) the quoted rate is based on the MSRP list price for the car. The whole point of this chapter is to help you avoid paying that price if you buy a car for cash; there is absolutely no reason to pay that price for a leased car.

So, let me reiterate: negotiate a great price for the purchase of the car, and *then* say, "Let's figure out the lease price for that car, based on the purchase price we just agreed to."

After you have brought down the purchase price of the car that is included in the lease formulation, there are at least three other numbers that should be factored into your analysis of the real cost of leasing a car: the down payment (sometimes euphemistically called "capital cost reduction" or other such bafflegab), any "lease origination" fees, and any end-of-lease "disposition" fees.

The down payment is a way to make the monthly payment seem lower by prepaying some of the interest costs. The origination or disposition fees are nothing less than pure profit padding, above and beyond the money that is made from interest on the loan that is at the heart of a lease agreement. In theory the disposition fee at the end of a lease pays for paperwork and cleaning of the car to prepare it for auction; a typical charge is $350, which pays for quite a few more hours of work than I'd bet is actually put in.

Remember that there is nothing to prevent you from attempting to negotiate any and every element of a lease agreement. I'd start with making an offer that removes the origination and disposition fees from the deal or cuts them down to size.

Estimate the Mileage You Will Put on a Leased Car and Make It a Part of Your Deal

Give thought to how many miles you will put on the odometer over the term of the lease. Nearly every lease agreement includes a fee for excess mileage.

Part of the calculation involved in a lease is a calculation of the resale value of the vehicle when you turn it back to the lender. A standard lease agreement penalizes lessors who put too many miles on the odometer; a typical contract allows 15,000 miles per year. The contract should spell out a specific charge per mile if you go over that amount.

Most leases allow for 12,000 to 15,000 miles per year, which matches pretty closely the average driver's use. If you are a salesperson and expect to drive 20,000 miles per year, however, you need to calculate the cost of those extra 5,000 miles. Some leasing agencies will increase the allowable miles for an additional charge payable in advance or as part of the monthly payment; compare this sort of arrangement to the cost of an excess mileage charge applied at the end of the contract.

On the other hand, if you expect to be putting only 8,000 miles per year on the odometer, ask for a low-mileage lease rate.

Learn How to Negotiate Automobile Financing

As with the lease process, keep all discussions of financing out of your early negotiations with the dealer. Once you have accepted a good price for the car you can move on to financing.

Actually, let's move back a few steps. Before you set foot in a car dealership, do the following:

1. Contact a few area banks to find their best auto-financing rates. The number you are looking for is the Annual Percentage Rate (APR), which is a federally defined cost of borrowing that can be compared from one lender to another. The APR may vary slightly based on the term (the number of months for the loan), and some lenders may require you to make a certain percentage down payment for the car.

2. Check with credit unions and other sources of financing, including auto clubs, for their rates. Your auto-insurance company may also offer a loan program.

Now, armed with a list of the best rates you can obtain outside the dealership, ask the salesperson for the best rate. Don't be surprised if the number you are quoted is higher than what you can get for yourself; the dealer is always looking for a way to boost its profit and that includes marking up financing. Tell the dealer you can do better at a bank or credit union and stand back and watch as (in most cases) the interest rate they quoted you magically reduces to meet or beat that rate.

Consider a Home-Equity Loan As an Alternate Source of Financing

Homeowners can usually obtain a relatively lower-cost loan by tapping into some of the equity they have built up in their home. And interest you pay on a home-equity loan may be tax deductible, reducing the cost by your tax bracket; consult your accountant or financial adviser. On the down side, there may be loan origination or closing costs on a home-equity loan, although you may be able to find no-cost deals. And, most important, you do not want to take out a home-equity loan if you have any uncertainty about your ability to repay it. In a worst-case scenario, defaulting on a home-equity loan could result in the loss of the roof over your head rather than merely losing the flashy new car in the driveway.

Compare the True Cost of a Lease to the Cost of a Purchase Before You Sign on the Bottom Line

In most circumstances, the true cost of a lease is higher than that of a purchase, although a lease may allow you to drive a newer car and perhaps a more expensive one than you would otherwise buy.

Here's one way to help you understand the true monthly cost of a lease: Start by adding any down payment and loan-origination fees and then dividing the total by the number of months of the lease agreement. Add the result to the monthly lease payment to learn your true out-of-pocket cost. If your lease calls for a $1,000 down payment and a $350 disposition fee, you can think of those costs as adding $56.25 per month over the course of a 24-month lease.

If you want to be even more precise, you should calculate the cost to you of the lost earnings on your down payment. For example, if you are being asked to make a $1,000 down payment on a three-year lease, you can use a financial calculator to determine how much money you would have earned if you had invested that money instead. For example, if you could have earned 6 percent on your money, that $1,000 would be worth $1,123.60 after two years. The loss of that money, then, adds another $5.15 per month to the real cost of the lease.

There are hundreds of variables that can make it difficult to compare a lease to a purchase. Following is a simplified calculation sheet you can use for rough numbers.

One more thing: If you lease the car and take good care of it and if resale values go in the right direction, you may end up in a situation where it makes sense to buy the leased car at the prenegotiated residual value and then either keep it for yourself or resell it at a higher price. You might also be able to buy the car at the residual value and then immediately trade it in for a higher price on another leased vehicle or a purchase.

If you purchase the car at the end of the lease period, add the purchase price to the Total Cost figure in the chart on the following page and then subtract from Total Cost the resale value of the car you then would own.

	Lease	Financing
Expenses at time of purchase		
Down payment, including trade-in	N/A	$
Capital reduction	$	N/A
Sales tax	$	$
Lease- or loan-origination fee	$	$
Security deposit	$	N/A
	PLUS	*PLUS*
Expenses over the course of the lease or loan		
Total of monthly payments for loan principal and interest	N/A	$
Total of monthly lease payments	$	N/A
Lost earnings on down payment or capital reduction over course of the lease or loan term	$	$
Lost earnings on security deposit over course of the lease or loan term	$	N/A
	PLUS	*PLUS*
Expenses due at the end of lease or loan period		
Disposition fee	$	N/A
Excess mileage fee	$	N/A
SUBTOTAL OF OUTLAYS	$	$
Recovered costs	*MINUS*	*MINUS*
Return of security deposit	$	N/A
Resale value of used car	N/A	$
Total Cost	$	$

Here's an example of the calculation using some sample numbers. The example is based on a real-world set of prices for a famous-name car; the manufacturer provided lease and purchase prices on their Internet Web page. The manufacturer, of course, based monthly payments on the MSRP of the car; readers of this book know better than to accept that sort of deal.

The manufacturer priced the car at $29,158 and included a $1,000 down payment in financing or a $1,000 capital reduction for leasing. The lease also required a one-month security deposit.

Example based on $29,158 purchase	Lease	Financing
Expenses at time of purchase		
Down payment including trade-in	N/A	$1,000.00
Capital reduction	$1,000.00	N/A
Sales tax	$1,458.90 (5%)	$1,458.90 (5%)
Lease- or loan-origination fee	$0	$0
Security deposit	$542.79	N/A
	PLUS	*PLUS*
Expenses over the course of the lease or loan		
Total of monthly payments for loan principal and interest	N/A	$30,533.28 ($1,272.22 times 24 months)
Total of monthly lease payments	$13,026.96 ($542.79 times 24 months)	N/A
Lost earnings on down payment or capital reduction over course of the lease or loan term	$123.60 ($1,000 at 6% interest)	$123.60 ($1,000 at 6% interest)
Lost earnings on security deposit over course of the lease or loan term	$67.09 ($542.79 at 6% interest)	N/A
Lost earnings on cash payment for car over 24 months	N/A	N/A
	PLUS	*PLUS*
Expenses due at the end of lease or loan period		
Disposition fee	$350.00	N/A
Excess-mileage fee	$	N/A
SUBTOTAL OF OUTLAYS	**$16,569.34**	**$33,115.78**
Recovered costs	*MINUS*	*MINUS*
Return of security deposit	$542.79	N/A
Resale value of used car	N/A	$19,000
Total Cost	$16,026.55	$14,115.78

What does this example show you? In this particular case, with the cost of a loan at 8 percent and an investment earning 6 percent in the bank, you'd save more than $2,000 by financing the car rather than leasing it. And at the end of the two years you'd own a car and not a memory. (The leasing counterargument: at the end of two years, you could lease a new car. But there is no guarantee that the new lease rate in two years will be as good as today's prices; over time, car prices head in only one direction, and it is not down.)

You've got to run the numbers with every deal you are offered. But in general, buying the car, with low-cost financing or with cash, is usually a better deal than leasing.

You'll also find an online version of a similar lease-versus-buy calculator at **http://www.financenter.com/newautos.htm**

Avoid Pressure Tactics, Misleading Statements, and Outright Fraud at the Finance Manager's Desk

Pay for the car on your terms. You should make your decision on how to come up with the scratch before you find yourself sitting across the table from the dealer's finance manager; it's his or her job to try to undo most of the savings you have made with your negotiations over the purchase price. At some car stores, this is the biggest profit center at the dealership.

There's a new high-tech show-and-tell presentation that may be appearing at a car dealership near you: a computer analysis that purports to show that you can save money by financing a car instead of paying cash.

Why would a dealer want to make this argument? Because they want you to use their financing, which is another source of profit for them in the form of a slice of the pie kicked back to them by the lender and by fees paid by the borrower.

Keep this in mind: Borrowing money with interest always costs more, unless you can find a way to invest your cash at an interest rate higher than the loan rate.

The computer program typically compares financing at one rate to investing the money not spent in a certificate of deposit at a lower rate.

What many of the programs leave out is the fact that when you pay cash, you have no monthly payments. If you were to invest each month an amount equal to the car payment, the total you accumulate will be more than the value of the CD.

There are, of course, valid reasons to take out a loan. Financing is one way, for example, to purchase a more expensive car than you could afford with the cash on hand. You may also want to keep cash available for other purposes.

One strong-arm tactic some buyers have reported is a claim by dealers that it is necessary to purchase an auto-service contract to qualify for financing.

Such a claim is probably not true; you can contact the lender yourself to check it out. If the lender does, in fact, require purchase of a service contract, this amounts to an increase in the cost to you of the financing. You can avoid that by going elsewhere for your financing or your car.

Watch out, too, for requests by some dealers and lenders that you purchase credit insurance. They'll claim this is to "protect" you if you should die or become disabled; actually, it's to protect their interests, not yours. You may already be covered for such eventualities under existing disability and life-insurance policies you have, and in any case the cost-per-thousand of credit life insurance is usually out of line with regular life insurance. You'd be better off increasing your life-insurance coverage by $20,000 instead of paying a car dealer for a small, separate policy. In any case, credit life insurance is not a requirement of financing.

Consider an Advantage of Leasing from a Dealer

Under a lease agreement, you are obliged to return your car in good condition so that it can be resold. Many lessors have unexpectedly found themselves being charged for all sorts of minor problems.

One way to improve your chances of good treatment at the end of a lease is to make your deal with a car dealer rather than a leasing company; the dealer may be more accommodating to you if you buy or lease another vehicle from it at the end of your contract.

You still want to strike the best deal you can for the lease terms, though.

Put Residual Value to Work for You: Obtaining Low Lease Prices on High-Priced Luxury Cars

Interestingly, one of the best places to obtain a good deal on a lease is at a luxury-car dealer. Many of the most expensive cars are good at retaining their resale values, making their residual value high and their relative leasing costs low.

In the best of cases you can lease a luxury car for the same monthly outlay as you would have to pay for a lesser vehicle.

Other types of vehicles that have held their value well in recent years include sport-utility vehicles (although there will be a glut of them off lease in coming years) and larger family vehicles such as the Chevy/GMC Suburban, Chevy Tahoe, GMC Yukon, and the Ford Expedition.

Know Where Borrowers in Trouble Can Obtain Help

If you find yourself too deep in debt, you may want to ask for some help from an organization such as the Credit Counseling Service. CCS is a nonprofit organization with more than 850 offices in every state. Counselors will work with you and your creditor to try to arrange a repayment plan; beyond that, you can receive help on setting up a budget for current and future expenses.

Counseling services may be offered free or for a minimal charge. Contact the National Foundation for Consumer Credit, Inc., 8611 Second Avenue, Suite 100, Silver Spring, Maryland 20910, (301) 589-5600 or (800) 388-2227.

What to Do When the Repo Man Cometh

If you are in default on an automobile loan, the laws in most states permit the lender to repossess your car at any hour without prior notice.

Read your loan agreement carefully to understand your rights and obligations.

In general, once your car has been repossessed, the lender has the option of keeping or reselling the car to recoup its value. Your contract, and state law, may allow you to buy back a repossessed vehicle by paying the full amount owed on it, plus reasonable expenses connected with its repossession.

Any personal property found inside the vehicle cannot be kept by the creditor and must be returned to you.

A "repo" company can generally take hold of your car anytime it is in a place where they have free access—a public street or a parking lot, for example. In general, most state laws prohibit entry into a locked garage or any threats of force or violence.

If you come to an arrangement with the creditor to extend or change your loan agreement because of a default, be sure to obtain a written statement of the new terms and be aware that this may constitute a new contract, voiding the terms of the original deal.

15 Maintaining Your Car

Every move you make, every trip you take . . . parts of your car are wearing out. Start with the obvious things like tires, which have a finite life based on miles driven and proper care along the way. Then consider things like the battery, which has a predicted life span of a certain number of months but can be affected by your style of driving and the condition of your vehicle's charging system.

Before we go into little things such as oil filters, though, I'll show you how to find out if there are any unofficial or unpublished warranties on new and used cars.

And finally, I also lay out the benefits of pumping your own gas and the potential cost of speeding.

✓ Take advantage of secret warranties on new and used cars.

✓ Save on auto insurance before you buy a car.

✓ Buy tires without being taken for a ride.

✓ How to buy a set of tires.

✓ Take charge of a battery purchase.

✓ Get the most mileage at the gasoline pump.

✓ Know the truth about octane ratings.

✓ Be wary of "miracle" fuel additives.

✓ Fill it up yourself.

✓ Maintain your car properly.

✓ Understand the real cost of speeding.

✓ Learn how to be a savvy driver in the parking lot.

Take Advantage of Secret Warranties on New and Used Cars

Has your new car run roughly from the day your drove it off the lot? Is the paint peeling over the hood? Has the dealer replaced the battery twice?

These problems are not supposed to happen to a new car, or to an older car properly maintained. And while the new-car warranty may pay for some or all of the cost, sooner or later there may come the point where it runs out—and you've still got a problem.

Ask the dealer if the manufacturer has issued any advisory about the problem; there may be a more permanent fix, paid for by the carmaker. It's to the dealer's advantage to get you out of their hair, especially if the manufacturer will pay the bill and make both of you happy.

Owners of any problematic cars should also check in from time to time with an organization that tracks so-called "secret warranties" issued by manufacturers to deal with problems. These extensions to the standard coverage are typically not widely publicized. Send information about your car, including its make and model year, with a stamped, self-addressed envelope to the Center for Auto Safety, 2001 S Street NW, Washington, DC 20009.

Save on Auto Insurance Before You Buy a Car

If you're not already in love with a particular model of car, consider calling your insurance agency with your list of finalists and ask for the cost of a policy for each.

You may be surprised to find wide differences in rates between different models; sometimes a more expensive vehicle warrants a lower premium than a lower-priced car. This is because insurance companies base their charges on information including the expense of repairing particular cars and the rate of theft for that model.

Buy Tires Without Being Taken for a Ride

How complicated can buying a tire be? After all, we're just talking about a black rubber donut, right? Wrong: The savvy shopper makes the proper selection of size, classification, performance, speed rating, load rating, and then moves on to issues of price and warranty. I'll try to help here.

We'll start with tire type. If you were to somehow magically confine all of your driving to a single set of conditions, the choice would be easy; instead, your goal must be to choose the type that most closely matches your driving.

- *All-season tires.* Long tread life and a smooth, quieter ride with only ordinary traction and handling. This compromise design comes at a relatively reasonable price.

- *Touring all-season tire.* Better performance and handling, with good tread life but greater noise and moderately harsh ride. More expensive than all-season tires.

- *Performance tires.* Wider tread and a lower profile, they are intended for high-speed precision driving. On the down side, they are not very predictable in rain and worse in snow, have a relatively shorter tread and body life, and deliver a harsh and somewhat noisy ride. And, all this comes at a premium in price.

- *Snow tires.* Good on snow-covered pavement, they are noisy and mushy on dry roads. Snow tires used to be common on all cars in wintry climates, but have been mostly replaced by all-season radials; they are installed on the driving wheels (the front on a front-wheel drive, or the rear on a conventional rear-wheel car.) Most drivers use them only in winter months, removing them in the spring.

  A variant of the snow tire is the studded snow tire, which adds metal studs that help on snow and ice; many states have banned studs because of the damage they do to roads.

  Another more high-tech variant is a group of snow tires that use special rubber compounds that are supposed to be soft and pliable even in winter cold, improving traction. These designs are noisy and somewhat unpredictable on dry pavement, and they wear out quicker than other tires.

- *Rain tires*. A specialty design that features a channel in the tread that moves water away from the tread, allowing good traction on wet roads.
- *Sand/off-road/high-flotation tires*. Balloonlike wide tires often used on 4WD and sport-utility vehicles for driving on sand and unpaved roads. They are squishy on paved roads, deliver poor traction on snow and ice, and should be used seasonally in cold climates.

Then there are some special features available on a number of tire types. They include:

- *Safety tires*. These are tires intended to either seal themselves against a puncture, or allow you to keep on driving with a hole long enough to get to a service station. They make good sense for drivers who have to pass through areas where they would rather not stop to change a tire or wait around for help.
  The variants include self-sealing tires, which use a flexible inner lining that seals around an object that punctures the outer tread and run-flat tires that have especially stiff sidewalls that can support the car even if the air has escaped.

The next questions are those of size and rating. You'll find information on your current tires molded into the sidewall; the manufacturer's range of sizes is also listed in the owner's manual and on a sticker on the driver's doorjamb.
  Modern tires are sized by their width (measured in millimeters), their aspect ratio (the relationship of the sidewall height to the tire width, also called the profile), a letter code for speed rating on some tires, an indication of construction type, and finally the diameter of the wheel on which the tire is mounted. Some tires add a load rating and other specifications.
  Here are two examples:

- *P215/60SR15*. This is a passenger-strength tire with a width of 215mm, a profile of 60 percent, an S speed rating (which I'll explain a bit later on), an R for radial construction, and a 15-inch wheel.

- *P245/70R16 105S M+S*. A passenger tire, it has a width of 245mm, a fatter profile, and a 16-inch wheel. Not all tires bear a speed rating;

you'll find that information on the sticker that is attached to the tire when new. The 106S label gives the load rating (explained later) and an S speed rating. Finally, this tire, mounted on my sport-utility vehicle, bears an M+S label indicating it is appropriate for mud- and snow-covered roads.

Speed ratings indicate performance at high speed; you're not likely to drive any car at the speeds the tiremakers use for their ratings, but the higher the rating the more stable the tire on the freeway (and often the more harsh the ride at slower speed). The codes are:

Q	99 mph
S	112 mph
T	118 mph
U	124 mph
H	130 mph
V	149 mph
Z	149 mph & over

The load ratings are a sliding scale. The ratings refer to each tire. Here are some of the numbers and their meaning:

75	853 pounds
85	1,135 pounds
88	1,235 pounds
91	1,356 pounds
93	1,433 pounds
105	2,039 pounds

Therefore the 105S rating means the tires can carry 8,156 pounds at 112 mph, which is faster and heavier than I ever expect to travel. I appreciate the safety margin, though.

Traction ratings indicate a tire's ability to stop in a straight line on wet pavement. Ratings run from AA (best) to A (good) to B (average) and C (worst).

One way to determine the expected life of the tire is to look for the Uniform Tire Quality Grade, also molded into the sidewall. The number is a relative comparison of one tire to another. A government reference standard for tire life is set at 100; a tire with a grade of 200 should last two times as long. Use these numbers to compare among various models in a tiremaker's line.

How to Buy a Set of Tires

Buy as good a set of tires as makes sense for your style of driving, type of car, and how long you expect your vehicle to last. If your car has 90,000 miles on it and you expect to deliver it to the junkyard within the next 10,000 miles, there is no point to buying top-of-the-line rubber. (You might want to look into buying good-quality used tires from a tire recycler or a junkyard.)

On the other hand, if you are replacing tires on a fairly youthful vehicle, use the information on tire type and ratings to choose the appropriate type.

Look for a tire from a major manufacturer, backed by a reasonable guarantee. Read the fine print carefully to understand how the warranty works; in most cases you will receive a prorated credit for the tire if it fails within the specified period.

You will generally find the best prices at discount stores and at tire dealers rather than at service stations. The last place I would shop would be the car dealer.

If you have some time, look for sales. And you can also find mail-order sources for tires; you'll have to arrange for the tires to be mounted at a service station or tire dealer when they arrive. (Compare the total cost of the tires, shipping, and installation to the price at the store.)

Take Charge of a Battery Purchase

When you buy a battery with a lengthy guarantee, be sure you understand exactly how the deal works. Some battery companies—including some of the largest sellers—offer guarantees that sound a lot better than they really are. (Many tire guarantees work in the same way.)

Here's an example: You might think that a battery that fails three years into a "five-year guarantee" would be replaced with a new battery; instead, the seller divides your purchase price by 60 months (for the five years in the guarantee) and then subtracts an amount equal to 36 times that amount (for the three years of use you have received). You are left with a credit worth two years of use. That's not great, but it gets worse: The guarantee may go on to require you to purchase a new battery using your credit toward the price. It all amounts to more of a battery rental program than a sale with a guarantee.

Some guarantees are more straightforward, promising to replace your battery with a completely new unit within the first few years of ownership, or even better, at any time during the full guarantee period. Caveat emptor.

Get the Most Mileage at the Gasoline Pump

Don't waste money on fuel that is too rich for your car. Gasoline makers offer several mixtures of fuel with different octane ratings, a measurement of the amount of antiknock ingredients in the fuel; there is no advantage to using a higher rating than your engine requires. Higher-octane fuel will not deliver substantial increases in miles per gallon or horsepower in a properly maintained engine.

With the proper fuel in your tank, knocking or pinging should be solved by proper tuning of the engine.

Most standard automobiles produced in the 1990s are designed and tuned for "regular" gasoline, which is usually 87 octane; perhaps only 5 percent of vehicles need premium fuels. Check the owner's manual of your car to find out its minimum rating.

In 1997, premium fuel sold for about 15 to 20 cents more per gallon than regular gas. If you drive 15,000 miles per year and burn fuel at a rate of 20 miles per gallon, you'd pay about $112 to $125 extra for premium; that money would be better invested in a tune-up or new tires every few years.

Another easy way to save gas: Keep your tires properly inflated.

Know the Truth About Octane Ratings

Don't rely on "regular" or "premium" ratings on gasoline grades, especially if you cross state lines. Generally, regular is an 87-octane fuel,
while premium is usually a 92-octane fuel; there are, however, no
national standards for labels applied to octane ratings. Instead, pay
attention to the actual octane amount posted on the pump.

Be Wary of "Miracle" Fuel Additives

It sounds reasonable: a chemical that supercharges your gasoline to
increase mileage. But in truth, according to the Environmental Protection
Agency and the Federal Trade Commission, most of the products are at
best a waste of money and at worst a potential hazard to your engine.

An EPA test of more than 100 products found only a few that actually improved mileage by a small amount. Think of it this way: If an
additive actually does deliver on claims of, let's say, a 10 percent boost
in mileage, that might save a dollar or two on a full tank full of gas; if
the additive costs $4, you have spent twice as much as you might pos-
sibly save.

Also of dubious value are hardware add-ons for your engine or
exhaust system. The FTC singled out an "air-bleed" device that pumps
more air (and therefore less fuel) into the mixture going to the cylin-
ders; this can cause some engines to misfire and eventually suffer damage. This is especially troublesome on older cars with carburetors. On
more recent cars with "feedback" carburetors and the newest models
with computer-controllers, the engine's brain will adjust the fuel mixture to compensate for the extra air, making the add-on device useless.

Fill It Up Yourself

And while we're on the subject of fuel, how about paying yourself every
time you visit the gas pumps, an option available in most states and
localities.

Saving a dime per gallon by filling your own tank at the gas station may sound like small change, but a typical driver putting 15,000 miles on the odometer at 20 miles per gallon can save $75 per year here. That'll pay for the deluxe set of fuzzy dice you've always wanted . . . or an evening out at a fine restaurant.

Maintain Your Car Properly

You can save money by waiting for longer periods between oil changes and other maintenance; in fact, your car will likely keep on moving for years . . . until it comes to a grinding and much more expensive halt.

Here's an example where I recommend you spend a bit more than necessary. A much more savvy strategy is to perform minor maintenance tasks early and often—meeting or exceeding manufacturer's recommendations. A typical recommendation from a new carmaker these days, for example, calls for a change of engine oil every 7,500 miles or 12 months and a replacement of the oil filter every 15,000 miles. Many car owners, though, change both the oil and filter every 3,000 to 5,000 miles—every three to four months for a typical driver.

You should be especially vigilant about shortening the interval between oil changes if you do a lot of stop-and-go travel, short trips, tow a boat or trailer, or operate your vehicle in extremes of weather—very hot, very cold, and very dirty or sandy environments. My sports utility vehicle, which lives outdoors near the beach, qualifies for extra TLC on all accounts.

The added cost of doubling your maintenance may be $40 to $50 per year, but may save you hundreds or thousands of dollars in engine repairs down the road.

The best deals on ordinary maintenance tasks including oil and filter changes, air filters, lubrication, and fluid checks of transmission fluid, transfer-case oil, coolant, and many other tasks are found at high-volume service operations such as Jiffy Lube and other companies of its type. Among their advantages are speed (a team of four or five members of a "team" descend on your vehicle), price (as little as half the price charged by a dealership), and the fact that you can witness the work being performed.

All that said, you should not rely on a "jiffy" or "minute" shop for major maintenance tasks such as engine tune-ups and suspension adjustments. Here you want to go to a specialist or to the dealer; you'll pay more for the work, but the complexity of modern cars demands the attention of a mechanic trained on a specific line of vehicles.

Understand the Real Cost of Speeding

Driving at 65 miles per hour instead of 55 mph increases fuel consumption by about 20 percent. Pushing the speedometer another 10 mph to 75 mph increases fuel consumption by another 25 percent.

If your car delivers 20 miles per gallon, here are your approximate per-hour gasoline costs, based on a gasoline price of $1.25 per gallon:

    55 mph $3.41 per hour
    65 mph $5.08 per hour
    75 mph $7.81 per hour

And, of course, if you find yourself the lucky winner of a $75 speeding ticket, the cost of a few miles per hour are even greater.

Learn How to Be a Savvy Driver in the Parking Lot

For most of us, the most dangerous place for our automobiles is not the superhighway but instead the supermarket parking lot.

The parking lot is a place with a lot of coming and going, runaway shopping carts, and some generally unusual traffic lanes. Another high-risk car park is at the airport, where people are always in a rush to come and go.

Parking lots are also common places for petty theft.

Here are a few things you can to do improve your chances in parking lots:

- *Back into your space.* First of all, it's an easier way to get into a tight space because it is the car's front wheels that do the steering. Then when you are ready to leave, you have a better view of obstacles and oncoming traffic. And a bonus: You're more likely to notice if you left your headlights on if you walk away from the front of the vehicle.

- *Park defensively.* Find a spot next to a wall or a support column to defend at least one side of the car from dings. If the lot is not crowded (and security is not an issue), park in the distant reaches where you may end up without company. Park next to an expensive car in good condition; owners of banged-up old heaps obviously care very little about their own wheels, so why should they watch out for yours when they open doors or pull out of a spot?

- *Protect against theft.* The safest strategy is to never leave anything of value in the car. If that's not possible, do whatever you can to make it not obvious that there is something worth a smash-and-grab. Keep items in the trunk; if you have a hatchback or station wagon with an open storage area, consider purchasing a tonneau cover that sits above the packages in the rear. In a pinch, throw a tarp or blanket over items.

    If you must rearrange items before you leave the car, consider doing so somewhere away from the parking lot or garage so that you don't draw attention to what you're doing.

To Your Health

Chapter

16 Health Care

When you think about it, you'll realize that your body may be the most expensive machine you own. You've got to maintain it, augment it, and fuel it for a lifetime.

In this chapter we talk about strategies for choosing a doctor, being a savvy consumer of prescription drugs, and offer some advice on saving money on hospital tests. Then we look at a few common augmentations: eyeglasses, contact lenses, hearing aids, and cosmetic surgery.

✓ Be a savvy consumer when you hire a doctor.

✓ Don't pay for brand-name drugs when a cheaper generic version is available.

✓ Sample your drugs before you buy them.

✓ Go halfsies on prescription drugs for a volume discount.

✓ Learn how to deal with an unexpected prescription switch.

✓ Hello operator? Medical help lines.

✓ Save on preoperative hospital tests.

✓ See your way to eyewear discounts.

✓ Cut contact-lens bills down to size.

✓ Buy contact lenses by mail order.

✓ Look into laser eye surgery.

✓ Listen to an independent expert on hearing aids.

✓ Protect the health of your bank account when you join a health spa.

✓ Think rationally about cosmetic surgery.

✓ Consult the experts about cosmetic surgery.

✓ Prepare yourself before going out in the midday sun.

Be a Savvy Consumer When You Hire a Doctor

You're reading this book because you're the sort of person willing to visit or call half a dozen stores to save money on a camera or a car; why would you just place an order for medical service without knowing the price?

But wait, let's back up one step. Here's what I want in a doctor: someone who knows what he or she is doing and someone who is willing and able to allow me to become an informed consumer of medical services.

How do you know if a doctor is competent? Ask your friends and coworkers for references. If you know a good surgeon, ask for the name of a general practitioner he or she respects. Other good sources of information: a pharmacist you trust, a school nurse, and even a good insurance agent. You want to talk to someone who talks to lots of other people about medical care.

In some states, you can request information from a state medical licensing board about the education of doctors and the results of any lawsuits.

Don't be afraid to inquire about the charges for a medical procedure at various specialists. You will almost certainly be amazed at the variations. (How much? A plastic surgeon quoted a rate of about $700 to remove a small mole, while a more general surgeon at my neighborhood hospital asked for $140.)

Call your medical-insurance provider and find out how much it will pay for a procedure. If the prices you've been quoted are at or below that level, you're in good (financial, at least) shape. If the insurance company's definition of customary prices in your area are well below the rates you have been quoted, you have three paths: you can ask a doctor on your list to accept what your insurance will pay, you can attempt to get the insurance company to adjust its payment in your favor, or you can challenge the insurance company to set you up with a physician who accepts its payments. (I'd still prefer to find a doctor I trust and attempt to bring the price down.)

Don't Pay for Brand-Name Drugs When a Cheaper Generic Version Is Available

Are you the sort of person who insists on buying Diamond Crystal salt or Domino sugar, or are you perfectly happy to buy salt or sugar in a plain paper bag and carrying the change home in your pocket?

Salt is salt, just as acetaminophen is Tylenol and diazepam is Valium. We're talking about generic prescription and over-the-counter drugs, which are pharmaceuticals that have the same active ingredients, strength, and dosage form as brand-name counterparts. For a drug to be therapeutically equivalent, it must be chemically the same and must also have the same medical effect.

When a new drug is approved, the company that develops it is given an exclusive right to market it under a brand name for a period of time; when that patent expires, other drug makers—and the original developer—can sell it under a generic name. About half the drugs on the market are available generically.

Therefore, if your prescription is for a hot new drug, you can expect to pay a high price for a brand name; if it is an older drug, you can hope to save money with a generic.

If your doctor does not write your prescription for a generic equivalent, ask if there is a reason he or she has ordered a more expensive version of the drug. Similarly, if a pharmacist substitutes a brand name for a permissible generic, find out why.

Sample Your Drugs Before You Buy Them

If your doctor writes a new prescription for you to try, especially if it is a relatively new pharmaceutical, here are a few money-saving tips to try:

- Let your doctor know that you want to try to keep your medication costs under control. If you pay for most or all of your drug bills, say so.

- Ask your doctor if he or she has any samples of the drug to try before you fill the prescription. Drug companies regularly give doctors sample packets in hopes the drug will become a regularly prescribed tool. You may be able to obtain a full course of treatment free, or at least enough of the drug to see if it has any effect or any unacceptable side effects before you fill a full prescription.

    Doctors sometimes also have stocks of over-the-counter medications and devices in sample sizes.

- Ask your pharmacist to only partially fill a prescription, again to see if the drug will work properly for you. You can always go back for the rest of the prescription or have the doctor's office call in a new order. The cost of buying two smaller quantities of some drugs may be higher per dose than a full order, but you should balance that against the cost of throwing away a medication that does not do the job.

Go Halfsies on Prescription Drugs for a Volume Discount

If you're taking pills (not capsules filled with powder, tiny pellets, or liquid), look into ordering them in higher-dosage size and then slicing them in half.

Double the dosage usually costs less than twice the price of the original dosage, and most pills can be sliced with a razor or an inexpensive pill splitter sold at many drugstores. Ask your doctor or pharmacist for advice.

Learn How to Deal with an Unexpected Prescription Switch

What should you do if your pharmacist tells you that your doctor has switched you to a new prescription? Ask why.

You'd like to assume, of course, that any changes to your regular regime of medication have been made with your best interests in mind:

an improved drug, or a medication with fewer side effects or long-term risks, for example.

Alas, those are not always the reasons. In some cases, an HMO or a medical-insurance plan may be suggesting to doctors or pharmacists that they substitute a less expensive drug. Sometimes these "suggestions" are accompanied by rebates or other financial incentives from the health organization or the drug company. Does this sound like bribery? It does to me, too, although it is in most cases perfectly legal.

But is it good for you? A better drug, or a less expensive equivalent drug, is fine. But a change that causes you new side effects, or is not as effective as the medication you are presently using is no deal at all.

Ask your pharmacist or physician: Will the new drug work as well as the previous one? Are there different side effects or risks? Are the dosage levels the same? Is there a business connection between the pharmacist and the drug manufacturer? Will the switch save you or your benefit plan money or cost you money?

If you are uncomfortable about making a switch, call the Food and Drug Administration, your local Department of Health, or your local Board of Pharmacy. They can help you decide whether it makes sense to change your medication.

Hello Operator? Medical Help Lines

Need some medical advice? Before you make an appointment with your doctor and pay a fee, see if there's a free help line in your area; some are offered by hospitals and other health organizations.

Call your health-insurance carrier to see if they have a program offering advice to their clients—it's to their advantage to help you avoid unnecessary bills.

Save on Preoperative Hospital Tests

If you are due to enter the hospital for elective (nonemergency) surgery, discuss with your doctor or surgeon about having necessary tests done at the doctor's office or at the hospital on an outpatient basis before you are admitted to the hospital. Having tests done in this way is almost always significantly less expensive than having them done as a patient of the hospital.

Once you are admitted, be an active participant in managing your account—don't go for the same test you've already taken as an outpatient.

See Your Way to Eyewear Discounts

Under the Federal Trade Commission's "Prescription Release Rule," eye doctors must give you a copy of your eyeglass prescription after an exam. You can use this prescription to shop for the best price on glasses at a store associated with the optometrist, or you can take the information to a competing optician.

Contact-lens prescribers, though, are not covered by the same federal law, although some state statutes may require them to give you a copy of your prescription. Ask for a copy anyway, and consider changing doctors if you are refused. You may be able to save money by ordering replacement lenses by mail.

You should also understand the differences among three types of eye-care specialists:

- *Ophthalmologists*. These are medical doctors or osteopathic physicians who specialize in diagnosing and treating diseases of the eyes. They can prescribe drugs, perform examinations and eye surgery, and dispense eyeglasses and contact lenses.

- *Optometrists*. Possessed of a doctor of optometry degree (O.D.), optometrists can examine eyes for vision problems and eye diseases and dispense eyeglasses and contact lenses. In some states, optometrists may diagnose and treat eye diseases and prescribe drugs; where they are not permitted to provide treatment, optometrists will generally refer patients to an ophthalmologist or a medical doctor.

- *Opticians* fill prescriptions for eyewear written by ophthalmologists and optometrists. In some states they are also permitted to fit and dispense contact lenses. They may not examine eyes or prescribe lenses. About half the states require opticians to be licensed.

Cut Contact-Lens Bills Down to Size

One hundred dollars for contact lenses! Of course, you'll need your reading glasses to decipher the tiny fine print at the bottom of the ad. You'll need to find out if the price includes any exams or fittings, and it is also worthwhile to determine the quality of the service provided.

Here are some important questions to ask about contact lenses:

1. What do you charge for an eye exam?
2. What are the charges for contact-lens evaluation, fittings, and follow-up visits?
3. What are the charges for lenses and a lens-care kit?
4. What is your refund policy? Not everyone is able to wear contact lenses, and some designs may not be appropriate for all users. Will you be able to receive a refund of some or all of your money if you are unable to wear contact lenses?
5. How much do you charge for replacement lenses? Do you offer "insurance" policies for lost or damaged lenses, and do they make economic sense? Compare the cost of the insurance policy to an ordinary purchase of replacement lenses, and read the fine print on the policy to see what restrictions it places on claims.
6. Will you give me a copy of my contact-lens prescription? You should be able to shop around for the best price on new or replacement contact lenses. Under FTC regulations, contact-lens specialists are not required to give you a copy, although some states insist they do. That doesn't mean you shouldn't ask for a copy; consider taking your business elsewhere if you are refused.

Buy Contact Lenses by Mail Order

With your prescription in hand, call one of these mail-order operations to check their prices:

Contact Lens Supply (800) 833-7525

Lens Express (800) 666-LENS

Ultimate Contact (800) 432-5367

Look into Laser Eye Surgery

Nearly one in four Americans is nearsighted, and most every one of us in that group wish we weren't. That's the power behind the lure of "laser" or "refractive" eye surgery, more properly known as radial-keratotomy (RK) or photorefractive-keratectomy (PRK) procedures.

These are medical decisions, and you should obviously seek competent, independent advice. Remember that important bit of buying advice: Don't seek an opinion from someone who is seeking to sell you something.

The Federal Trade Commission and the Food and Drug Administration both point out that this type of elective surgery is not for everyone and is not always perfect in its effects. And most patients will still need reading glasses for close-up work after the surgery.

RK and PRK are both intended to reduce nearsightedness. In an RK procedure the surgeon uses a diamond knife to make incisions in the cornea in a radial or spokelike pattern, causing the cornea's curvature to flatten, changing the way it focuses light on the retina. In PRK, the surgeon uses a computer-controlled excimer laser to sculpt the surface of the cornea, changing its shape and the way light is refracted to the retina.

The U.S. Food and Drug Administration recommends eyes be done one at a time, with a three-month waiting period between PRK operations. Many RK patients and a small percentage of PRK patients will also need or want additional "enhancement" surgery to fine-tune the results of the initial operation. Finally, there is some uncertainty about long-term effects of the surgery.

Clinical studies submitted to the FDA by one laser manufacturer reported side effects within six months after surgery including corneal haze (2.3 percent of patients), a loss of best vision achieved with glasses (6.8 percent), minor glare (10 percent), and mild halos around images (9.7 percent).

Neither RK nor PRK is considered a medically necessary procedure because the operation is performed on a healthy organ. As a result, the surgery usually is not covered by health insurance.

Here are some savvy questions to ask:

1. What are the risks associated with this procedure? What are the chances my eyesight will not be improved, will become worse, or fail?
2. What is the full cost of the procedure and aftercare? Does that fee cover possible complications after the surgery? What if an enhancement operation is required?

You can obtain more information about the procedure from the National Eye Institute, Building 31, Room 6A32, 31 Center Drive MSC 2510, Bethesda, MD 20892-2510, or call them at (301) 496-5248.

Listen to an Independent Expert on Hearing Aids

Never go to a hearing-aid salesperson for advice on whether you need a hearing aid. Their self-interest lies in selling you a device.

And if a salesperson attempts to pressure you into making a purchase, walk away . . . and call your state's consumer-protection agency.

If you feel you have hearing loss, begin with a medical evaluation to determine the nature and extent of the problem; your doctor may refer you to an audiologist for testing.

More than 21 million Americans suffer from some type of hearing impairment, and many of these people can benefit from the use of a hearing aid.

The two basic types of hearing loss are conductive and sensorineural. Conductive hearing loss involves the outer and middle ear. It can result from a blockage by wax, a punctured eardrum, birth defects, ear infections, or heredity. Conductive hearing loss can usually be corrected medically or surgically.

Sensorineural or "nerve" hearing loss involves damage to the inner ear. It can be a natural effect of aging, or be caused by viral and bacterial infections, heredity, trauma (such as a severe blow to the head), exposure to loud noises, the use of certain drugs, fluid buildup in the inner ear, or a benign tumor in the inner ear. Only in rare cases can sensorineural hearing loss be medically or surgically corrected. It is the type of hearing loss that is most commonly managed with a hearing aid, and often the device can be specifically tuned or adjusted to compensate for particular sound frequencies where help is needed.

Regulations of the Food and Drug Administration require hearing-aid dispensers to obtain a written statement from a licensed physician, dated within the previous six months, certifying that the patient's ears have been medically evaluated and that the patient is cleared for fitting with a hearing aid. However, and this is a huge loophole, an adult patient (age 18 or older) can sign a waiver for the medical examination.

The FDA requires that dispensers not encourage patients to waive the examination and that they advise the customer that waiving the examination is not in their best health interest. An unscrupulous salesperson, though, may try to gloss over these requirements.

Here are some steps to help you be a savvy consumer in buying a hearing aid:

1. Check the reliability and service offered by local hearing-aid dispensers. Ask your doctor, friends who use hearing aids, and check with the Better Business Bureau in your area and your state's consumer-protection agency.

2. Look for a trial period; this is required in some but not all states. The dispenser or manufacturer may give a 30-day or longer period in which the unit can be returned without charge, or for the payment of a small service fee. This is your best protection to obtain a proper fit.

3. Find out full details about service and adjustments as well as warranties. Is the warranty honored by the manufacturer or by the dispenser? In some cases the manufacturer may not honor a warranty if the hearing aid is purchased from an unauthorized seller. Will the dispenser offer you a "loaner" if your hearing aid needs to be repaired?

4. There are no federal laws against mail-order or door-to-door sales of hearing aids, although some states have banned this practice. Buying from a stranger at your door is a bad idea. Buying by mail order is risky because of the difficulties in getting a proper fit and in obtaining service. One exception might be buying a replace-

ment unit for one properly dispensed in the past; you should nevertheless obtain a current test and prescription.

Protect the Health of Your Bank Account When You Join a Health Spa

Health spas can be good for your heart and waistline and damaging to your bank account. The danger comes with the long-term commitment demanded by many of the spas.

Here are some questions to ask yourself and the salesperson at a health spa:

1. What are the terms of the membership contract? Take it home and read it at your leisure, away from the pressure of the salesperson's office.

2. Is there a free trial period during which you can try out the club?

3. Can you cancel the contract and receive a refund if you change your mind or find the club unacceptable? Can you quit the deal if you move from the area? What happens if you become disabled and cannot use the club? Check with your local consumer-protection agencies and the Better Business Bureau to find out if there are complaints about the spa.

4. How many members belong to the spa, and what is its reasonable capacity? Is there a limit to the number of people who can join? Visit the spa during the hours you would normally use the facility to see if it is overcrowded during that period.

5. What are the qualifications or special training of instructors?

6. Before you sign the contract, is everything the salesperson promised written in the contract? If a problem arises after you join, the contract will probably govern the dispute.

7. Calculate the actual cost per day of being a member of the club, including sign-up fees, monthly charges, locker-room fees, and any interest charged on annual charges.

Think Rationally About Cosmetic Surgery

Cosmetic surgery, even more so than other forms of surgery, is more of an art than a science. Because it is usually not performed on an emergency basis, it is even more important that you make yourself a savvy consumer before going into the operating room.

Here are some steps to take:

- Consult with several surgeons who specialize in the type of cosmetic surgery procedure you want. You may have to pay a consultation fee, but that cost is minor compared to problems you could suffer as the result of a poorly done operation.

- Avoid any doctor who does not give you straightforward answers to all your questions, and especially one who tries to sell you a procedure you don't want.

- Ask the surgeon whether he or she has training in the specific cosmetic-surgery procedure you are after. Find out if the doctor is certified by an appropriate medical board. Ask if the doctor has hospital privileges, even if the procedure will be performed in the office; hospital privileges are an indication that the doctor has been reviewed and accepted by peers.

- You can ask for the names of patients who have undergone similar procedures; the doctor is not going to give you the names of patients without their permission, though, and is not likely to refer you to someone who had a bad experience. You might ask among your friends for unbiased references.

- Ask if the doctor will perform the surgery, or whether he or she will use interns or other doctors. There is nothing necessarily wrong with these other surgeons, but there's not much point in becoming comfortable with the skills of a doctor who will not be treating you.

- Ask what percentage of patients have needed additional surgery or have suffered complications. Ask, too, about potential side effects. You're looking for an honest answer, not a feel-good reply.

- Finally, ask for a full disclosure about fees for preparation, surgery, anesthesia, recovery, and post-operative treatment. Most insurance plans will not reimburse you for elective cosmetic surgery, and fees can greatly vary from doctor to doctor. Find out if the quoted fee includes further procedures that may be necessary in the event of complications.

Consult the Experts About Cosmetic Surgery

Here are some independent resources:

The federal Food and Drug Administration offers publications about surgeries including breast implants, collagen injections, and liquid-silicone injections. To obtain this information, send a postcard to: "Breast Implants" or "Collagen and Liquid Silicone Injections," FDA, HFE-88, 5600 Fishers Lane, Rockville, MD 20857. The FDA also has a toll-free hotline on breast implants: (800) 532-4440.

To check whether a doctor's private surgical suite in his or her office has passed an inspection from a national medical association, call one of the following: the Accreditation Association for Ambulatory Health Care, Inc. (708) 676-9610; the American Association for Accreditation of Ambulatory Plastic Surgery Facilities (708) 949-6058; or the Joint Commission for the Accreditation of Healthcare Organizations (312) 642-6061.

After surgery, if you have a problem that cannot be resolved with the physician, contact your county medical society, state medical board, or your local consumer-protection agency; or if you feel malpractice may have been involved, consult with your local bar association for the name of an attorney with a medical specialty. (And check out the attorney just as thoroughly as you would a surgeon.)

Prepare Yourself Before Going Out in the Midday Sun

When I was growing up, a suntan was considered "healthy." We'd look forward to the arrival of summer and long afternoons cooking on a blanket at the beach. A good sunburn was a mark of a vacation well spent.

Today, a suntan—and especially a burn—is the sign of poor judgment and a warning of impending bad health. Every year, some three quarters of a million Americans are diagnosed with skin cancer, making it the most common form of the disease; left untreated, skin cancer can be life threatening. Your chances of developing skin cancer are greater if you had numerous blistering sunburns as a child, a family history of skin cancer, or if you have light-colored skin, hair, and eyes. Check with your family doctor or a dermatologist at the first signs of a change in size, shape, or color of a mole. At best, overexposure of the skin to sun causes wrinkles, permanent discoloration, and other cosmetic problems.

Tanning salons and booths are little better than exposure to the sun itself, and may be worse if not properly monitored. Consult with your doctor, not a health-spa salesperson, before using one.

Enough with the lecture; here's what you can do to protect yourself from the rays of the sun:

- Be especially vigilant between the hours of 10 A.M. and 3 P.M.

- Keep infants under six months old out of the direct sun.

- Make liberal use of a sunscreen, buying a lotion with an SPF rating of 15 or higher. The SPF number is a relative indication of the protective ability of the lotion; if you would normally burn in 10 minutes without a sunscreen, an SPF 15 lotion will give you about 15X protection, or 150 minutes. As noted, the rating is based on liberal application, about an ounce per application.

- Apply the sunscreen about one half hour before going out in the sun to give your skin a chance to fully absorb it.

- Reapply sunscreens after swimming or perspiration. Waterproof lotions offer some additional protection while you are in the water, but you should still reapply the sunscreen when you are on dry land.

- Even sunscreens with high SPF numbers do not provide full protection from two types of ultraviolet light, UVA and UVB; there is no rating system yet for ultraviolet-light protection.

- If you are taking medications, ask your doctor or pharmacist if these medications will sensitize your skin to the sun and aggravate sunburn or rashes. Common drugs that may do this include certain antibiotics, birth-control pills, diuretics, antihistamines, and antidepressants.

- Do your shopping based on the SPF rating. The most expensive sunscreens of the same rating are no better at protecting you from the sun; the added cost may provide some skin moisturizers or fragrances or may just go to pay for the expensive advertising and packaging.

17 The Expense at the End of Life

Hidden behind the unctuous solicitude of most funeral directors is the knowledge that they are selling a high-priced service to people at a moment of great vulnerability. After all, who wants to seem to be cheap when it comes to laying a loved one to rest?

If you've got the heart for it, though, you should not hesitate to inquire about prices, ask for less expensive options, and otherwise act like a savvy consumer. You might also want to delegate a trusted friend or a clergyperson to make arrangements on your behalf, instructing him or her about your needs and wants.

If you won't have the heart then, you should consider doing some thoughtful prearrangements now. Some people even choose to arrange for their own funeral services and burial.

By the way, it also pays to know something about the ownership of funeral homes; more than 15 percent of these establishments are now owned by national corporations and local homes. Though they bear different names, they may have the same management and prices. Two of the biggest chains are the Loewen Group and Service Corporation International (SCI).

✓ Know your rights as a funeral customer.

✓ Know where to seek help with funeral questions.

✓ Understand the casket shell game.

✓ Consider prepaying for funerals to save money.

✓ Preplan for funerals without prepaying.

✓ Order a casket by mail.

✓ Rent a casket for the final day.

Know Your Rights As a Funeral Customer

Here are some things you should know:

The Federal Trade Commission's Funeral Rule requires a funeral home to disclose its prices for individual services and items. If you inquire in person, the funeral home must give you a written price list of available goods and services; you should ask about packages of services as well as individual ones. The elements include embalming, cremation, caskets, and use of the home for services.

You can also call a funeral home to ask about terms, conditions, or prices of funeral goods and services, and the FTC rule requires the provider to reveal prices over the phone.

Under the Funeral Rule, a funeral provider must disclose in writing that embalming is not required by law, except in certain special cases, and may not charge a fee for unauthorized embalming. You must also be told of your right to choose direct cremation or immediate burial instead of embalming. (On a practical note, embalming is usually recommended or required if the body is going to be viewed.)

Funeral homes are also required to inform you if they add a markup to items they may procure for you, such as flowers, clergy, and obituary notices.

If you choose cremation, you should ask for a cost-saving alternative container made of cardboard, fabric, or pressed wood; the container will be incinerated with the body and there is no reason to buy an expensive casket for the purpose. In fact, the Funeral Rule requires providers to disclose in writing your right to buy an unfinished wood box or an alternative container for a direct cremation, and they must make these available to customers.

In general, the funeral provider must disclose the specific state law that requires you to purchase any particular item on your itemized statement of goods and services selected.

About caskets: The funeral provider may not refuse, or charge a fee, to handle a casket you bought elsewhere. And the provider is barred from making claims that caskets or vaults will keep out water or dirt unless that can be proven, or that embalming will preserve a body indefinitely.

Know Where to Seek Help with Funeral Questions

Most states have a licensing board that regulates the funeral industry. You may contact the licensing board in your state for information or help.

If you want additional information about how to make funeral arrangements and the options available, you may want to contact interested business, professional, and consumer groups. Some of the largest include:

The AARP publishes a free pamphlet called *Pre-Paying for Your Funeral?* Write to American Association of Retired Persons, AARP Fulfillment, 601 E Street, N.W., Washington, DC 20049.

You can also contact the Funeral and Memorial Societies of America, P.O. Box 10, Hinesburg, VT 05461. This consumer organization offers information on funeral alternatives including advance planning. You can call them at (800) 458-5563.

The Cremation Association of North America offers information about cremation and can refer you to members. Contact them at CANA, 401 North Michigan Ave., Chicago, IL 60611, or call (312) 644-6610.

For information about Jewish burial ceremonies, contact the Jewish Funeral Directors of America, Seaport Landing, 150 Lynnway, Suite 506, Lynn, MA 09102, or call (617) 477-9300.

You can also seek advice from the National Funeral Directors Association, 11121 West Oklahoma Ave., Milwaukee, WI 53227, or call (414) 541-2500.

And if you have an unresolved problem with a funeral service or bill, contact the Funeral Service Consumer Assistance Program, National Research and Information Center, 2250 E. Devon Ave., Suite 250, Des Plaines, IL 60018, or call (800) 662-7666.

Understand the Casket Shell Game

Caskets are often the most expensive single item at a funeral, a pricey piece of furniture that has a very short useful life. And as we've already noted, a coffin may not be necessary at all if the body will be cremated or if an immediate burial is planned.

The FTC has demanded that funeral homes refrain from making claims that caskets are watertight or airtight unless this can be proven; in truth, nearly every casket will eventually rust, warp, or deteriorate.

Metal caskets often are described as having gaskets or sealers or other protective devices. The FTC points out that these systems serve only to delay the penetration of water. Wooden caskets are usually not gasketed and do not carry a long warranty period.

Many cemeteries require a burial vault or a grave liner to enclose the casket in a grave; the purpose of this cement device is to prevent the ground from caving in as the casket deteriorates.

Consider Prepaying for Funerals to Save Money

If you choose to prepay for funeral arrangements, be sure you know what you are paying for.

Here are the questions to ask:

1. Is the arrangement for a product such as a casket and vault, or does it include funeral services as well? Am I fully protected against price increases at the funeral home?

2. How is your prepayment safeguarded? Some states require that money be placed in trust accounts; in some states you are entitled to the interest proceeds. What are my protections against the funeral home going out of business?

3. Do I have the right to cancel the contract and receive a refund of funds on deposit? What if I move from the area?

If you do enter into a prearrangement for yourself or a loved one, be sure that others in your family are fully aware of the details so that they don't make arrangements of their own in the event of death.

Preplan for Funerals Without Prepaying

It is not necessary to prepay for funeral arrangements to save on expenses. You, or your loved one, can meet with a funeral home and put all funeral desires on record, including choice of casket and services. This will eliminate some of the pain of arranging for a funeral after death and allow for a more dispassionate decision.

Order a Casket by Mail

You'll likely find caskets just like the ones available at funeral homes at about half price if you do your shopping from a mail-order catalog. Yes, really.

After shipping (slow freight and overnight express are both available), you can expect to save several hundred dollars for basic models and as much as several thousand dollars on fancier boxes. If you're preplanning a funeral, standard shipping should suffice. To meet an unexpected need, express freight service should still save money.

Here are some mail-order (and Internet!) sources:

Catskill Casket Co. (888) 531-5151.
   http://www.simpworld/casket/

Consumer Caskets USA. (800) 611-8778.
   http://www.consumercasket.com

Destiny Casket Co. (800) 659-6065.
   http://www.destinycasket.com

Illinois Casket Company. (773) 483-4500.
   http://www.illinoiscasketco.com

Rent a Casket for the Final Day

Here's an even stranger one, but a sure-fire way to save hundreds or even thousands of dollars on a funeral: Rent a casket. When it finally comes down to it, there is not a whole lot of difference between a $750 wooden box and a $3,000 polished-aluminum casket with a velvet lining. And if the family has chosen cremation, the casket serves no purpose other than putting on a good appearance at a viewing or service.

Ask the funeral director or a casket company about renting a fancy casket for the service. You can then purchase a much simpler casket for burial, or a cardboard or plywood casket for cremation.

SECTION VI

Real Estate

18 Buying and Selling a House, and Moving

Buying and selling a house is another example of a task that is simple at its heart and in practice is often maddeningly complex. Here's an example: You've put your old house up for sale and have begun shopping for a new and better place to live. What if you sell your old house before you find a new one to move to? What if you find the house of your dreams before you sell the one that will help pay for it? What if you can't get someone to offer a fair price for your old home or accept a reasonable offer for a new one?

There is, alas, no simple answer to any or all of these knotty problems. There is, however, one piece of savvy advice for all homebuyers or sellers: Don't become emotionally involved in the purchase or sale. What does that mean? Set a reasonable price that will result in a reasonably quick sale, and accept the fact that sometimes local real-estate values go down instead of up.

On the buying side of the equation, guard against falling in love with just one house. You could end up paying too much for it or put yourself in a situation where the loss of a potential deal becomes a catastrophe instead of merely a minor detour in the road toward a real-estate closing.

Here are some savvy tips for selling and buying a home, and moving your stuff once you know your new address.

✓ Market your home with style.

✓ Get your broker to lower the fee.

✓ Give yourself some breathing room with a preapproved mortgage.

✓ Hire a buyer's broker.

✓ Take a test drive around your would-be neighborhood.

✓ Research the future of the neighborhood.

✓ Hire your own home inspector.

✓ Timeout on timeshares.

✓ Move smartly when you hire a mover.

Market Your Home with Style

Do something to make your house stand out from the half dozen others the real-estate agent showed prospective buyers on the day of their visit. Use a readily available computer-based design program to prepare a one-page brochure about the house, with a floor plan and a description of some of the benefits that come with it. You can insert a black-and-white photo in the brochure, or make up a stack of prints at your neighborhood photo processor.

Don't rely on your real-estate agent to do this for you. It may or may not get done to your satisfaction, and in any case it may end up as one of a group of near-identical offerings.

One of the tried-and-true secrets of the homeseller is to fill the house with the smell of baking bread, an odor that seems to advertise family values. Even easier: Place a small drop of vanilla extract on a *cold* light bulb and then turn on the lamp. As the bulb heats, it will fill the area with another pleasant homey odor.

Other suggestions: It is difficult to sell an empty house. Even if you haven't vacated the premises, you may want to rent or borrow some spectacular furniture to fill out the common areas of the house. Upgrade the things a buyer may touch: Bright, good-quality doorknobs and hardware are a good place to start.

Get Your Broker to Lower the Fee

Nearly every part of a real-estate transaction is open to negotiation, and there is no reason why you shouldn't try to get the real-estate agent selling your house to accept a fee below the 6 percent that is standard in many parts of the country.

Here are two situations where you can move the power to your side of the table:

1. When the real-estate market is booming and selling your house will be relatively easy and prices are good, the agent is likely to have to spend less time and money and be able to apply the fee to a higher selling price.

2. When the real-estate market is in a slump and prices are plummeting, you're going to receive less for your house, and the agent is likely to be anxious to bring in whatever business is possible. Put it this way: 4 or 5 percent is better than nothing.

If you're planning to sell your home to trade up to another in the same area, here's a way to sweeten the deal for your agent: Tell the agent you will employ him or her as your agent when you buy a new house. This adds back 3 percent or so to the agent's take on the two deals.

Give Yourself Some Breathing Room with a Preapproved Mortgage

One valuable way to ease the strain of house hunting is to get yourself prequalified for a mortgage loan. You'll know exactly how much money you can expect to borrow, you'll be able to pounce quickly when you find the home of your dreams, and you'll also make your offer much more attractive to the seller.

That last benefit may even save you a bit of money. A seller anxious to be rid of a house may accept a slightly lower offer from a buyer who can take possession a month or two earlier.

The prequalification from a bank or mortgage broker is not quite the same as a loan in the hand, though. The lender still has to appraise the house you are proposing to buy and agree that your offer is a reasonable one, and you may be subject to changes in the interest rate between the time you apply and when you lock in the loan. Finally, the bank will want to know that your financial situation has not significantly changed between the time you applied and closing time.

Hire a Buyer's Broker

Few real-estate agents will make it clear to the buyer that when push comes to shove, their loyalty lies with the seller and not with the buyer. That's right: Even though you have approached a real-estate agent to help you find the house of your dreams at a price you can afford, in most locales his or her legal responsibility and self-interest lies in helping the seller get as much money from you as possible.

For that reason, you should never tell a real-estate agent anything you don't want the seller to know. If you want to offer $200,000 for a house but secretly are willing to go as high as $220,000, keep that second number to yourself. Tell the agent only what you want him or her to present to the seller.

There is, however, a developing class of brokers who are more on your side. "Buyer brokers" are supposed to be working just for you, although most still receive their income from a commission on the selling price.

Take a Test Drive Around Your Would-be Neighborhood

Before you make an offer on a house, explore the local area. How far is it to the supermarket, and will you be happy with shopping there? If you make regular trips to the post office, make a test run there.

If your children will be walking to school, park your car and try out the route with them.

Research the Future of the Neighborhood

If one of the appeals of the area is the undeveloped land all around, don't rely on statements about the future of the area made by the broker or developer.

Instead, pay a visit to the town or city offices and ask the planning or zoning department about permitted uses. Are there plans for a smelly factory? Is a subdivision plan for dozens of cookie-cutter homes on the books?

Hire Your Own Home Inspector

Hiring a qualified engineer or inspector to check a house you are proposing to buy is an excellent idea. Make sure, though, that the inspector works for you and not for the seller or the real-estate agent.

Think of it this way: Although you hope that the house you want to buy is perfect in every way, you do want the unvarnished truth about any problems or shortcomings in construction, maintenance, and mechanical systems. If you go out and find an inspector, he or she has no questions about where loyalty should be directed.

On the other hand, if you rely on your real-estate broker to engage an inspector, you are setting up a conflict of interest. The agent wants you to buy the house, and the engineer wants to keep the agent happy and receive future jobs.

You should be seriously skeptical about any representations made by the seller or by an inspector engaged by the seller.

Timeout on Timeshares

There are few areas of real estate and vacationing that engender such black-or-white responses: Timesharing is either the greatest innovation in vacations since the luggage tag or the most egregious rip-off since, well, the luggage tag.

Here's the pitch made by timeshare salespeople:

You go on a vacation every year, and you love [fill in the name of the location]. Here's your chance to own your very own vacation home, at a price about the same as renting a luxury hotel room. And that's at today's prices. Hotel rates are always going up, but your time-share will stay the same. And because you own your timeshare, you

can always sell it and between you and me, there's a price increase
coming along in a few weeks that is sure to make timeshares even
more valuable in the future.

I could write a whole book about the misstatements and problems
with this sort of concept. Here are a few comments, though. First of all,
you don't really own a piece of property. Instead you own a right to use
a portion of a property for a specific part of the year; in some plans you
won't even have rights to a particular suite or room at the timeshare
resort.

What do you do if you grow tired of the same place for a vacation
every year? What do you do if you change jobs or otherwise are unable
to take a vacation during your designated week? The timeshare sales
staff will likely tell you about vacation clubs that allow you to swap
your share; what if there isn't space available when you want to go?
And couldn't you just book your own vacation in the location of your
choice?

Next there is the question of prices: Don't accept someone else's
estimation of room rates. You know full well how much you are paying
for a hotel room, and if you are a regular visitor to an area you know
how much or how little hotel rates have changed over the years. (At the
most popular of tourist destinations, including Florida and Las Vegas,
room rates have remained stable over the years because of the tremendous level of competition for visitors.)

And then there are little things such as maintenance and repairs.
Timeshare owners must contribute to the upkeep of their own units
as well as to the building itself. This can be no more than ordinary
upkeep—painting the walls and shampooing the rugs in early years—
to more significant and expensive repairs. What if the heating or air-
conditioning system fails? What if the elevator in a high-rise fails? The
older the building, the more likely high maintenance costs will be
passed along to timeshare holders; by that time the original management company—the one that made all sorts of promises to buyers—is
likely to be gone. And in its place will be a company that makes its profit from maintenance and management fees.

The salesperson's claim that you can always sell your share
includes a few massive assumptions: First, that there will be any market for your share, and second, that prices will go up. In fact, the history of many timeshares in this country is just the opposite. Resales are

difficult and typically involve a significant drop in value. Check area newspapers or real-estate agents to see if there are any resales offered by current owners. (If you are still determined to buy a timeshare, consider buying in the secondary market to benefit from the depreciated value of the share.)

As I said, I could go on and on. Put me down firmly in the camp of the nonbelievers here.

Move Smartly When You Hire a Mover

One in six Americans will move this year; according to an industry association, the average bill from a professional mover is nearly $3,000.

Moving companies take most of the heavy lifting and hassle out of relocating your stuff from one place to another, but the bad news is that for many of us a mover's bill is one of those inscrutable transactions (like auto repair and medical diagnosis) where we sometimes have to accept more on faith than we really want to.

Your bill from the moving company is based on four major elements: time, weight, distance, and supplies. For most of us, it is the charge for weight that is the most problematic: Do you really know how much the contents of your house weigh? There is room for misunderstanding, errors, and even fraud in the entire element.

Here are some ways to keep the costs down and protect your property:

- Research moving companies. A brand-name moving company's advertising campaign and reputation is interesting, but the fact is that most movers are local companies who have a franchise or contractual agreement with the national company. Ask for recommendations from neighbors, or check with your employer if he or she is paying some or all of the bill.

- Throw away that moth-eaten old sofa, your lifelong collection of telephone books, and consider whether those unopened boxes of stuff in the basement from your last move really should be introduced to the landfill. Get rid of as much as possible before you invite the moving company representative to give you an estimate.

- Put the job out to bid. Obtain estimates from several companies; don't be afraid to tell them you are seeking prices from other movers. Be sure to compare apples to apples—include the same services (options such as packing, unpacking, extra insurance) in all the estimates.
- Look carefully at the prices quoted for packing and materials. Put a value on your time for the same job and obtain a price for boxes, tape, and packing material you can buy on your own. (The U-Haul rental system and some major office-supply stores sell packing materials. You may also be able to obtain free boxes from super- markets and liquor stores.)

  If you do allow the mover to do the packing, you should go through your possessions and house beforehand and throw away anything you don't want moved. It's the job of the packer to go through the place like a locust, putting away everything including garbage you'd rather leave behind.

  One advantage of using a professional packer is the stronger position it puts you in if you have to file a claim for broken items.
- Be sure you understand the nature of the quote. Most movers will quote either a binding price or a nonbinding estimate. A binding price is a firm figure, while a nonbinding estimate is a ballpark fig- ure that will not be final until the truck is weighed. Some moving companies will guarantee that the nonbinding estimate will not go up more than a ceiling price—usually 10 percent of the estimate.

  Moving-company estimators are pretty good at their job; you're probably safest in accepting the binding price unless it is more than the ceiling price.
- If you opt for a nonbinding estimate, discuss with the company your interest in being present (or sending a representative) to the weighing of the load.

  (A true story: A number of years ago, I made my first transfer using a moving company. As a business reporter, I thought I knew all the angles. After the truck had loaded all of my possessions, I told the driver that I wanted to witness the weighing of the vehi- cle; he looked at me with a cool, appraising eye and then invited me to follow the truck across town to a commercial scale. I watched as the driver and his two helpers drove the truck onto the scale and sat there as the operator calculated the weight. I was handed a printout of the numbers—before loading, after loading, and the difference. Quite satisfied with myself for my careful guardianship of my limited funds, I paid the bill when the moving van arrived at my new apartment 500 miles away. It was a few months later before I fully replayed the scene in my mind and realized that I had most probably paid for the weight of the driver and two helpers—perhaps 600 pounds. Another easy trick to inflate the weight of a shipment is for the driver to stop off to fill up the fuel tank between the preload and post-load weighing.)

- Consider shipping heavy books by cheap (and slow) book rate at the post office. Once you have obtained the per-pound cost for moving your stuff, check with the U.S. Postal Service for the current price for book rate. Pack small quantities of books in small boxes to save your back.

- If you are flexible on when you have to move, try to wait for the off-season when rates are usually lower. In most parts of the nation, the high season for moving is the summer.

- Read the policy carefully to understand the mover's obligations on a delivery date. You may be entitled to a payment for expenses if your possessions do not show up within a few days of the contracted date.

  You should also be aware of your obligations. Under most moving contracts, the driver will not unload the truck unless you or your representative meets them with an acceptable form of payment. (Pay by credit card if possible, or by check.)

- Be sure you understand the insurance offered by the mover and don't pay for more coverage than you need. Consult your insurance agent to see if your homeowner's or renter's policy covers your possessions in transit from one place to another. If you purchase special insurance from your agent or from the moving company, consider paying extra for a "full-value" or "replacement-value" policy. Without such coverage, loss or damage payments will be based on the depreciated value of items. For example, if a three-year-old television set is destroyed in the move, a standard policy would pay for the set minus the value it has lost while you owned it; a replacement-value policy will issue a check equivalent to the price you would pay to purchase a new set today.

- If you do suffer a loss, file your claim—in writing—quickly. Be sure you read and understand the terms of your agreement with the mover. Hold onto damaged boxes and packing materials until the claim is settled.

  In general, a mover must acknowledge your written claim within 30 days and must make an offer of settlement or deny the claim within 120 days. You have the right to object to a denial of your claim or protest the amount offered.

Chapter

19 Mortgaging Your Future

Before you think about obtaining a mortgage from a bank, divide your decision into two parts: Consider how much of a house you want or need, and then decide how much of a mortgage you can obtain and afford.

There are some important variables in that decision, of course. A $300,000 house in Boston may be an ordinary bungalow, while that much money might buy a mansion in Memphis, and a shack in Santa Monica. The amount of mortgage you qualify for, though, does not vary because of the price of the house but instead depends on your annual income and other debts.

✓ Choose the best available mortgage.

✓ Know how much of a mortgage you can expect to receive.

✓ Shorten your mortgage term to save thousands.

✓ Refinance your mortgage when it makes sense.

✓ Take advantage of streamline refinancing.

✓ Consider reverse mortgages in your senior years.

Choose the Best Available Mortgage

For almost all of us, the single largest expense in our lives—and the largest loan we ever take out—is a home mortgage. It's a frightening procedure, and as in most situations where there are bankers and lawyers, it is unnecessarily complicated.

In general, the best mortgage deals include the following:

- The lowest possible interest rate.
- No prepaid points or a low prepayment.
- The smallest possible down payment.
- The least possible closing costs.

You'll want to consult your accountant or financial adviser to discuss any special circumstances.

Here are some ways to save hundreds of dollars each month, and tens of thousands across the term of a mortgage loan:

- Think of obtaining a mortgage as the most important shopping you do. Don't sign up with your neighborhood bank because that's where you keep your savings and checking accounts or because you like the free jelly beans on the counter. Be loyal to them if—and only if—they reward you with the best deal. Put your business out to bid by contacting half a dozen banks and mortgage companies in your area.

- Consult listings of mortgage rates published by some major newspapers in their real-estate sections. And read the ads in search of special deals.

- Remember that mortgage loans are negotiable. When you find the best combination of interest rate, application fee, prepaid points, and other elements, don't hesitate to discuss that deal with other lenders. Tell them: Here's the best deal I've found. Can you do better?

- Understand your own finances and consider your long-term goals. Are you 20 years away from retirement and living in a home you expect to keep after you're no longer employed? In that case, you may not want to sign up for a 30-year mortgage that will demand monthly payments when your income has been reduced. Are you just starting out and would rather put away a few hundred dollars a month into an investment that will (or should) earn more than the money you would pour into a mortgage loan? In that case, you should consider a 30-year loan.

Here's an example: I have a 30-year mortgage at 7 percent interest. Much as I would like to reduce the term and the interest paid, my accountant asks the following: Can't you earn more than 7 percent on your money in a mutual fund or the stock market? The answer, for now, is yes, and therefore it makes more sense for me to pay more (tax-deductible) interest to the bank and earn more (taxable) interest on my investments.

- Understand how mortgages work and how the interest rate and the length of the repayment schedule (the term) affect your monthly payment and the total amount of interest you will have to pay over the course of the contract. In the chart that follows you'll find a quick comparison of the effect of a difference of two points in interest and 15 years in loan term.

Principal Rate	Interest Term	Monthly Payment	Total Amount	Repaid
$100,000	8%	30 years	$733.76	$264,153.60
$100,000	10%	30 years	$877.57	$315,925.20
$100,000	8%	15 years	$955.65	$172,017.00
$100,000	10%	15 years	$1,074.61	$193,429.80

This example does not deal with other variables, such as prepaid points. This is a way to reduce the amount of interest you pay by giving the bank some up-front profit on the deal.

I'd recommend you work with one of the capable mortgage calculation software programs available as stand-alone packages, as part of personal finance programs such as Microsoft Money or Quicken, or at online stops on the Internet. And be sure to run your information by your accountant or financial adviser for a second opinion.

- Be sure you understand all the fine points of an adjustable mortgage. Here are some pitfalls:

Is the initial rate artificially lower than the market rate to serve as a come-on to customers? (This is a common tactic, but one that a savvy consumer can make good use of; some buyers happily refinance their loans every few years to take advantage of initial rates.)

How soon after the loan starts will the rates be adjusted?

What index will be used as the basis of the new rate?

How much can the rate go up when it is adjusted? Is there an annual cap and a lifetime cap? (Ask yourself if you could afford to pay the mortgage if the rate were to go up to its maximum level.)

Know How Much of a Mortgage You Can Expect to Receive

Here's an exercise you should run at home before you go to a bank or mortgage broker; it's pretty much the same process they will use.

Total your gross salary, bonuses, and other income and then divide the amount by 12; then multiply that figure times 28 percent (0.28). For most lenders, that is the minimum monthly mortgage payment—principal and interest—they want to permit. FHA-backed loans are figured on the basis of 29 percent of gross income, while certain other guaranteed loans such as VA financing go even higher.

Remember that we're talking about gross salary—salary before taxes are held back.

Most lenders also look at another number, 36 percent, as the maximum amount of your gross income they want to see going to total debt, including mortgage, auto loans, and credit-card debt. If you don't have any other debt, or if your debt is relatively low, you may be able to get the lender to increase your mortgage eligibility slightly.

When you come up with the monthly payment a bank is likely to allow you to make, you can look at other ways to increase the actual loan amount: reducing the interest rate (by getting a better deal, or by buying it down by prepaying points), or by adjusting the number of years of the loan.

Shorten Your Mortgage Term to Save Thousands

A relatively easy way to save tens of thousands of dollars on a typical mortgage is to switch to biweekly payments instead of monthly, or to make the equivalent of a thirteenth monthly payment per year.

Here's how it works: Let's say you have borrowed $200,000 for 30 years at 8 percent; the monthly payment would be $1,467.53. At the end of 30 years you will have paid (are you sitting down?) $328,309.52 in interest over and above the $200,000 in principal.

Now, let's look at the same loan and interest rate converted to biweekly payments. Take the monthly payment and divide it in half, to $733.77, and send that amount to the bank every two weeks. First the loan will be paid off five years early, in 24 years and 7 months to be exact; and the amount of interest paid will be nearly $100,000 less, at $233,516.14.

This is not sleight of hand. You are making 26 payments a year, the equivalent of an extra month's payment. The extra money, which many borrowers will find almost painless to come up with, goes straight to reducing the principal of the loan.

You should be able to set up a biweekly schedule when you initiate a loan from a major bank or mortgage company. If you already have a loan in effect, talk to your bank about converting it to a biweekly schedule.

An alternate route to the same destination is to stay on a standard monthly schedule but add an additional amount to each payment to go to the bottom line. Using our same example, let's say you sent the bank an additional $125 per month, for a payment of $1,592.53. The loan would be paid off in 22 years and 8 months with a total interest cost of $235,126.22.

Be sure that your bank will allow prepayment of a loan without penalty; most contemporary mortgages permit this. And then keep a close eye on your monthly or annual statements from the bank to make sure your extra payments are being properly credited against the outstanding principal of the loan.

Refinance Your Mortgage When It Makes Sense

Use a mortgage-calculation program and consult your accountant before making a final decision on refinancing a mortgage to obtain a new loan. One of the pitfalls is the hidden cost of application fees, points, and closing costs.

As a general rule of thumb, though, experts say that you should consider refinancing your mortgage if the new rate is at least one percentage point lower than your existing mortgage rate and if you plan to keep the new mortgage for several years or more. (Keeping the mortgage for several years allows you to spread out the cost of refinancing against the money you will save at the new rate.)

Take Advantage of Streamline Refinancing

If you have a mortgage insured by the FHA or held by Fannie Mae (Federal National Mortgage Association) or Freddie Mac (Federal Home Loan Mortgage Corporation) and some other federally managed programs, find out if your loan includes the option for a "streamline refinance." This is a nearly painless and low-cost refinancing that dispenses with redundant charges for surveys, title insurance, and other fees.

Consider Reverse Mortgages in Your Senior Years

If you're retired or about to be, you may want to consider—carefully— the option of signing for a reverse mortgage as a source of income.

A reverse mortgage is a form of home-equity loan that pays a lump sum or a monthly payment drawn against the equity in your house; the owner of the home retains title to the property, albeit with a reduced equity.

It is an interesting retirement solution for someone who is house-rich and cash-poor, facing medical bills, or for retirees who don't plan to pass along the equity in their home to others when they die. You can use the money for any purpose, and in most cases do not have to make any repayment of the loan, interest, or fees until the house is sold by you or your heirs. You will, though, be responsible for maintaining the house, paying taxes, and keeping an insurance policy in effect.

Depending on the terms of the loan agreement, the amount of money paid out becomes due—with interest—when the owner dies, when the house is sold, or at the end of a particular period of time. Your heirs, if you have any, can pay back the loan with the proceeds of the sale of the house, or they can take out a new standard mortgage and use the funds from that loan to pay off the reverse mortgage.

Reverse mortgages are rising-debt loans, meaning that the interest due on the loan is added to the principal balance each month, increasing the total amount due over time.

There is one important safety net in most reverse-mortgage arrangements: Your legal obligation to pay back the loan is limited by the value of your house at the time the loan is repaid. In other words, you or your heirs should not end up owing more money than the value of the house at the time it is sold; of course, most lenders will take this into account and limit the amount of money they will lend based on your age, life expectancy, and an estimation of the future value of your house.

This sort of arrangement should not be undertaken lightly; consult with your attorney, financial advisers, and members of your family before signing for the loan. In general, reverse-loan advances are not considered income and are therefore nontaxable and do not affect the amount of Social Security or Medicare benefits you receive. In most states, recipients of Supplemental Security Income or Medicaid benefits are not affected as long as they spend reverse-mortgage payments within the month they are received.

In any case, the one thing you certainly do not want to do is to create a threat to your ownership of a roof over your head in your retirement years. Proceed with caution.

Banking and Personal Finances

20 Shopping for a Loan

Don't think for a moment that a bank is doing you a favor by making you a loan. Actually, it's the other way around.

Banks exist to make loans; it's the primary way most of them make their money. They are constantly looking for new ways to give their money to customers and then collect interest. That's why your mailbox fills up with offers for credit cards and equity loans.

Now, with this in mind, you also need to recognize that almost everything in commerce is negotiable. Apply for a loan at several banks and institutions and analyze the offers for the best rate and terms. Then don't hesitate to call a few loan officers and tell them you're giving them a chance to improve on their deal; tell them the best rate you've been offered and ask them to do better.

✓ Know what a banker looks for in someone asking for a loan.

✓ Know what's in your consumer credit report.

✓ Don't waste your credit line.

✓ Don't cosign a loan unless you're willing to pay it off.

Know What a Banker Looks for in Someone Asking for a Loan

First, as we've already noted, get over the feeling that you're trying to get the bank to do you a favor. Remember that a bank makes most of its money from lending money to individuals and businesses; if no one approached them looking for a loan, they'd soon be out looking for a job.

All that said, you will still have to satisfy some criteria that make the bank comfortable with the prospect that you will repay the loan. Think of it as establishing a business relationship rather than merely a banking process.

Personal loans are usually based on collateral—a car, a boat, or a portion of the equity you have put into your house purchase. A banker will want to see that you have sufficient income to repay the loan, but he or she will also be comforted by the fact that the bank will hold onto the title of your car or boat or file a lien against your house in case you can't make the payments.

Business loans are more complex, since they are usually based on an assumption that an investment will eventually yield a profit.

Here are some tips for people seeking loans for small businesses:

- Be prepared. Come in with all your documents to support your business's income and expenses, lists of assets and liabilities, and perhaps most important, a business plan that explains what you hope to do with the money you borrow and how you expect to produce income to repay the loan within the term.

    The more money you are asking for, the more detailed the business plan should be.

    If you are starting a new business, or are in a new area for an existing business, share some of the research you have performed that convinces you that this new direction is a viable one.

    Bring along information about yourself. You're not applying for a job, but your employment history is a good indicator to the bank of your trustworthiness.

- Demonstrate the equity you plan to put into the business. The more of your own money and assets, as well as time (so-called "sweat equity") you are putting into the business, the more the bank will feel comfortable with you.

- Be prepared to pledge collateral for the loan, especially if your business is new or unknown to the bank. You may have to put up some of the company's assets including real estate and business equipment as a guarantee of repayment. And you may be asked to put up personal property, such as your home, as collateral; be careful here. You don't want to lose your business and your home if your deal goes sour.

  Collateral will likely be discounted, based on the fully depreciated value the bank would expect to receive if it were forced to sell it quickly to repay a loan. Therefore, you might have to put up a lot more in collateral as you value it than is the amount of the bank loan.

- Look into subsidized or guaranteed loans, such as those offered by the Small Business Administration and other agencies. Some of these loans go through the banks; ask the loan officer for information.

Know What's in Your Consumer Credit Report

They're out there, and they're watching you: the keepers of information at consumer credit-report agencies. What can they put in those records?

Identifying information: your name, nicknames, current and previous addresses, Social Security number, year of birth, and current and previous employers. In most instances, your spouse's name and his or her financial information is not listed on your report. Source: primarily drawn from your responses on credit applications.

Credit information: specific information about each account including date opened, credit limit or loan amount, balance, monthly payment, and payment pattern during the past several years. The report will also indicate if there is a cosigner, including your spouse, who is also responsible for the loan. Source: companies that do business with you.

Public record information: federal-district bankruptcy records; state and county court records, tax liens and monetary judgments; and, in some states, overdue child support. Source: public records.

Inquiries: the names of any companies, agencies, or others who have obtained a copy of your credit report for any reason. Note that there are several credit-reporting agencies, and this may not reflect all requests for information about you. Inquiries are kept on record for two years. Like it or not, inquiries by federal law-enforcement agencies are not listed on the version of your record you are allowed to check.

Positive information—your successful use of credit—remains on your report indefinitely.

Here's what's *not* supposed to be in your credit report: your race, religious or political preference, medical history, personal lifestyle, medical history, friends, criminal record, or any other information unrelated to credit.

And your past mistakes are not supposed to hang over your head forever. Federal law requires that most negative information be erased after seven years. Forgettable occurrences include late payments, accounts turned over to collection agencies, and judgments filed against you in court.

A Chapter 7, 11, or 12 bankruptcy remains on your credit report for ten years; most credit-reporting agencies will remove a reference to a Chapter 13 bankruptcy—which sets a court-approved repayment plan for debt—after seven years.

The three major credit-reporting services are Equifax, Experian (TRW), and Trans Union. Each of the services has procedures to allow you to obtain copies of your report. The most cooperative is Equifax, which allows you to order your profile by toll-free telephone, by mail, or over the Internet. There may be a service charge for your report; the agencies are required to offer a free report if you have recently been denied credit.

Equifax: To use the Internet, your browser must support SSL (Secure Sockets Layer) encryption; current versions of Netscape Navigator and Microsoft Internet Explorer meet that requirement. To order by phone, call the Equifax Information Service Center at (800) 997-2493 using a touch-tone phone. To order by mail, write to the Equifax Information Service Center, P.O. Box 740241, Atlanta, Georgia 30374-0241. Include the following information: full name,

Social Security number, current and previous addresses within the last five years, date of birth, home telephone, and your signature. You'll also need to include applicable service charges. For general information and to learn about service charges for Equifax, call (800) 685-1111.

Experian (TRW): Call (800) 682-7654 or write to Experian, P.O. Box 2104, Allen, TX 75013-2104.

Trans Union: Call (800) 916-8800 or write to Trans Union, P.O. Box 390, Springfield, PA 19064.

Don't Waste Your Credit Line

Credit-card companies want you to use the credit they extend to you; once you prove yourself a trustworthy customer, they're almost certain to increase the credit line without your even asking.

And you are almost certain to receive dozens of offers for new credit cards, many of them free of an annual charge and offering all sorts of giveaways as enticements to just put their piece of plastic in your wallet.

It is true that no one will force you to use a card. But it is also true that having an unnecessarily large credit line or too many credit cards could end up costing you money when it comes time to apply for a mortgage or personal loan.

When you apply for a loan, the bank or institution will use a formula that relates your income to your debts. Your credit history will indicate all open lines of credit—credit cards, equity lines of credit, automobile loans, and personal loans—as part of your total possible indebtedness.

You could end up in a situation where a lender could decide against making a loan, or rank you as a higher risk (and charge a higher rate) because of the debt you could amass using lines of credit.

Cancel any cards or lines of credit you don't intend to use. It also pays to check your credit history at least once a year in search of errors and to know of open lines of credit you don't intend to use. If you cancel a line, be sure to ask the lender to notify credit-reporting agencies.

Don't Cosign a Loan Unless You're Willing to Pay It Off

Think twice . . . and maybe three or four times . . . before you cosign someone else's loan. Think about it this way: If you are being asked to cosign, you're being asked to take a risk that a professional lender won't take. If the borrower met the criteria, the lender wouldn't be asking for a cosigner.

Under a standard loan agreement, the cosigner may be required to pay up to the full amount of the debt if the borrower does not meet obligations. You may also have to pay late fees or collection costs.

But wait, it gets worse: In some states, the creditor can collect an overdue debt from the cosigner without first trying to collect from the borrower.

The creditor can use the same collection methods against you that can be used against the borrower, such as suing you or garnishing your wages. And the fact that the debt went into default may become a part of your credit record.

Even if you're not asked to repay the debt, your liability for the loan may keep you from getting other credit because creditors will consider the cosigned loan as one of your obligations.

If you do choose to go ahead as a cosigner, you may be able to negotiate the specific terms of your obligation. For example, you may be able to have the lender modify the language to limit your liability to the principal on the loan, and not include late charges, court costs, or attorneys' fees.

Ask the lender to agree, in writing, to notify you if the borrower misses a payment. That will give you time to deal with the problem or make back payments yourself without having to repay the entire amount immediately.

Finally, make sure you get copies of all important papers, such as the loan contract, the Truth-in-Lending Disclosure Statement, and warranties. You may need these documents if there's a dispute between the borrower and the seller.

21 Savvy Credit-Card Use

Credit cards, used properly, are among the greatest conveniences available to the savvy consumer. Here are three good reasons why:

1. They're safer than cash. If the card is lost or stolen, your liability is minimal once you notify the issuer.
2. They help you keep track of where you spend your money, useful information for budgeting and tax purposes.
3. Some cards offer special perks including rebates, frequent flyer mileage, free rental car or airline insurance, and other features.

Notice what is missing? In my opinion, the "credit" side of the credit card is its least appealing feature. It is going to be a tax-free day in Washington before I willingly pay 18 percent interest, or more, on a meal I ate six weeks ago, a play I went to a month ago, or a pair of shoes I haven't taken out of the box yet. And I'm not inclined to give back 18 percent on that television set on which I spent so much time negotiating the best price in town.

Credit cards are among the worst loan deals, right up there with pawnbrokers. Their worst feature is the "revolving-loan" provision; if you owe $100 one month and charge another $300 in the next month, you owe interest on $400, not just on the amount that is outstanding from the first due date.

Now, I realize that some consumers feel they have no choice but to pay for their purchases on credit. But I would suggest that you do whatever you can to avoid long-term outstanding balances; you are better off taking money out of your savings to pay bills or carefully use other lower-cost sources of loans including home-equity or life-insurance loans.

In this section I explore some strategies to help you be a savvy consumer of credit-card service.

- ✓ Choose the best card for your needs.
- ✓ Understand your credit-card company's fine print.
- ✓ Avoid credit-card pain.
- ✓ Squawk! Complain about unjust charges.
- ✓ Get out from under a revolving balance.
- ✓ Lower your interest rate.
- ✓ Play off one bank against another for special rates.
- ✓ Move your balances around to maximize your benefits.
- ✓ Take every bonus you can.
- ✓ Watch out for credit-card blocking.
- ✓ Pay off your highest-cost loans first.

Choose the Best Card for Your Needs

Analyze your credit behavior before using a particular credit card. If you always pay off your bill in full when it is due (the best policy to follow), you can be less concerned about the annual percentage rate on outstanding balances and pay more attention to annual fees and special perks that may be offered.

See the discussion of special features of credit cards in Chapter 1 of this book.

If you're like most consumers, your mailbox is stuffed almost daily with offers for credit cards, most of them trumpeting claims of low rates. First, be sure to read the fine print on offers: Many cards offer a legal form of bait-and-switch. The rates are low at first and then climb to the upper reaches. Other cards are tied to the prime rate, or to another index; read the details to learn how the rate is calculated and whether there is a cap to the rate.

Several companies track interest rates. You can subscribe to newsletters from companies such as Bankcard Holders of America (703) 389-5445, or CardTrak from RAM Research Corp. (800) 344-7714. Both also have listings on the Internet.

Understand Your Credit-Card Company's Fine Print

Before you use a new credit card, there are a few important bits of small print on the agreement that you should understand:

1. *The annual fee.* Typical charges range from free (usually accompanied by a higher-than-typical interest rate) to about $80 (usually for a card that delivers some special benefits such as frequent-flyer airline mileage).

   A free card with a higher interest rate is a good deal only if you pay off your bills each month as they come due.

2. *The annual percentage rate.* Lower is better than higher, of course. Pay attention to the small print on adjustable-rate schemes, where you want to know how often and how much the rate can change.

   Again, this is not important if you pay off your bills when due.

3. *Late charges.* Many cards add insult to injury, applying a fixed late charge as well as starting the interest meter any time you fail to make a minimum payment.

4. *The grace period.* This is the period between the date the bill is drawn up and the date the account must be paid. A typical period is just under a month, 25 days. The longer the grace period, the more advantage the card gives you.

   If you come across a card that has no grace period, tear up the offer or cut the card to pieces. And warn your friends. This is a bad deal—a credit card that makes you pay interest on every purchase you make, as soon as you make it.

Avoid Credit-Card Pain

The best thing about a credit card is that it can be treated as an interest-free short-term loan. Buy something today, wait for the bill to arrive in a few weeks, and then wait until a week or so before the due date to pay off the entire balance.

If you use your card in that way, you have the equivalent of an automatically renewing interest-free loan. You can think of that as saving 15 to 20 percent on whatever balance you carry . . . actually the cost is even more. I prefer to think of it as a way to hold onto my money for as long as I can, playing the float to earn interest on my investments instead of paying a bank.

It's important to understand just how awful a "revolving" credit line is. It works like this: If you carry over an unpaid balance from one month to the next—even just a few dollars—you not only pay interest on that amount but also on every other purchase you make once the line of credit has been opened.

A true story: My wife made a mistake on the check to pay off a balance, sending 20 cents less than the amount due. The next month, we received a bill with an interest charge of $80, representing the charge for that pair of dimes as well as all of the charges made after that.

You can rest assured that we reached for the telephone immediately and spoke with customer service; an agent recognized that we were justifiably outraged savvy consumers and removed the charges quickly.

Squawk! Complain About Unjust Charges

Even if it is your fault, call the credit-card company's customer-service line and complain about any charges that you consider unfair, like the $80 charge on the 20-cent mistake. Assuming you don't do this every month, the card company is almost certainly going to remove the interest charge from your account if you make a reasonable complaint. They'd much rather keep you as a customer—a threat you should follow through on if they don't give you back your money.

There are many more credit-card offers than space in your wallet for new cards.

Get Out from Under a Revolving Balance

If you end up in a situation where you are paying interest when you don't intend to carry a balance, you'll need to do a few things to shut off the meter:

1. Call the credit-card company's customer-service department and find out your current balance, including interest charges.
2. Hold off on any further charges on that card until you can zero-out your balance.
3. Send in a check to pay off the balance, including an extra amount of money to cover any charges you may have put on the account since the last payment—ask customer service for advice on just how much to overpay.

   Any extra payment you make will be credited to your account and will be applied to purchases you make once you have the account back under control.

Lower Your Interest Rate

You may not have to go to a new credit-card company to obtain a lower interest rate. Try calling the issuer of your current card and ask for a reduction.

Why might this work? First, credit-card companies want your business—the average account brings in more than $300 per year in interest payments, plus the money earned from fees charged to merchants for your purchases. Second, credit-card companies know that it costs them money—about $100 to $150—to acquire new clients.

Tell the card company about any offers you have received in the mail, or have seen in the paper. Ask for a break on interest rates, annual fees, and anything else offered by a competitor. If they say no, be prepared to take your business elsewhere.

Play Off One Bank Against Another for Special Rates

If you maintain a loan balance and subscribe to a card with a special rate that is in effect for only a limited period of time, be prepared to move on to another card when the rates go back up. A typical offer: 5.9 percent for six months and then a boost to prime rate plus 2 points, which is about double that rate. Just before the six months are up, contact the card company to see if they will drop the rate to keep your business—or move on to the next attractive offer.

Move Your Balances Around to Maximize Your Benefits

Many card users are fond of rebate programs or cards with frequent-flyer-program affiliations; the more you charge the more points you earn. That's the good news. The bad news is that most rebate or affiliation cards charge a higher interest rate.

If you maintain a monthly loan balance, here's one way to have your cake and eat it, too: Make your charges to the account that earns you rebates or mileage and then transfer your balances to a credit card with a lower interest rate. Most credit-card companies are happy to allow you to transfer outstanding balances from a competitor's account. Contact customer service for your credit card for assistance.

Take Every Bonus You Can

Many mileage-program and rebate cards offer special bonuses when you open an account. If you want to milk the credit-card companies for every possible bonus, sign up for new cards and transfer your balance or make a major purchase to receive the bonus. Be sure you read the conditions of any offer carefully. If a card has a maximum on the amount of rebate or mileage you can earn each year, consider obtaining a second card from another issuer and make your charges on both accounts.

Charge! You might be amazed at what you can place on your credit card these days: In recent days I've flashed my card at doctors and dentists, the U.S. Postal Service, supermarkets, and automobile-parking attendants. Remember that you don't want to run up an unnecessary loan balance, but why not take advantage of a few weeks of a free ride to earn mileage or rebate points.

We installed a new oil-furnace heating system in our home this year. The contract with the oil company called for payments of $3,000 on agreement, another $3,000 when the system was installed, and a final payment of $3,000 one month after it was up and running. The oil company took credit cards for fuel delivery; I told them I would use plastic for the furnace payments. The net result: I spread out the payments for almost four months, paid the bills when due so that I didn't owe any interest, and earned 9,000 miles on my frequent-flyer account.

Watch Out for Credit-Card Blocking

When you rent a car, rent a pair of skis, or check into a hotel you may be putting down a deposit without realizing it. It's called credit-card "blocking," and it is a term for a temporary hold on your credit line.

For example, a hotel may block an amount equal to the expected bottom line on your stay, and in some cases may add other expected charges including meals, drinks, and incidentals. The block is removed when you pay your actual bill. Merchants want to use the blocks to be certain that your credit line will be available to them when you actually do check out.

Why does this matter? If you are close to the credit-line limit on your card, you could end up in an embarrassing situation without realizing it; you should also be vigilant when your credit-card bill arrives to make sure that you are not double-billed for a hotel stay or car rental.

If you pay your bill with a different credit card from the one originally presented, or use cash, be sure to ask the clerk to release the block.

Pay Off Your Highest-Cost Loans First

If you've got to choose among various outstanding bills, pay the one that has the highest interest rate—almost always a credit card or personal bank loan.

For the same reason, financial experts advise against reducing the size of your mortgage with extra payments when you have outstanding credit-card loans. Mortgage rates are usually lower than those of credit cards, and interest on home mortgages, including home-equity loans, is tax-deductible.

And again, within reason, you are better off paying your credit-card bills even if you have to dip into your savings. Compare the money you earn on your savings to the money you lose on the interest to see why. If you're worried about impoverishing yourself by spending your savings, you're asking the wrong question. Instead, ask yourself: Why are you going into debt if you are unable to pay off your loan without spending your savings?

22 Saving Money at Your Bank

The most important thing to remember about a bank is this: Though they often don't act as if they know this, they need you more than you need them. They need you to make deposits; they need you to take out mortgages and open credit-card accounts and buy mutual funds and insurance and all of the other "products" that banks now sell.

That's right, a bank is selling something, and you are the buyer. Be a savvy one!

✓ Pay the least and earn the most on your checking account.

✓ Save money on check printing.

✓ Get the most bang for your bucks in savings and investment accounts.

✓ Pay attention to insurance guarantees on your accounts.

✓ Watch out for the demise of the float.

✓ Save money with a credit union.

✓ Use your ATM card smartly.

✓ Don't pay twice for safe-deposit-box insurance.

Pay the Least and Earn the Most on Your Checking Account

When you open a new checking account you should spend the time to select the program that results in the lowest monthly or annual fees. Be sure you understand any minimum-balance requirements and charges for bank services. A half hour at the banker's desk could save you $100 or more per year.

Here are some more ideas to maintain your edge:

- Once you have an account, sit down with an officer at your bank at least once a year to review current policies. It may make sense to switch to a new plan if your operations—or the bank's—has changed.

- Keep an eye on the offerings of competitors to your bank. Ask your banker to match any special offers, or be willing to walk across the road to save banking fees. Why should you be loyal to a bank if they are not loyal to you?

- Look into having your paycheck directly deposited into your account. Your bank might reward you with a break on fees, and in any case you will have access to your money more quickly and easily.

Save Money on Check Printing

Your friendly neighborhood bank will be happy to order a full set of checks and deposit slips for your new account and provide you with new materials when you run out. Did you realize, though, that the typical bank marks up the cost of checks by 100 percent or more?

Individuals and businesses can order checks from several national firms; the checks you receive will be accepted just as readily as "official" checks. Not only will you save $5 to $10 or more per order, but you may also be able to choose from a much larger selection.

Here are three mail-order check-printing companies: Current (800) 533-3973; Checks in the Mail (800) 733-4443; Designer Checks (800) 239-9222.

Get the Most Bang for Your Bucks in Savings and Investment Accounts

Compare savings and CD rates at several banks before forking over your cash.

The difference between 6 percent and 7 percent interest is a lot more than it seems. Think of it this way: the higher rate represents about 16.6 percent more interest per year. And then the extra interest gets compounded.

Pay Attention to Insurance Guarantees on Your Accounts

Be sure you understand whether your accounts are insured by the federal government, a private group, or not at all. While savings and CD accounts are usually protected, some mutual funds and annuities may be "bare." Next, you need to find out if there is a limit on the amount of insurance; if you have a very large account, you may want to diversify your investments across several accounts or several banking institutions to obtain full coverage.

Watch Out for the Demise of the Float

Smart investors—and sloppy bookkeepers—used to keep their checking accounts afloat by "playing the float." It was a process that involved moving money around from account to account to pay bills and earn interest, taking advantage of the fact that it used to take several days to a week for checks drawn on out-of-area banks to clear.

Today, though, the advances of technology have all but eliminated most of this "float." Most checks clear on the same day they are deposited for settlement.

Therefore, it makes more sense these days to maintain overdraft protection at your bank. This amounts to a short-term line of credit that will protect you from bouncing a check and from the sometimes-outrageous fees banks and stores may charge for a returned check. Be sure you understand the terms of the overdraft account, including the interest rate charged. And when you are notified by the bank that a check has been paid by the overdraft account, pay off the full amount immediately to avoid paying interest for an extended period.

Save Money with a Credit Union

Banks are the very underpinning of our capitalist society; that's not a knock, it's just a way of explaining the fact that bankers are in it for the money. They seek every possible way to make a profit on the money you put on deposit as well as the services you use. Seen many poor bankers?

That's why you should look into a credit union if one is available in your area or through your place of employment. In theory, and in general practice, credit unions are not-for-profit organizations that offer many of the same services as banks. You may be able to save hundreds of dollars on checking accounts, credit-card accounts, and personal loans.

Banks often spread the cost of special services—and fancy buildings—across their entire clientele. And they must produce a profit to pay their shareholders.

Ask for a copy of the fee structures for financial institutions you want to compare; the Truth-in-Savings law requires all financial institutions to provide this information.

Call any credit unions in your area and find out if you are eligible to join.

Use Your ATM Card Smartly

Most of us are big fans of our ATM card, that other little piece of plastic in our pocket that has allowed us to carry a lot less cash and permits us to do many banking tasks without entering a teller line. But using the card is not without risk or cost. Here's some advice, some obvious and some not:

- Be sure you understand your bank's policies on charges for use of ATMs. Some banks allow unlimited free use of their local machines for ordinary deposits and withdrawals, while others apply fees on some or all services. That doesn't mean it still isn't worth a $1 charge to make an emergency cash withdrawal on a Sunday, but you might want to think twice about using the machine in the lobby of the bank when the teller's cage is open inside.

  Nearly all banks apply charges—sometimes rather steep—on the use of their cards at "foreign" machines. This can be the competing bank next door, or one halfway around the world. Be sure you understand the current fee schedule before you use the machine.

  And don't assume that there is only one price list, either. Ask your banker about better deals for customers with multiple accounts or a minimum balance.

- Keep your PIN (Personal Identification Number) secret. Never disclose your code to a merchant or to a telephone caller; if you are asked for the code by an officer of your bank for a good reason, be sure to change the code immediately.

- Always take your ATM receipt. It contains information about your account.

- Report a lost or stolen card to your bank at once.

- Check your receipts against your monthly statement and immediately inform your bank of any transactions you did not authorize or do not recognize.

- Be aware that ATM terminals have become a favorite site for robberies. Always look around before approaching an ATM; if you are arriving by car, park close to the terminal but don't block the view of the machine with your vehicle.

  As you enter your PIN, block the view of the keypad so that someone else cannot see your code. Similarly, do not make a big show of checking the amount of money received; it is better to do so away from the machine in your car or elsewhere.

  If an ATM is hidden from view or poorly lit, go elsewhere. If you are a regular user of banking machines, spend the time to locate ones that seem safe. Try to find ATMs located within businesses, such as supermarkets and malls.

If you see anything suspicious, cancel your transaction and leave immediately. If someone follows you from an ATM, head for a busy, well-lighted place and call the police.

Don't Pay Twice for Safe-Deposit-Box Insurance

Read your bank's bill for your safe-deposit box carefully. Some banks automatically add a fee for insurance on the contents of the box, which you may not need if you have a properly drawn homeowner's or renter's policy. Check with your insurance agent.

If you are already covered for loss, inform your bank that you will be declining the insurance and pay only the rental fee and any tax.

There is no point to double coverage; you cannot collect twice for the same loss.

Chapter

23 Savvy Personal Investments

This book is mostly about savvy ways to spend your money, but I didn't want to miss the chance to pass along some of my favorite conservative ways to build up more cash to spend. There are dozens of weighty tomes with detailed suggestions on ways to earn more on your investment; some of them even make sense.

Here are some savvy tips:

✓ Build your nest egg through market highs and lows.
✓ Watch out for mutual-fund gotchas.
✓ Almost always on Friday: a good day to sell stocks.
✓ Leverage a charitable gift.

Build Your Nest Egg Through Market Highs and Lows

There is only one sure way to make money in the stock market: Buy low and sell high.

But if you're a conservative investor willing to take a small amount of risk, there is an investment scheme that almost always works out to the benefit of the long-term investor. And it is a scheme that works when the market is skidding downward.

It's called dollar-cost averaging, and it works like this: you determine a specific amount you intend to invest on a regular schedule and then you apply it to the price of a stock or mutual fund each time.

For example, let's say you intend to invest $1,000 per month in a mutual fund. When you start out, the shares are selling for $10 each, and you buy 100. A month later, the market has gone through a spectacular rise and the shares are selling for $20 each; you buy 50. A few months down the road, the market has come back to earth and shares sell for $5 each; you by 200.

By buying more shares when prices are low, and fewer when they are high you are establishing a moving average price. So long as you end up selling your shares at a price above that average, you're going to make some money on your investment. And the fact is that over time nearly every stock and mutual fund increases its value.

Another advantage of dollar-cost averaging is the fact that some mutual-fund companies will allow you to make investments below their ordinary minimums if you sign up for an automatic withdrawal plan from your checking account.

Some investment experts say that dollar-cost averaging is a particularly good strategy if you are buying a highly volatile stock—one that goes up and down a great deal over time—or even a volatile commodity such as gold.

Perhaps the best thing about dollar-cost averaging, though, is the fact that it fits in well with human nature and society. Although a lump-sum investment in a quality stock almost always yields a substantial profit over time, most investors (starting with me) receive much more pain from losses than they do pleasure from gains. We want to reduce risk as much as we can, and that is one of the beauties of dollar-cost averaging.

Another advantage of dollar-cost averaging is that it sets up a pattern of regular investing, like a car payment or a mortgage. You don't have to make an investment decision each month; in fact, you might want to set up an automatic money transfer from your checking account or your paycheck to a brokerage or mutual-fund account for the purpose.

And an automatic plan forces you to keep investing in a falling market, which goes against the natural instinct to pull out. Since our economy generally operates on the assumption that the stock market will go through cycles that go up and down, toughing it out through a fall and then holding on until shares recover their value is a good way to build a nice portfolio.

Watch Out for Mutual-Fund Gotchas

I'm a big fan of mutual funds because I long ago decided that I was better at earning money than I was at keeping track of my investments. My basic strategy is to find a good, diversified group of mutual funds and then stay with them and add to them over time.

But here are some important mutual-fund "gotchas" you should be aware of:

- When you own stock in a particular company, you are liable to pay capital-gains taxes on the shares when you sell them; if you hold onto shares for ten years, the tax is calculated on the difference between the price you paid when you bought the shares and the price you received when you sold them (you should be able to rely on the assistance of the mutual-fund company in tracking the *cost basis* of your shares, but it also pays to hold on to the paperwork from the investment company as you make purchases).

- But when you own a mutual fund that invests in shares of stock, as most do, the managers of that fund may be buying and selling shares daily, resulting in capital gains or losses. If the gains outweigh the losses, the fund must distribute those gains to investors, and the holders of the mutual fund end up with a tax liability.

    Even worse, if you buy into a mutual fund late in the year, you can end up owning a piece of that capital gain even though you did not profit from the run-up in share value.

    This doesn't mean you shouldn't buy into a good mutual fund. But if you're investing near the end of the calendar year you might want to find out when distributions are made and buy in after that date.

- In this electronic age, it is tempting to try to time the market by switching from one mutual fund to another to try and catch the latest and greatest wave. You may make more money—on paper— in this way, but you are also building up a series of capital gains even though you have stayed fully invested. Each transfer, including those within a family of funds offered by one mutual-fund company, is considered a sale for tax purposes.

Almost Always on Friday: A Good Day to Sell Stocks

You can't quite take this to the bank, but in the absence of a stock-market crash or some unusually bad news of the moment, the best day to sell stocks has historically been Friday. Perhaps it's the approach of the weekend, or more likely the perceived need of mutual-fund managers to be fully invested instead of leaving money sitting around on the table, but in any case across history the stock market more often goes up on Friday than it goes down. And if you're into precise timing, markets more often head upward at the start of the day and again in the final half hour of trading. This won't help you if you're selling mutual funds, since sale proceeds are based on prices after the close of trading.

Leverage a Charitable Gift

Here's a way to increase the amount of your contribution to charity (or reduce the out-of-pocket cost of a contribution) and increase the tax benefits to you:

- Make a donation of an appreciated asset such as a block of shares or a mutual fund. (You must have held the investment for a year or more.) Let's say you paid $1,000 for 100 shares several years ago; today the shares sell for $20, and your investment is worth $2,000. Your donation will be worth $2,000 to the charity, you will be able to declare a $2,000 tax-deductible contribution, and you will not have to pay capital-gains taxes on the run-up in share values.

- You can also come out ahead on a loss: Sell off an investment you have held for more than a year that has depreciated in value and give the proceeds to a charitable institution. You will be able to deduct the value of the contribution and the capital loss from the investment.

  Be careful not to give the asset directly to the charity in this case; if you do so you will not be able to deduct the capital loss.

24 The Tax Man Cometh

There are bookshelves full of tips on tax strategies; I'm not sure even the authors fully understand everything they've written.

Since this book is about consumer strategies, though, let's look at tax tips in that way: It does not seem to make any sense to me to spend the time to fully understand every facet of the tax code. Instead, I recommend you buy yourself the good advice of a competent accountant or financial adviser.

I'd advise you to seek a relationship where you are paying for time and services, and not paying a commission on stock or mutual-fund trades or other management of your money. When you can separate the advice from the buying and selling you are removing a dangerous conflict of interest.

The second bit of critical advice is this: Understand the difference between tax avoidance and tax evasion. It is perfectly legal to avoid paying certain taxes by structuring your holdings or income; for example, you can invest in tax-free federal or state bonds rather than taxable stocks and bonds. It is not legal, though, to evade taxes by hiding income or holdings or by simply not paying your bill when it comes due.

I don't like paying taxes any more than the next guy does, but I'd rather work a little harder and spend my income like a savvy consumer rather than picking a fight with the IRS.

Here, though, are a few important bits of information for the savvy consumer. Included is a warning about a particularly poor deal on a loan attached to tax refunds and another a way to dig yourself out (just once) from a tax hole.

✓ Run away from tax-refund rip-offs.

✓ Seek IRS grace.

✓ Hold onto those tax documents.

Run Away from Tax-Refund Rip-Offs

Be very wary of "rapid refund" or other schemes that promise to deliver your tax-refund check ahead of its delivery from the Internal Revenue Service. These amount to thinly disguised consumer-loan programs that carry very high interest rates and can end up putting you in a deep hole if the IRS delays your refund or disagrees with the claims you make on your tax form.

In 1997, New York City's Department of Consumer Affairs settled a lawsuit against the nation's largest tax chain for claims that the company misled consumers about the program and charged interest rates for short-term loans that worked out to as much as 700 percent on an annual basis.

The absolutely worst example of this sort of program I have ever seen was inside a Nevada casino, where a lender was offering instant cash for anticipated refunds just steps away from the blackjack tables and slot machines.

In any case, remember that you should structure your withholding schedule so that you are owed as little in refund each year as possible. It's your money—why should you lend it to the federal government (without interest) over the course of the year?

Seek IRS Grace

If you end up with a frightening tax bill to the IRS, you may be able to work out an installment plan with the feds—special deals are usually available to taxpayers who have not had problems in the past and owe less than $10,000. If the bill is higher, you can attempt to make a deal with the IRS, something called an "offer in compromise." This is a reduced lump-sum payment, again usually available on a one-time basis.

Speak to your accountant and the IRS before you make any irrevocable moves about your taxes.

Hold onto Those Tax Documents

One corner of my office is devoted to a set of files that haven't been touched in years . . . and I'm reasonably happy about that. These files hold the documentation for my tax filings, and I'd rather have them than not even if the IRS hasn't asked to see them.

In general, a law-abiding taxpayer needs to keep documents for at least six years. The law says you need to keep materials for three years in most cases. If you managed (innocently) to underreport your income by 25 percent or more, you may need to show documents going back six years. And if you filed a fraudulent return or didn't file at all, the IRS can follow you to your grave to collect.

If you ever need to lay hands on an old tax return, you can pay the IRS about $14 for a copy. Returns for the past two years, in computerized form, are free to filers. Contact the IRS at (800) TAX-FORM.

Hold onto documents for house purchases and sales over the course of your lifetime. This is important in establishing a basis price for a house to avoid paying taxes on gains with every sale.

Consult your accountant for any specific details related to your particular situation and to keep abreast of any changes in tax laws.

SECTION VIII

Travel

25 Air Travel

In some ways, air travel is an example of our modern technological society at its best. You can get from just about anywhere on earth to almost anywhere else in a matter of hours.

In other ways, air travel is free enterprise at its worst, a confusing Turkish bazaar with prices changing by the hour. In the introduction to this book, I use the real example of two people seated next to each other on the same plane; one pays $804 for a ticket and the other $309, and they both have to suffer through an airline meal.

The savvy consumer, of course, is the one who pays the lowest possible price for an airline ticket.

In this chapter, I pass along some savvy tips on the best times to call an airline-reservations system, how to use frequent-flyer miles smartly, and how to choose an on-time flight and the best seat on the plane. I also tell you how to cancel a noncancelable ticket. You also learn how to make yourself comfortable in the air and fight off jet lag when you land.

✓ Take advantage of airline specials.

✓ Use a computer—or a good travel agent with a computer—to track airfare changes.

✓ Know how and when to call an airline.

✓ Learn some sneaky tricks.

✓ Use your frequent-flyer miles to your best advantage.

✓ Consider buying airline tickets from a consolidator.

✓ Know the meaning of airline on-time rankings.

✓ Know how to improve your chances of arriving on time.

✓ Try to avoid changes of airline en route.

✓ Learn the first thing to do when a flight is canceled at the airport.

✓ Bump me, please!

✓ Know your rights as an airline passenger.

✓ Pick the best airline seat.

✓ Do what you can about airline safety.

✓ Learn the tricks to avoid a seatmate.

✓ Make yourself comfortable in midair.

✓ Fight against jet lag.

✓ Learn how to cancel a noncancelable ticket.

✓ Know the dangers of buying someone else's airline ticket.

✓ Play the currency game to save on foreign travel.

✓ Tourist Information

Take Advantage of Airline Specials

Read the newspapers, study those annoying inserts in your credit-card bills, listen to the radio and television ads, and consult the online computer travel agencies regularly in search of airline specials.

A common deal: "companion" tickets. These specials allow you to purchase a second ticket for a companion for a deep discount or even for free. They are generally good deals, but you'll have to read the fine print carefully. In some cases, the offer is valid only if you purchase a certain class of ticket; sometimes they are tied to the cheapest fares. I have seen other offers that give you a break only if you purchase much more expensive business-class or first-class tickets. Watch out, too, for excluded travel periods.

And if you see a great deal on American but would prefer to fly with Delta, don't hesitate to call Delta's reservations line. Most major airlines match any offer made in their territory.

Use a Computer—or a Good Travel Agent with a Computer—to Track Airfare Changes

On a typical day, airlines may make 20,000 changes to airfares. That is not a typographical error. In addition to the generally wild pricing swings of the highly competitive industry, airlines also practice something called "load management" in which they adjust prices based on how heavily booked an upcoming flight is.

There are two ways to make the most of these fluctuations: One is to use one of the online computer services such as Microsoft's Expedia or Travelocity; you'll see promotions for them on most online services. You can easily check fares as often as you want. And several of the online agencies offer automated "fare-tracker" services; you can enter several city pairs (departure and arrival airports) and ask to be notified by E-mail any time the published fares change.

You can also put your faith in a state-of-the-art travel agency that can perform the same sort of fare-tracking process. You will, though, have to rely on the travel agent to call you when there is a significant change.

Here are some of the best online travel agencies; most offer free membership and often feature special deals:

Microsoft Expedia: **http://www.expedia.com**

Reservations: **http://www.reservations.com**

Travelocity: **http://www.travelocity.com**

Know How and When to Call an Airline

If you choose to buy your airline tickets directly from an airline, you should do what you can to get a reservationist who is willing to spend some time looking for the best fares and schedule. Here are some tips:

- Call late at night or early in the morning. Agents are generally less busy and more willing to put in some serious finger clicks on their computer terminal.

- Sound as if you know what you are talking about. Do some research on the Internet, in newspapers, and in schedule books. Ask for particular bargain-rate classes you have seen offered and then ask the agent to try to do better.

- Do something to make the day (or night) of the person on the other end of the line—it might be enough just to be unusually pleasant. Or tell a joke. You're not likely to get a free flight, but you just might get a better deal.

Learn Some Sneaky Tricks

First, these tricks are not illegal, although they may violate the terms of an airline's contract with its customer. Second, you'd have to be very unlucky or very obvious to get caught. And finally, I think the airlines deserve everything we savvy consumers toss at them because of the incredibly complex thicket of obstacles they place in the way of travelers and especially those who must travel on short notice or during a business week.

Here are some strategies to consider:

Nested Tickets

This scheme generally works in either of two situations—where regular fares are more than twice as high as excursion fares that include a Saturday night stayover, or in situations where you plan to fly between two locations twice within less than a year.

Let's say you want to fly from New York to Los Angeles, departing on a Monday and returning on a Thursday. The quoted fare for this flight is $804. With a bit of research, you find that an excursion fare that includes a Saturday night stayover is just $329.

Here's how a nested purchase works:

1. Buy a $329 excursion ticket from New York to Los Angeles departing on Monday [call this coupon A] and returning to New York a week later on Thursday [call that trip coupon B].

2. On a separate call, buy another $329 excursion ticket, this time from Los Angeles to New York, departing on Thursday [coupon C]

and returning to LA on the other side of the weekend on Monday [coupon D].

Then head out to the airport for your first flight. Fly to Los Angeles using coupon A on Monday, and then return to New York using coupon C. Be careful not to present the wrong ticket.

If you end up throwing away the return coupons on both tickets, you would be (in this example) ahead by $126.

Even better: Set the return dates on both tickets several weeks or months later and earn yourself a free round trip. Just sit down with a calendar and plan the travel dates carefully so that the trips are properly nested with each other and then fly on coupons D and then B.

By the way, some travel agents may be willing to assist you in constructing a nested pair of tickets.

Split Tickets

The vagaries of fare wars and other forms of competition sometimes result in supercheap fares through a connecting city. For example, an airline seeking to boost traffic to and from a hub in Pittsburgh might set up a situation in which buying a round-trip ticket from Boston to Pittsburgh and a second ticket from Pittsburgh to Seattle might work out to be considerably less expensive than a single ticket from Boston to Seattle even if it makes a stop in Pittsburgh.

Once again, this is a perfectly legal ploy. The possible fly in the ointment involves missed connections; be sure to book a schedule that allows enough time between flights and offers backups.

A good travel agent should be able to help you construct a split-ticket arrangement.

Use Your Frequent-Flyer Miles to Your Best Advantage

Use your frequent-flyer mileage to buy expensive tickets, not fares on deep discount. The number of miles required for a domestic flight varies from program to program—generally from about 20,000 to 40,000 miles—but whatever the number of miles you should value the free ticket at the price of a standard excursion fare—at the time of this writing, about $400 to $500.

Consider Buying Airline Tickets from a Consolidator

On a recent trip to Europe, I saved about $800 on four tickets by buying tickets from a consolidator. These companies, less flatteringly known in the industry as "bucket shops," buy blocks of tickets from airlines at deeply discounted rates and then resell them to the public or travel agencies at rates typically about 10 to 35 percent lower than advertised rates.

Look for ads from consolidators in the classified sections of many Sunday-newspaper travel sections. You may also find that your travel agency will offer you consolidator tickets, marked up a bit from the price you might be offered if you bought the tickets directly.

Consolidator tickets are usually purchased from major airlines—my tickets were on American Airlines—although you may sometimes be offered seats on more obscure carriers such as Icelandic Air or Air Saudi Arabia. I would imagine that these proud national carriers operate a fine airline and may be rather interesting to fly; from my point of view, though, I would not recommend accepting a ticket on an airline that you do not feel comfortable flying.

Here are some other shortcomings of consolidator tickets:

- They are usually available only for the most popular routes and more commonly for long-distance flights than for short hauls. For example, you're likely to find plenty of tickets from New York to London, or Miami to Rio de Janeiro. Less likely would be Akron to Fiji.

- Not every flight may be available. A consolidator may specialize in flights from Boston to Paris on Friday nights returning on Sunday mornings.

- The tickets may be noncancelable, or subject to very stiff cancellation penalties since the consolidator may be forced to eat the cost of any unsold or returned seats. Here is a good reason to consider trip-cancellation insurance to cover any possible loss; be sure the policy covers consolidator tickets.

- Be sure to pay for your trip with a major credit card and examine your tickets when they arrive. Then call the airline directly and confirm that you have been properly booked on the flight.

Know the Meaning of Airline On-Time Rankings

One innovation in air travel has been the publication of national statistics on the on-time record for particular flights. You can obtain this information from a travel agent, from the airline itself, or from various online services. The number is presented as a rating from 0 to 10, with 9 meaning that 90 percent of the trips for this particular flight are on time.

What does this mean to you? If you are traveling from one point to another on a fairly loose vacation schedule, it shouldn't matter whether a particular flight operates on time 70 percent or 80 percent of the time. But if you must make a tight connection midway on a flight, you might want to stay away from an initial flight with a 50 percent rating.

We can make the assumption that all airlines want to have their planes fly on time. It's good marketing, plus a delay on one flight can quickly cascade into a systemwide hang-up later in the day. But certain types of airlines are more prone to delays: commuter carriers that make lots of little hops from one busy major airport to another and those that operate in areas subject to bad weather.

Know How to Improve Your Chances of Arriving on Time

There are no guarantees in this life, and that especially applies to airline schedules. But there are some things you can do to improve your chances of arriving at your destination more or less on time. It starts with doing some savvy things to enhance the likelihood of taking off on time:

- Select the first flight out in the morning. First, there is a good chance that the airplane will be sitting at the gate after having come in late at night. Airlines rarely schedule departures between 1 A.M. and 6 A.M., allowing for some time in the schedule to make up for delays of the day before.

  Delays almost always cascade throughout the schedule. If a midday flight is an hour late, all of its later arrivals and departures will be at least that much late; problems with gates and air-traffic control can multiply the delays.

(I almost always take the 6 A.M. flight out of the small airport on the island where I live. The airport regularly closes because of morning fog, blocking all incoming traffic for hours. But the one plane that comes in overnight is almost always able to rise above the pea soup and be on its way.)

- Choose a nonstop flight if possible. The more takeoffs and landings, the more chances for delays.

- If you can't get a nonstop, try for a direct flight, which in most cases is a plane that goes from your departure city to your destination but makes one or more stops. With a direct flight, at least you will have possession of a seat on a plane with the best of intentions of delivering you to your destination. (Pay close attention to the schedule, though; some airlines have what they call direct flights with a single flight number but a change of planes is required at one of the stopover points.)

- If you must choose a flight with stopovers, see if there is a connection that takes you through a less-congested airport or one less likely to have weather delays. For example, a flight with a connection through Chicago may be more prone to delays than one through Cincinnati; a flight with a change of planes in Denver in the winter may not be as reliable as one that uses Dallas as a hub.

- Consult the on-time rating for the flight, which is available from the airline, a travel agency, or an online reservations service. You don't want to fly in on a flight with a rating of "5" (on-time for only 50 percent of its flights) to meet a flight with a rating of "9."

Try to Avoid Changes of Airline en Route

Try to stay on the same airline if you have a multistop trip. You have the best chance of arriving at a distant destination if you stay on a single carrier instead of changing from one airline to another in the course of a day.

For example, if you are making a connection from one American Airlines flight to another and your inbound flight is delayed, American will likely be aware of that delay and make alternate reservations for you on a later flight.

On the other hand, if you are coming in on a USAir flight to pick up a Delta plane in Boston, neither airline may notice that you are likely to miss your connection because of the delay. And to make things worse, neither airline is likely to take the blame here: USAir is not obligated to get you to your final destination, and Delta may consider you a no-show if you don't check in on time.

Learn the First Thing to Do When a Flight Is Canceled at the Airport

Most of us have been there—first the plane is late, and then the takeoff is delayed, and finally comes an announcement: "We're sorry to inform you that Flight 189 has been canceled. If you will line up at the check-in desk we will rebook you on another flight."

A full planeload of unhappy to angry passengers dashes across the lounge to queue up in front of one or two agents at the desk.

The savvy consumer, though, heads in another direction. Here are some better options:

- Look for a telephone and call the airline's toll-free reservations number; you'll save time and you may be able to snare one of a dwindling few remaining seats on the next flight.

- Find a customer-service desk for the airline or a helpful agent at another airport gate who is not otherwise engaged in loading another flight.

- If you are a member of the airline's airport club, go there for priority service.

- If you purchased your ticket through a good travel agent, call the agency and ask for immediate assistance on rebooking.

Most airlines will attempt to rebook you on another of their own flights so that they can hold onto the revenue; if there are no more seats available, they may be willing to book you on a competitor's plane. Stand your ground and ask for a reasonable solution to your joint problem.

Bump Me, Please!

Airlines love to fly their planes with every seat occupied by a paying customer; in fact, most companies count on flying sardine cans for the largest portion of their profit.

It is also true that a certain percentage of travelers holding airline reservations fail to show up at the gate.

And so airline companies have put their computers to work to come up with formulas that say something like: Flight 131 on Monday mornings usually has a 3 percent "no-show" rate, which can translate to 12 seats on a 400-seat jumbo jet. The computer records might show higher rates of absence on early-morning flights, or on particular days of the week.

Some accountant somewhere came up with a strange solution: If there is a historical no-show rate of 3 percent to a particular flight, then the airline should sell 103 percent of tickets for that plane. It's called "overselling."

If everything works out properly the no-shows won't show and the people who bought a ticket for a seat that didn't exist will walk onto the plane without ever knowing they were in danger of being bumped.

But if things don't follow the computer projection, the airline is put in the position of having to refuse a seat to some of its paying customers. It's called, rather inartfully, "bumping."

Here's the way it usually works: The airline will offer an incentive to volunteers who are willing to give up their seats and take a later flight. Travelers might be offered $100 or $200 in vouchers that can be exchanged for future air travel. The more overbooked the flight, the more desperate the gate agent becomes; the next step up in offers is a free roundtrip ticket. If you accept that, you are at least doubling the value of your current ticket. (My best-ever deal was $1,000 in travel vouchers for each of four tickets (which cost me $400 each) plus a suite in a four-star hotel, dinner, and breakfast for the family.)

Think of the process as a reverse auction. Put a value on your time and inconvenience and judge how desperate the airline is for your seat and how much competition you can expect from other travelers.

If the power is on your side of the table—more oversold seats than volunteers—you can push for a better deal.

And if you want to increase your odds of winning a chance to be bumped, travel on a Friday afternoon when businesspeople are anxious to get home, or at the start or end of a holiday period such as the days around Memorial Day, Labor Day, Thanksgiving, or Christmas.

Know Your Rights As an Airline Passenger

If your flight is delayed by weather or mechanical problems, or is even canceled for those reasons, the airline is not obligated to do anything more than give you its best wishes and an offer to take you to your destination at its next convenience.

If, however, you were bumped from an oversold flight against your will, the airlines must compensate you for the inconvenience. Note that you are not considered to have been bumped if you arrive late at the gate or otherwise fail to check in on time.

If the airline books you on another flight that gets you to your destination within an hour of your original appointed time, they owe you nothing, although an airline will rarely stiff its customers in that way. According to federal rules, if you are delivered one to two hours late, the airline must pay you an amount equal to your one-way fare; if you are more than two hours late, the airline must pay twice the amount of the one-way fare.

Pick the Best Airline Seat

You've got to sit somewhere, so why not go for the best seats in the house . . . or the airplane.

In today's crowded travel market, there's not always a lot of choice available to travelers, especially within a few weeks of departure.

Here's a guide to some of the pros and cons of various seats in the plane:

- *Safety.* The wing area is the strongest part of the plane, and on most planes there is a wing exit. As a bonus, the exit seats usually offer a bit more legroom. Note that you have to be willing to accept the assignment as part of the safety crew and be able to open the heavy door on the instructions of the flight attendants. Children under the age of 15 and disabled travelers cannot use these seats.

- *Comfort.* Some flyers insist on an aisle seat because you can more easily get up and walk around on the plane. You may have a better view of the in-flight movie, too. If you're not in an exit row, the aisle seat is a bit safer than a window or middle because you're in a better position to sprint to the emergency exit. And in any case, you're the first to get up into the aisle when the plane lands safely.

  On the down side, in an aisle seat you're more likely to be bumped by the food cart and others walking the aisles, and you may be disturbed by others in your row when they want to get up.

  Other flyers, including me, prefer the window seat. First, although I have flown millions of miles, I still enjoy the view. The light through the window helps me work with my papers or laptop computer. I can lean up against the wall to sleep. And no one will disturb me when they get up for a walk.

  The shortcomings of the window seat include the fact that there is a bit less legroom because of the curvature of the plane, and the under-seat storage area is narrower for the same reason.

  There are no good reasons to recommend the middle seat in a three-across row.

- *Quiet.* The noisiest part of the plane is alongside and behind the engines. If the engines are on the wings, the entire back half of the plane will hear their roar. If the engines are mounted at the back of the plane and on the tail, you're likely to find quiet from there forward.

  You also may want to sit away from the galleys and the bathrooms.

- *Ride.* Some travelers are immune to turbulence while others swear they can tell the difference between a seat at the back (supposedly the most prone to bouncing) and one over the wing (perhaps a bit more stable because it is at the fulcrum of most movements of the plane).

Do What You Can About Airline Safety

Airplanes crash. That's a fact. It's also true that it is significantly more dangerous to drive to the airport than it is to take off and fly halfway around the world.

The likelihood of surviving a major crash is not good, although some people do limp away. There is often not a great deal of logic about who makes it and who doesn't. (If it makes you feel better, though, consider the fact that the people up front in first class and the pilots usually arrive at the scene of the accident first.)

Anyway, here are some things you can do to try to improve your odds on an air flight:

- *Choose your airline wisely.* Although the Federal Aviation Administration says it won't allow an unsafe airline to take to the skies, you can still pay attention to news reports and industry sources. Although the FAA has come under some strong criticism over its oversight of upstart airlines such as Valujet, the fact is that American airlines are closely monitored—much more so than those of most other nations.

  If you are flying overseas, you can enhance your safety by sticking to American carriers, followed by major national carriers of foreign nations.

- *Choose the right seat.* The window seat in the exit row over the wing is generally considered the safest place to sit. Second to that are aisle seats in rows near an exit row.

- *Listen to the preflight patter.* Though you've heard it all before, pay attention to the safety briefing to see if there are any unusual features to the plane you are on. Locate the nearest exits in front or behind you and count the rows to them so that you'll know where to go in a smoky, dark emergency.

- *Dress sensibly.* Wear comfortable shoes; leave high heels in your luggage. Wear natural-fiber fabrics, less likely to catch fire or melt in flames.

- *Take care of baby.* If you are traveling with an infant, the baby is a lot safer if you purchase a seat for him or her and bring along a car safety seat that can be belted into place on the airplane.

Learn the Tricks to Avoid a Seatmate

Let's face it: Sometimes you just want to be alone. You want to stretch out and sleep on a long return trip, you want to do some work on your laptop computer, you want to read the potboiler you bought in the airport newsstand. You know what you don't want: a nervous neurotic who wants to discuss his life story with you, the life-insurance sales-woman who thinks it is appropriate to investigate the details of your life and financial situation, or the unpleasant dropout from the school of good manners and good grooming.

Here are some savvy tips on how to improve your chances of sitting next to nobody:

- Try to select a flight that is not fully booked. A basic rule of physics: If there are no empty seats on the airplane, your chances of sitting next to one are slim. Choose a flight that leaves at an off-peak time (midmorning or early afternoon on a midweek, non-holiday-period flight, or some but not all overnight flights). Ask the reservations clerk or your travel agent how many seats are available.

- If you are traveling with someone else, book the aisle and window seats in a row. The middle seats are the last ones assigned, and if you end up with someone in the middle, you should have good success in convincing that unlucky soul to trade for one of your seats to reunite your party.

- Ask for a seat toward the back of the plane, an area that is usually filled last.

- When you arrive at the gate, ask the agent if the seat next to yours is vacant; if it is not, politely ask if you can be moved. You may have to wait for the last moment to board, but a friendly gate agent may be able to hold a row open for you and might even decide that you're such a swell person you deserve to be upgraded to business or first class.

Make Yourself Comfortable in Midair

An airplane cabin is not to be confused with a health spa. The air is extremely dry and not well refreshed. Just about anything in the air—from smoke to odors to germs—is moved efficiently through the cabin.

Here are some things you can do to maintain your health onboard an airplane:

- *How dry you are.* Sharply increase your intake of water and juices to combat dehydration; water may also help combat jet lag and altitude sickness when you arrive. Avoid alcohol and caffeine (coffee, tea, and cola drinks), which work the other way.

- *Keep your pipes clear.* Ascent and especially descent can be painful to your ears. It's caused by an imbalance in your sinuses, a condition that can be cleared up by opening the Eustachian tube, which runs from the middle ear to the nasal passages.

    I am old enough to remember how stewardesses (that's what they were called) used to walk the aisles offering chewing gum as a plane was about to come in for a landing. That's still a good idea, especially for children. Another way to open the tube is to pinch your nose, close your mouth, and attempt to breathe out through your nose; if you do it right, you'll feel a relieving pop in your ears.

    Consult your doctor about taking an over-the-counter or prescription decongestant, especially if you have a cold. The downside to decongestants: They may make you drowsy, which could be a problem if you need to drive when you arrive or make a business presentation.

- *Smoke gets in your eyes (and lungs).* All U.S. flights are smoke-free, as are most international flights from and to the United States; elsewhere in the world, the record is spotted. In some parts of the world, smoking is unregulated. If a smoke-free environment is important to you, inquire of the airline about its policies.

- *Keep your blood flowing.* It's not a good practice to be completely sedentary for long periods of time, especially if you have any type of circulatory problems. If you suffer from any significant medical conditions, consult your doctor before taking a long flight. Try to get up and walk around several times on the flight. It is also a good idea to dress in loose-fitting clothing.

Fight Against Jet Lag

The human body was designed well before the day when one could walk into an airport in Boston at breakfast time and step off in London for dinner, or depart London at dinner and arrive in New Zealand for breakfast.

We pay for this wondrous ability with something called jet lag, our body's reaction to zooming across time zones with abandon. For most of us, it feels like something between a hangover and mild case of the flu: exhaustion, dizziness, headaches, and a general failure to compute.

Here are some tips to get the edge on jet lag:

- Skip the alcohol and coffee on your flight; substitute an extra ration of water and juices.

- Try to get onto local time as quickly as possible, even if it means fighting off sleep for hours until it is bedtime at your destination. Switch your meals to the local schedule, too, but eat a light dinner before bedtime to help you fall asleep. For most people, carbohydrates (sugars and starches) help promote sleep, while protein (a slab of steak) can keep you up.

- Reset your body clock with a walk in bright sunlight in the morning.

- Discuss with your doctor taking melatonin, a food supplement sold at many health-food stores. Melatonin is a chemical that is naturally produced by your body at bedtime, and some studies indicate you can set your internal clock by taking a dose at the appropriate time for bed. (You can get a head start by starting on melatonin a few days before your trip and gently adjusting your bedtime and morning alarm in the direction of your new time zone.)

Learn How to Cancel a Noncancelable Ticket

Yes, I know that the ticket says it cannot be canceled or refunded, but here's what that really means in most cases:

- If you decide you need to change the departure date or flight before you begin your trip, you can do so for a fee (currently $50 on most airlines). You can't choose another destination, and you may have to pay an increase in fare if seats are not available at the same rate as your original ticket. If you have purchased a 30-day or 14-day advance-discount ticket, this will almost certainly mean you will have to pay a higher rate or wait another 14 or 30 days before you can fly.

Most airlines will also permit you to adjust your return date or time on a trip already underway, with the same sort of restrictions we've already covered.

- If your flight was canceled for any reason, or if the airline caused you to miss your flight (a changed time, terminal, or missed connection) you should be entitled to a full refund or a free rescheduling. Your rights should be spelled out on the Conditions of Carriage fine print on the back of the ticket.

- You may be able to reschedule or obtain a refund if you are unable to travel because of a call to military duty, jury duty, or other official business.

- Most airlines have a policy that allows you to reschedule a flight or sometimes be given a full refund if you miss a flight or must change your plans because of serious illness or death in your immediate family. You may need to present a note or documents from a doctor, hospital, or funeral home.

No matter what the reason, don't hesitate to call your travel agent or the airline to discuss your options and don't be afraid to ask to speak with a supervisor if you don't feel you've been offered a reasonable way out of your dilemma. Most airlines want to keep their customers and the travel agent happy, and supervisors have a great deal of discretion to bend the rules if you have a good story.

Know the Dangers of Buying Someone Else's Airline Ticket

It used to be that domestic travelers could treat their airline tickets in the same way as tickets to the theater: They could be given, traded, or sold to someone else in private transactions without any problem.

Today, though, nearly every airline asks for proof of identity when you check in at the counter. This began as part of an effort to improve security at airports; along the way it has been embraced by airlines as a way to cut down on the resale of nonrefundable tickets.

Some airlines are more diligent in checking for ID than are others, and at some airports the check-in takes place at the ticket counter and not on the supposedly secure side of the metal detectors: It might be possible to finesse the arrangement.

I cannot recommend you buy a ticket with someone else's name on it, however. Consider it a part of the price of security.

It may be possible, though, for the rightful owner of the ticket to get the airline or travel agency to reissue the ticket in a new name; there may be a fee assessed for such service.

Play the Currency Game to Save on Foreign Travel

Currency-exchange rates go up and down; one unpleasant experience for the traveler is to watch the value of the U.S. dollar decline in the months leading up to an international trip. It's like watching your vacation price go up, minute by minute.

If you think the rate will continue to go up, here are two things you can do to lock in your expenses:

1. Prepay for airfare, hotels, car rentals, and other elements of your trip, using a credit card from a bank or agency that will give you a fair exchange rate.

2. Convert cash into foreign denomination travelers' checks now. Again, you will be able to lock in the current exchange rate.

How can you be sure that the exchange rate will continue to worsen? You can't. But here's one thing that is generally true about things economic: Rates go up faster than they go down.

Tourist Information

Some people like to travel as if they were the first explorers of an undiscovered land; that's a lot of fun and a guaranteed way to be part of all sorts of unexpected experiences. Some of them might even be fun, although personally I wouldn't want to parachute unknowingly into a Civil War or backpack my way into an active volcano zone.

Remember that the first man on the moon was merely executing something that had been planned down to the microsecond by thousands of engineers and scientists—the equivalent of a lunar travel agency. On a more familiar plane, when I set foot in London or Orlando or Montreal or any of the places I visit as part of my work or vacation travel, I find great pleasure in knowing what there is to see and then setting forth in search of accidental tourism.

Here's how to research your travel before you leave: Seek the counsel of a competent and knowledgeable travel agent (alas, not always easy to find), collect brochures and publications from government agencies and tourism associations (and read them with a jaundiced eye), and consult a good, current guidebook for a critical review of what's hot and what's not (full disclosure: I write the *Econoguide* travel-book series).

Here's a collection of government tourism agencies and some private operators around the world. Many have Web pages that give instant access to information; if you don't have a computer with an Internet account, see if your local library or school offers access. (Some of the Web pages are published by the official tourist bureaus, while others are unofficial sites maintained by residents, expatriates, or enthusiasts; check to determine who is behind a Web page to help you gauge the accuracy of the information provided.)

If the tourism agency has an office in the United States, you'll find that listed here, too, along with a domestic telephone number. I've also included phone numbers for Caribbean destinations, in the 809 area code.

Remember that these groups present the *official* line. Be sure to supplement the information you receive from them with research from an independent source. And, though the Web pages, phone numbers, and addresses were correct when we researched them, there are certain to be changes; be persistent in your exploration, though, and you'll eventually be rewarded.

NOTE: In this book, ⚑ signifies American offices for foreign tourist bureaus.

AFGHANISTAN

Afghan Tourist Organisation (ATO)
Ansari Wat, Shar-i-Nau
Kabul, Afghanistan

Afghan Cultural Information Center
http://enterprise.aacc.cc.md.us/~haq/

ALGERIA

National Office of Tourism
25–27 Khelifa Boukhalfa
Algiers, Algeria

Arab Net
http://www.arab.net/algeria/algeria_con-
tents.html

AMERICAN SAMOA

American Samoa Office of Tourism
P.O. Box 1147
Pago Pago, AS 96799
American Samoa

ANDORRA

Andorra Tourism
6800 N. Knox Ave.
Lincolnwood, IL 60646
http://www.andorra.ad/
http://www.xmission.com/~dderhak/
    andorra.htm

ANGOLA

National Tourist Agency
CP 1240, Palácio de Vidro
Luanda, Angola

ANGUILLA

Tourist Information
The Social Security Building
The Valley
Anguilla, BWI
809-497-2759; 800-553-4939
http://www.candw.com.ai/~atbtour
http://www.news.ai

ANTIGUA & BARBUDA

Dept. of Tourism
Thames St.
P.O. Box 363
Saint Johns, Antigua
809-462-0480
http://www.interknowledge.com/
    antigua-barbuda/

Antigua & Barbuda Tourist Board
610 Fifth Ave. #311
New York, NY 10020
212-541-4117

ARGENTINA

Argentina Tourism
Suipacha 1111
Buenos Aires, 1071 Argentina
http://www.artour.sudnet.com.ar/
    infoarge/infoar.htm

Argentina National Tourist Council
12 W. 56 St.
New York, NY 10019
212-603-0443

ARMENIA

http://www.earthlink.net/~hamoarb/
    armenweb.html

ARUBA

Tourist Authority
172 L. G. Smithe Blvd.
P.O. Box 1019
Aruba
http://www.interknowledge.com/aruba

Aruba Tourist Authority
2344 Salzedo St.
Miami, FL 33134
954-767-6477

AUSTRALIA

About Australia
http://www.about-australia.com/

Guide to Australia
http://www.csu.edu.au/education/
   australia.html

Traveling Australia
http://www.travelaus.com.au/

AUSTRIA

Oesterreich Information
Margaretenstrasse 1 (Rilkeplatz 5)
A-1040 Vienna, Austria
http://www.anto.com
http://www.austria-info.at/oew.html

Austrian National Tourist Office
500 Fifth Ave.
P.O. Box 1142
New York, NY 10108-1142
212-944-6880; 800-474-9696

BAHAMAS

Tourist Office
212-758-2777
http://www.interknowledge.com/
   bahamas

**Nassau/Cable Beach/Paradise
Promotion Board**
800-327-9019

BAHRAIN

Bahrain Tourism Company
P.O. Box 5831
Manama, Bahrain

BANGLADESH

Bangladesh Parjatan Corporation
(National Tourism Organization)
233 Old Airport Road
Tejgaon, Dhaka 1215, Bangladesh
http://www.asel.udel.edu/~kazi/
   bangladesh/bd.html
http://www.servtech.com/public/
   outcast/tour/

BARBADOS

Board of Tourism
P.O. Box 242
Bridgetown, Barbados
809-427-2623; 212-986-6516;
888-BARBADOS; 800-221-9831
http://barbados.org/

BELGIUM

Tourist Information Bureau
Town Hall of Brussels
Grand Place
Brussels 1000, Belgium
http://www.eunet.be

Antwerp City Tourist Office
Crote Markt 15
Antwerp B-2000, Belgium

Brussels
212-758-8130
http://www.interpac.be/G7/brussels/
   brussels.html

BELIZE

Tourism Industry Assn.
99 Albert St.
P.O. Box 62
Belize City, Belize
http://www.belize.com/home.html

Belize Tourist Board
421 7th Ave. #1101
New York, NY 10001
212-563-6011; 800-624-0686

BENIN

Societe Beninoise pour la Promo. du Tourism
B.P. 1508
Cotonou, Benin

BERMUDA

Department of Tourism
Global House, 43 Church St.
Hamilton HM BX, Bermuda
http://www.bermudatourism.com/

Bermuda Department of Tourism
310 Madison Ave., Suite 201
New York, NY 10017
212-818-9800; 800-223-6106,
800-BERMUDA

BHUTAN

Bhutan Tourism Corporation Ltd. (BTCL)
P.O. Box 159
Thimphu, Bhutan

Bhutan Travel Inc.
120 E. 56 St., Suite 1130
New York, NY 10022
212-838-6382; 800-950-9908

BOLIVIA

Ministerio de Industria, Comercio & Tourismo
P.O. Box 20299
La Paz, Bolivia
http://www.boliviaweb.com/

Bolivian Consulate
3014 Massachusetts Ave. N.W.
Washington, DC 20036
202-232-4828

BONAIRE

Government Tourist Office
12 Kaya Simon Bolivar
Kralendijk, Bonaire
http://www.interknowledge.com/bonaire

Bonaire Gov. Tourist Office
444 Madison Ave., Suite 2403
New York, NY 10022
212-832-0779; 800-266-2473

BOTSWANA

Department of Tourism
Private Bag 0047
Gaborone, Botswana

BRAZIL

Embratur Brazilian Tourism Board
Rua Mariz e Barros, 13
Rio de Janeiro 20270, Brazil
http://www.embratur.gov.br/home.htm

BRITISH VIRGIN ISLANDS

Tourist Board
Social Security Building
Wickhams Cay I
Road Town, BVI
809-494-3134

British Virgin Islands Tourist Board ▣
370 Lexington Ave., Suite 1605
New York, NY 10017
212-696-0400; 800-835-8530

BRUNEI

http://jtb.brunet.bn/index.htm

BULGARIA

Association of Tourism & Recreation
1 Lenin Square
Sofia, Bulgaria
http://www.cs.columbia.edu/~radev/
bulginfo.html
http://pisa.rockefeller.edu:8080/Bulgaria

BURKINA FASO

Ministry of Environment & Tourism
P.O. Box 624
Ave. de la Resistance du 17 Mai
Ouagadougou, Burkina Faso

BURUNDI

Office National du Tourisme
BP 902
2 Ave des Euphorbes
Bujumbura, Burundi

CAMBODIA

Direction General of Tourism
Achar Mean Blvd.
Phnom Penh, Cambodia
http://www.cambodia.org/

CAMEROON

**Société Camerounaise de Tourisme
(SOCATOUR)**
BP 7138
Yaoundé, Cameroon
http://www.compufix.demon.co.uk/
camweb/

CANADA

Canadian Tourism Commission
http://xinfo.ic.gc.ca/Tourism/

Travel Alberta
10155 102 St., 3rd Floor
Edmonton AB, T5J 4L6 Canada
403-988-5455; 800-661-8888
http://www.gov.ab.ca/dept/edt.html

Tourism British Columbia
1117 Wharf St.
Victoria BC, V8W 2Z2 Canada
604-683-2000 Vancouver,
604-387-1642 Victoria; 800-663-6000
http://www.gov.bc.ca/tourism/tourism.
html

Manitoba Tourist Information
Legislative Building
7-1455 Waverly St.
Winnipeg MB, R3B 5C3 Canada
204-945-3777; 800-665-0040
http://www.gov.mb.ca/itt/travel/

New Brunswick Tourism Inquiries
P.O. Box 6000
Fredericton NB, E3B 5W1 Canada
506-452-9500 Fredericton,
506-658-2990 St. John; 800-561-0123
http://www.gov.nb.ca/tourism/index.htm

**Newfoundland & Labrador
Department of Development**
Tourism Branch
Box 8730
St. John's NF, A1B 4K2 Canada
709-729-2830; 800-563-NFLD
http://www.gov.nf.ca/

**Northwest Territories Economic
Development & Tourism**
Box 1320
Yellowknife NT, X1A 2L9 Canada
403-873-7200; 800-661-0788
http://info.ic.gc.ca/Tourism/Canada/
    nwt.html

Nova Scotia Department of Tourism
Box 130
Halifax NS, B3J 2M7 Canada
902-424-5000; 800-341-6096
http://info.ic.gc.ca/Tourism/Canada/
    nb.html

Nova Scotia Tourism
136 Commercial St.
Portland, ME 04101
http://ttg.sba.dal.ca/nstour/halifax/
    geninfo/general.htm
http://www.webcom.com/morandan/
    generalStf.html

Ontario Travel
Queen's Park
Toronto ON, M7A 2E5 Canada
416-965-4008, 613-954-3980;
800-ONTARIO
http://www.gov.on.ca/MBS/english/
    its_ontario
http://info.ic.gc.ca/Tourism/Canada/
    ont.html

**Toronto Metropolitan
Convention & Visitors Assn.**
1 Brinkman Ave.
Buffalo, NY 14211-2503
416-367-9088; 800-965-9128
http://www.math.toronto.edu/toronto/

**Prince Edward Island Department of
Tourism & Parks**
Box 940, Department 1
Charlottetown PE, C1A 7N8 Canada
902-892-7411; 800-565-0267
http://www.gov.pe.ca/vg/index.html
http://info.ic.gc.ca/Tourism/Canada/
    pei.html

Tourism Quebec
C.P. 979
Quebec QC, H3C 2W3 Canada
514-873-2015; 800-363-7777, 800-361-6490,
800-363-1990, 800-443-7000
http://www.gouv.qc.ca/anglais/
    tourcult_e/tc_intro_e.html
http://info.ic.gc.ca/Tourism/Canada/
    quebec.html

Tourism Quebec
1 Rockefeller Plaza, 26th Floor
New York, NY 10020-2102
212-397-0200

**Greater Montreal Convention &
Tourism Bureau**
1555 Peel St., Suite 600
Montréal QC, H3A 1X6, Canada
514-844-5400

Tourism Saskatchewan
1919 Saskatchewan Drive
Regina SK, S4P 3V7 Canada
306-787-2300; 800-667-7191
http://www.gov.sk.ca
http://info.ic.gc.ca/Tourism/Canada/
    sask.html
http://www.virtualsk.com

Yukon Tourism
P.O. Box 2703
Whitehorse YT, Y1A 2C6 Canada
403-667-5367
http://www.touryukon.com
http://info.ic.gc.ca/Tourism/Canada/
    yukon.html

CARIBBEAN AREA

Caribbean Tourism Organization
20 E. 46 St.
New York, NY 10017
212-635-9530
http://www.caribtourism.com/
http://www.cpscaribnet.com

CAYMAN ISLANDS

Department of Tourism
Gov. Tower Bldg.
George Town, Cayman Islands
809-949-0623
http://cayman.com.ky
http://www.caymans.com/

**Cayman Islands
Department of Tourism**
420 Lexington Ave., Suite 416
New York, NY 10017
212-682-5582

CHAD

**Direction du Tourisme des Parcs
Nationaux et Réserves de Faune**
BP 86
N'Djaména, Chad

CHILE

**National Tourism Board of Chile
SERNATUR**
Providencia 1550
P.O. Box 14082
Santiago, Chile
http://www.brujula.cl/turismo/

CHINA

China National Tourist Office
350 Fifth Ave., Suite 6413
New York, NY 10118
212-760-9700

COLOMBIA

Corporacion Nacional de Turismo
Calle 28 No 13A-15, Piso 16
Santefe de Bogotá, Colombia
http://www.presidencia.gov.co/htm/
colomb11.htm

Colombia Government
Tourist Office
140 E. 57 St.
New York, NY 10022

COMOROS

**Société Comorienne de Tourisme et
d'Hôtellerie (COMOTEL)**
Itsandra Hotel
Njazidja, Comoros

PEOPLES REPUBLIC OF CONGO

**Ministere du Tourisme des Loisires et
de l'Environnement**
BP 456
Brazzaville, Congo

COOK ISLANDS

Cook Islands Tourist Authority
P.O. Box 14
Avarua, Rarotonga, Cook Islands

COSTA RICA

Instituto Costarricense de Turismo
Calles 5 y 7 avenida 4
P.O. Box 777-1000
San Jose, Costa Rica
http://www.ticonet.co.cr/costa_rica/
tourism_info.html
http://www.cocori.com/

Costa Rica
National Tourist Bureau 🏳
1100 Brickell Ave.
B.I.V. Tower #801
Miami, FL 33131

CÔTE D'IVOIRE

Plateau in Immeuble de la Corniche
Blvd. de Gaulle
Abidjan, Ivory Coast
http://www.africaonline.co.ci/

Côte d'Ivoire 🏳
Tourisme Côte d'Ivoire
2424 Massachusetts Ave. N.W.
Washington, DC 20008

CRETE

Greek National
Tourist Organization 🏳
645 Fifth Ave.
Olympic Tower
New York, NY 10022
212-421-5777
http://www.forthnet.gr/crete/

CROATIA

Croatian Convention Bureau
Ilica 1a
41000 Zagreb, Croatia

Croatian Embassy 🏳
2343 Massachusetts Ave. N.W.
Washington, DC 20008
202-588-5899
http://tjev.tel.etf.hr/hrvatska/
    Welcome2Croatia.html

CUBA

Cubatur
156 Calle 23
Vedaado, Havana, Cuba
http://caribbean.cun.net/

Cuban Interests Section 🏳
2639 16th St. N.W.
Washington, DC 20009
202-797-8609; 800-752-9282
http://www.cybercuba.com

CURACAO

Tourism Development Bureau
19 Petermaai
Curacao
http://www.interknowledge.com/curacao
http://www.dcwww.com/curacao/

Curacao Tourism
Development Bureau 🏳
400 Madison Ave., Suite 311
New York, NY 10017
800-3-CURACAO

CYPRUS

Tourist Organization
18 Th. Theodotou Str.
P.O. Box 4535
Nicosia, Cyprus

Cyprus Tourist Organization 🏳
13 E. 40 St.
New York, NY 10016
212-683-5280

CZECH REPUBLIC

Czech Tourist Authority
Prague 1, Narodni 37
Czech Republic
http://www.infotec-travel.com/
cznavbar.htm

Prague Convention Bureau
Rytirska 26, 110 00 Prague 1
Czech Republic

Cedok,
The Czechoslovak Travel Bureau
1109-1111 Madison Ave.
New York, NY 10028
212-288-0830

DENMARK

Danish Tourist Board
Vesterbrogade 6 D
Copenhagen, 1620 Denmark
http://www.dtb.dt.dk
http://info.denet.dk/denmark.html

Danish Tourist Board
655 Third Ave.
New York, NY 10017

REPUBLIC OF DJIBOUTI

Ministere du Commerce,
Transports et du Tourism
B.P. 79
Djibouti
http://www.intnet.dj/

DOMINICA

Tourist Bureau
Valley Road, P.O. Box 73
Roseau, Dominica, WI
http://www.delphis.dm/home.htm

DOMINICAN REPUBLIC

Ministry of Tourism
Ave. George Washington
Santo Domingo, Dominican Republic
809-689-3655
http://www.dominicana-sun.com/
Dom-info/dominfo.htm

Dominican Republic
Tourist Information
1501 Broadway #410
New York, NY 10036
212-575-4966

DUBAI

Dept. of Tourism &
Commerce Marketing
8 Penn Center
Philadelphia, PA 19103

ECUADOR

Ecuador Tourist Information
7270 N.W. 12th St. #400C
Miami, FL 33126
305-477-0041; 800-553-6673

EGYPT

Egypt Tourism
630 Fifth Ave.
New York, NY 10111
212-332-2570

EL SALVADOR

San Salvador Convention & Visitors
Bureau
73 Av Sur y Av Olimpica Edif
Olimpic Plaza L-28, Col Escalon
San Salvador, El Salvador

El Salvador-Consulate
46 Park Ave.
New York, NY 10016
212-889-3608
http://www.ecst.csuchico.edu/~william

ERITREA

Eritrean Tour Service (ETS)
P.O. Box 889
61 Harnet Ave.
Asmara, Eritrea

ESTONIA

Estonian Tourist Board
Pikk Street 71
Tallinn, Estonia
http://www.ciesin.ee/ESTONIA/

ETHIOPIA

Ethiopian Commission for Hotels & Tourism
P.O. Box 2183
Addis Ababa, Ethiopia
http://www.EthiopiaOnline.Net/

FAROE ISLANDS

http://www.ozemail.com.au/~skuvadal

FIJI

Fiji Visitors Bureau
Thomson St., P.O. Box 92
Suva, Fiji
http://www.usp.ac.fj/

Fiji Visitors Bureau
5777 W. Century Blvd., Suite 220
Los Angeles, CA 90045
310-568-1616

FINLAND

Finnish Tourist Board
Toolonkutu 11, P.O. Box 625
Helsinki, Finland
http://www.travel.fi/

Helsinki City Tourist Office
Pohjoisesplanadi 19, 00100
Helsinki, Finland
http://www.hel.fi/english/index.html

Finnish Tourist Board
655 Third Ave.
New York, NY 10017
212-949-2333; 800-FIN-INFO

FRANCE

Maison de la France
8 avenue de L'Opera
Paris, France
http://www.francetourism.com/
http://www.franceguide.com
http://www.franceway.com

Chamonix/Mont Blanc Bureau du Tourisme
Place de l'Eglise
74400 Chamonix
Mont Blanc, France

French Government Tourist Office
444 Madison Ave.
New York, NY 10022
212-838-7800; 800-391-4909

FRENCH CARIBBEAN

http://www.frenchcaribbean.com/

FRENCH GUIANA

http://www.frenchcaribbean.com/

FRENCH WEST INDIES

French West Indies Tourist Board
444 Madison Ave.
New York, NY 10022
212-838-6887
http://www.frenchcaribbean.com/
http://www.cieux.com/~philip/fwi.html

GABON

Gabon Tourist Information Office
347 Fifth Ave. #810
New York, NY 10016
212-447-6701

GAMBIA

Ministry of Information & Tourism
New Administrative Bldg., State House
Banjul, Gambia
http://www.sas.upenn.edu/
    African_Studies/Country_Specific/
    Gambia.html

GERMANY

German National Tourist Office
122 E. 42 St.
New York, NY 10168-0072
212-661-7200

GHANA

Tourist Board
National Culture Centre
Kumasi, Ghana
http://www.uta.fi/~csfraw/ghana/
    gh_tourist.html

GIBRALTAR

Gibraltar Information Bureau
1156 15th St. N.W. #1100
Washington, DC 20005
202-452-1108

GREECE

Greek National Tourist Organization
2 Amerikis Str.
Athens, Greece
http://www.vacation.forthnet.gr/
    first.html
http://www.stepc.gr/yannis/hotlist/
    sailing.html

**Greek National
Tourist Organization**
645 Fifth Ave.
Olympic Tower
New York, NY 10022
212-421-5777
http://www.forthnet.gr/crete/

GREENLAND

Qasigiannguit Touristservice
Box 155
3951 Qasigiannguit
Greenland
http://www.greenland-guide.dk/
    qasigiannguit-tourist

GRENADA

Tourist Board
Carenage
St. George, Grenada
809-440-2279

Grenada Tourist Board
820 Second Ave. #900D
New York, NY 10017
212-687-9554; 800-927-9554

GUADELOUPE

Office of Tourism
5 Square de la Banque
Pointe-a-Pitre, Guadeloupe
http://www.frenchcaribbean.com/

Guadeloupe Office of Tourism
888-4-GUADELOUPE

GUATEMALA

Guatemala Chamber of Commerce
10a Calle 3-80, zona 1
Guatemala City, Guatemala
http://www.guateconnect.com/
http://www.greenarrow.com/guatemal/
    guatemal.htm

Guatemala Tourist Commission
299 Alhambra Circle #510
Coral Gables, FL 33134
305-442-0651; 800-742-4529

GUINEA BISSAU

Centro de Informacao
Avenida Domingos Ramos
Bissau

GUYANA

Guyana Consulate
866 U.N. Plaza, Suite 304
New York, NY 10017
http://www.guyana.org/

HAITI

National Office of Tourism
Ave Marie-Jeanne
Port-au-Prince, Haiti
http://www.haitionline.com/

Haitian National Office of Tourism
18 E. 41 St. #1602
New York, NY 10017

HONDURAS

Honduras Chamber of Commerce
Edificio San Miguel
Tegucigalpa, Honduras
http://www.hondurastur.com/

Honduran Consulate
1612 K St. N.W. #310
Washington, DC 20006
202-223-0185

HONG KONG

Hong Kong Tourist Association
35/F Jardine House
Central Hong Kong
http://www.hkta.org

Hong Kong Tourist Association
590 Fifth Ave.
New York, NY 10036
212-869-5008

HUNGARY

Hungarian Tourist Board
Vigado 4.6
Budapest H-1051, Hungary
http://www.fsz.bme.hu/hungary/
    intro.html

Hungarian National Tourist Office
150 E. 58 St.
New York, NY 10155
212-355-0240; 800-367-7878

ICELAND

Tourist Information Center
Bankastreti 2 101
Reykjavik 101, Iceland
http://www.centrum.is/icerev/page2.html
http://islandia.nomius.com/

Iceland Tourist Board 🏳
655 Third Ave.
New York, NY 10017
212-949-2333; 800-346-3436

INDIA

India Tourist Office 🏳
30 Rockefeller Plaza
Suite 15, North Mezzanine
New York, NY 10012
212-586-4901
http://www.india-travel.com/

INDONESIA

**Indonesian Tourist
Promotion Office** 🏳
3457 Wilshire Blvd., Suite 104
Los Angeles, CA 90010
213-387-2078
http://www.sino.net/asean/indonesa.html

IRAQ

Iraq Tourism Board
P.O. Box 7783
Baghdad, Iraq
http://www.liii.com/~hajeri/iraq.html

IRELAND

Tourist Board
Baggot St. Bridge
P.O. Box 273
Dublin 8, Ireland
http://www.iol.ie/~discover

Irish Tourist Board 🏳
345 Park Ave.
New York, NY 10154
212-418-0800; 800-223-6470,
800-SHAMROCK

ISLE OF MAN

Tourist Board
http://www.isle-of-man.com/index.htm

ISRAEL

Government Tourist Office
http://www.infotour.co.il

Israel Government Tourist Office 🏳
350 Fifth Ave.
New York, NY 10118
800-596-1199

ITALY

**Ente Nazionale Italiano per il Turismo
(ENIT)**
Via Parigi 11, 00185
Rome, Italy
http://www.initaly.com/
http://www.mi.cnr.it/IGST/InfoTurist.html

Tuscany Convention Bureau
Via Borgognissanti 8, 50123
Florence, Italy
http://www.arca.net/florence.htm

**Azienda di Promozione Turistica di
Venezia**
Castello, 4421
Venice, Italy

Italian-Government Travel Office 🏳
630 Fifth Ave.
New York, NY 10111
212-245-4822

JAMAICA

Tourism Centre
21 Dominica Dr.
Kingston 5, Jamaica
809-929-9200
http://www.jamaicatravel.com/

Jamaica Tourist Board 🏴
801 Second Ave., 20th Floor
New York, NY 10017
212-856-9727; 800-233-4582

JAPAN

Tourist Information Center
Yuraku-Cho 2-10-1, Chiyoda-ku
Tokyo, Japan
http://www.jnto.go.jp

**Japan National
Tourist Organization** 🏴
Rockefeller Plaza
630 Fifth Ave.
New York, NY 10111
212-757-5640

JORDAN

Ministry of Tourism & Antiquities
P.O. Box 224
Amman, Jordan
http://www.iiconsulting.com/jordan/

Jordan Information Bureau 🏴
2319 Wyoming Ave. N.W.
Washington, DC 20008
202-265-1606

KENYA

Kenya Tourist Office 🏴
424 Madison Ave.
New York, NY 10017
212-486-1300

SOUTH KOREA

South Korea National Tourism Corp.
10 Tadong, Chung-gu C.P.O. Box 903
Seoul, Korea
http://mic.go.kr/VISIT/visitkor.htm

Korea National Tourism Corp. 🏴
Two Executive Dr., 7th Floor
Fort Lee, NY 07024

LAOS

Vientiane Tourist Office
Thanon Sithan Nua Building II
Thanon Luang Prabang
Vientiane, Laos
http://www.asiatour.com/laos/
    content1.htm

Lao Tourism
P.O. Box 2912
Vientiane, Laos

LATVIA

Tours
Kalpaka bulvaris 1
Riga, Latvia
http://www.EUnet.lv/

Latvia Centre for Overseas Tourism
29/31 Bruninieku str
Riga, Latvia LV1001

LEBANON

Ministry of Tourism
550 Central Bank St.
P.O. Box 11-344
Beirut, Lebanon
http://www.lebanon.com/tourism/
    index.htm

LESOTHO

Tourist Board
P.O. Box 1378
Maseur, Lesotho
http://uts.cc.utexas.edu/~jrubarth/world/
lesotho/lesotho.html#Lesotho

LIBERIA

National Bureau of Culture & Tourism
P.O. Box 3223
14th St. & Cheeseman Ave.
Monrovia, Liberia

LIECHTENSTEIN

Liechtenstein National Tourist Office
Postfach 139, Im Stadtle 7
Vaduz, Liechtenstein
http://www.travel.org/liechtens.html

LITHUANIA

Vytis International Travel SVC
2129 Knapp
Brooklyn, NY 11229
718-769-3300

LUXEMBOURG

Luxembourg National Tourist Office
P.O. Box 1001
Luxembourg, Luxembourg
http://www.restena.lu/luxembourg/
lux_welcome.html

MACAU

Macau Tourist Information Bureau
3133 Lake Hollywood Dr.
Los Angeles, CA 90068-1541
213-851-3402; 800-331-7150

MACEDONIA

http://spidey.cs.rit.edu/~bvs4997/faq/

MADAGASCAR

**La Maison du Tourisme de
Madagascar**
B.P. 3224
Antananarivo 101
Republic of Madagascar

Madagascar Tourist Office
124 Lomas Santa Fe Dr. #206
Solana Beach, CA 92075
619-792-6999; 800-854-1029

MALAWI

Malawi Department of Tourism
P.O. Box 402
Blantyre, Malawi
http://spicerack.sr.unh.edu/~llk/

MALAYSIA

Tourist Development of Malaysia
6,17,24027 Menara Dato Onn
Putra World Trade Centre
45 Jalan Tun Ismail
Kuala Lumpur 50480, Malaysia
http://www.tourism.gov.my

**Malaysia Tourist
Promotion Board**
595 Madison Ave. #1800
New York, NY 10022
212-754-1113; 800-KLUMPUR

MALTA

Malta National Tourism Organization
Harper Lane
Floriana, Malta
http://www.fred.net/malta/

Malta National Tourist Office
Empire State Building
New York, NY 10118
212-695-9520

MARSHALL ISLANDS

**Marshall Islands Ministry of
Resources & Development**
Division of Tourism
P.O. Box 1727
Majuro, Marshall Islands

MARTINIQUE

Martinique Tourism
Blvd. Alfassa
Fort-de-France, Martinique
http://www.martinique.org
http://www.frenchcaribbean.com/

MAURITANIA

**Société Mauritanienne de Tourisme et
d'Hôtellerie (SMTH)**
BP 552
Nouakchott, Mauritania
http://www.sas.upenn.edu/
    African_Studies/Country_Specific/
    Mauritania.html

MAURITIUS

Mauritius Government Tourist Office
Emmanuel Anquetil Building
Sir Seewoosagur Ramgoolam Street
Port Louis, Mauritius
http://www.barint.on.ca/mauritius/
    t_tourism.html
http://www.idsonline.com/usa/
    mauritius.html

**Mauritius-Government
Tourist Office**
8 Haven Ave.
Port Washington, NY 11050
516-944-3763

MEXICO

**Mexico Government Tourist Office
SECTUR**
Aguascalientes
Direccion Estatal de Turismo
Departamento de Atencion al Publico
Edif. Continental
Equador 202 P.B.
Mexico
http://mexico-travel.com/

MICRONESIA

Federated State of Micronesia
Liaison Office, P.O. Box 10630
Main Facility, Guam
http://darkwing.uoregon.edu/~robertsr/
    micro.htm

Federated State of Micronesia
Liaison Office
3049 Ualena St. #409
Honolulu, HI 96819-1946
808-836-4775

MOLDOVA
http://www.info.polymtl.ca/Moldova

MONACO

**Government Tourist & Convention
Bureau**
Direction du Tourisme et des Congrès de
   la Principauté de Monaco
2a boulevard des Moulins
Monaco, Cedex
http://www.monaco.mc/monaco/
    guide_en.html

**Monaco Government
Tourist & Convention Bureau**
565 Fifth Ave.
New York, NY 10017
800-753-9696
http://www.monaco.mc/usa

MONGOLIA

**Juulchin (Mongolian Foreign Tourism
Corporation)**
Chinggis Khan Avenue 5B
Ulan Bator 210543, Mongolia

Nomadic Expeditions
1 Deerpark Dr., Suite M
Monmouth Junction, NJ 08852
732-274-0088

MONTSERRAT

Dept. of Tourism
P.O. Box 7, Church Rd.
Plymouth, Montserrat
809-491-2230

Montserrat Information Bureau
485 Fifth Ave.
New York, NY 10017
212-818-0100

MOROCCO

National Marocain de Tourisme
31 angle avenue Al Abtal
Zankat Oued Fes
Rabat, Morocco
http://www.dsg.ki.se/maroc/

Moroccan National Tourist Office
20 E. 46 St. #1201
New York, NY 10017
212-557-2520

MOZAMBIQUE

Empresa Nacional de Turismo (ENT)
(Mozambique National Tourism Company)
CP 2446
Avda 25 de Setembro 1203
Maputo, Mozambique

MYANMAR

Travel & Tours
P.O. Box 559
Yangon, Myanmar

Myanmar National Tourist Office
2514 University Dr.
Durham, NC 27707

NAMIBIA

Namibia Tourism
P/Bag 13346
Windhoek, Namibia

NEPAL

Nepal Tourist Information
820 Second Ave. #202
New York, NY 10017
212-370-4188
http://www.travel-nepal.com/

NETHERLANDS

Netherlands Board of Tourism
Amsteldijk 166
1079 LH Amsterdam
The Netherlands
http://www.nbt.nl/holland/home.htm

Netherlands Board of Tourism
355 Lexington Ave., 21st Floor
New York, NY 10017

NEVIS

Nevis Tourist Office
Main St.
Charlestown, Nevis
809-469-5521
http://www.interknowledge.com/
    stkitts-nevis

NEW ZEALAND

New Zealand Tourist & Publicity
P.O. Box 95
Wellington, New Zealand
http://discovernz.co.nz
http://nz.com/

Rotorua
http://nz.com/Rotorua

New Zealand Tourism Board
One United Nations Plaza,
25th Floor
New York, NY 10017-3515
800-388-5494

NICARAGUA

Nicaraguan Consulate
1627 New Hampshire Ave. N.W.
Washington, DC 20009
202-939-6531
http://www.greenarrow.com/nicaragu/
    nicaragu.htm

NIGER

Office National du Tourismo
Ave. Luebke
Niamey, Niger
http://www.orstom.fr/bani/cartes/
    documents/Niger.html

NIGERIA

Tourist Board
Blocks 378 & 381, Zone 4
P.O. Box 167
Abuja, Nigeria
http://www.sas.upenn.edu/
    African_Studies/Country_Specific/
    Nigeria.html

NORTHERN IRELAND

(see also United Kingdom)

Northern Ireland Tourist Board
River House, 48 High St.
Belfast BT1 2DS, Northern Ireland
http://www.interknowledge.com/
    northern-ireland

Northern Ireland Tourist Board
551 Fifth Ave. #701
New York, NY 10176
212-922-0101

NORWAY

NORTRA
Langkaia 1
Postboks 499—Sentrum
0105 Oslo, Norway
http://www.sn.no/norway/
http://www.uit.no/norge/tourist.shtml

Oslo Tourist Office
City Hall
Oslo, Norway

Norwegian Information Service
825 Third Ave.
New York, NY 10022
212-421-7333

Scandinavian Tourism
655 Third Ave.
New York, NY 10017
212-949-2333; 800-346-3436

PAKISTAN

Tourism Dev. Corp
House No. 2, Street 61
P.O. Box 1465
Islamabad, Pakistan

PANAMA

Tourism Office
1110 Brickell Ave.
Miami, FL 33131
http://www.pa/

PAPAU NEW GUINEA

Tourism Dev. Corp.
P.O. Box 7144, Boroko
Port Moresby, Papua New Guinea
272521

PARAGUAY

National Tourism Office
Edif Ministerio de Obras Publicas y
  Comunicacionses
Asuncion, Paraguay
http://www.magma.ca/~embapar/
  p-eng.html

PERU

Tourist Office
1000 Brickell Ave. #600
Miami, FL 33131
305-374-0023; 800-854-0023
http://www.foptur.gob.pe/
http://www.rcp.net.pe/

PHILIPPINES

Philippine Convention & Visitors Corp.
4th Fl., Legaspi Towers 300
Roxas Blvd., P.O. Box EA-459
Metro Manila, Philippines
http://www.sino.net/asean/philippn.html

Philippine Center
556 Fifth Ave.
New York, NY 10036
212-575-7915

POLAND

Orbis Head Office
ul. Bracka 16
Warsaw, Poland
http://plwww.fuw.edu.pl/index.eng.html

Polish Tourist Association
ul. Senatorska 11
PL-00-075 Warszawa
Poland

Polish National Tourist Office
275 Madison Ave.
New York, NY 10016
212-338-9412

PORTUGAL

Portuguese National Tourist Office
590 Fifth Ave.
New York, NY 10036
212-354-4403

PUERTO RICO

Puerto Rico Tourism Co.
Old San Juan
San Juan, Puerto Rico
809-721-2400
http://www.discoverpuertorico.com

San Juan-Puerto Rico Convention Bureau
59 Del Cristo St.
Old San Juan, Puerto Rico 00901
809-725-2110

Puerto Rico Tourism Co.
575 Fifth Ave., 23rd Floor
New York, NY 10017
212-599-6262

ROMANIA

Carpati National Travel Office of Bucharest
7 Blvd. Gral Magtheru
Bucharest, Romania
http://www.eunet.ro

Romania National Travel Office
342 Madison Ave.
New York, NY 10173
212-697-6971

RUSSIA

Russian National Tourist Offices
800 Third Ave., Suite 3101
New York, NY 10022
212-758-1162
http://www.russia-travel.com/

St. Petersburg
http://www.spb.su/

RWANDA

Office of Tourism & National Parks
B.P. 905
Kigali, Rwanda
http://www.sas.upenn.edu/
    African_Studies/Country_Specific/
    Rwanda.html

SABA & ST. EUSTATIUS

Tourist Office
Windwardside, Saba
http://www.turq.com/saba

Saba & St. Eustatius Tourist Office
516-425-0900

ST. BARTHELEMY

Town Hall
Rue August-Nyman
Gustavia, St. Barthelemy
http://www.cieux.com/~philip/stb.html
http://www.frenchcaribbean.com/

ST. KITTS & NEVIS

Tourist Office
Main Street
Charlestown, Nevis
809-469-5521

St. Kitts & Nevis Tourist Office
414 E. 75th St.
New York, NY 10021
800-582-6208

ST. LUCIA

Tourist Board
Pointe Seraphine, Box 221
Castries, St. Lucia
809-452-4094
http://www.interknowledge.com/st-lucia/
http://www.candw.lc/stlucia/tboard.htm

St. Lucia Tourist Board
820 Second Ave.
New York, NY 10017
212-867-2950; 800-456-3984

ST. MAARTEN

St. Maarten Tourist Office
Cyrus W. Wathey Square
Phillipsburg, St. Maarten
http://www.frenchcaribbean.com/

St. Maarten Tourist Office
275 Seventh Ave., 19th Floor
New York, NY 10001-6788
800-STMAARTEN

ST. VINCENT & THE GRENADINES

Tourist Office
Egmont St.
Kingston, St. Vincent
809-457-1502

**St. Vincent &
The Grenadines Tourist Office**
801 Second Ave., 21st Floor
New York, NY 10017
212-687-4981; 800-729-1726

SCANDINAVIA

Scandinavian Tourist Board
655 Third Ave.
New York, NY 10017
212-949-2333; 800-346-3436

SCOTLAND

(see also United Kingdom)

Scottish Tourist Board
23 Ravelston Terrace
Edinburgh, Scotland
http://www.efr.hw.ac.uk/EDC/
   Edinburgh.html
http://www.linnet.co.uk/linnet/tour/
   links.htm

**Greater Glasgow Tourist Board
& Convention Bureau**
35/39 St. Vincent Place
Glasgow G1 2ER, Scotland
http://www.glasgow.gov.uk

SENEGAL

Senegal-Tourist Office
888 Seventh Ave.
New York, NY
800-HI-DAKAR
http://www.refer.sn

SERBIA AND MONTENEGRO

http://www.yugoslavia.com/Culture/
   HTML/yu.html

SEYCHELLES

Ministry of Tourism & Transport
Independence House, Box 47
Seychelles, Indian Ocean

Seychelles Tourism
820 Second Ave. #900F
New York, NY 10017
212-687-9766

SIERRA LEONE

National Tourist Board of Sierra Leone
P.O. Box 1435
International Conference Centre
Aberdeen Hill
Freetown, Sierra Leone

SINGAPORE

Singapore Tourist Promotion Board
Raffles City Tower #38-00
250 N. Bridge Rd.
Singapore 0617
http://www.singapore.com
http://www.sino.net/asean/spore.html

**Singapore Tourist
Promotion Board**
590 Fifth Ave.
12th Floor
New York, NY 10036
212-302-4861

SLOVAKIA

Slovak Tourist Club
Junácká 6
83280 Bratislaval
Slovakia
http://www.eunet.sk/slovakia/travel.html

SLOVENIA

Centre for Tourism Promotion
Dunajska 156
61000 Ljubljana, Slovenia
http://www.ijs.si/slo/

Slovenia Tourism
122 E. 42 St. #3006
New York, NY 10168

SOUTH AFRICA

Cape Tourism Authority (CAPTOUR)
Tourist Info Centre, Adderly St.
Cape Town 8000
South Africa
http://osprey.unisa.ac.za/south-africa/
http://www.travel.co.za/travel.html

**South African
Tourism Board SATOUR**
500 Fifth Ave.
Suite 2040
New York, NY 10110
212-730-2929; 800-822-5368

SPAIN

Tourist Office of Spain
666 Fifth Ave., 35th Floor
New York, NY 10103
212-265-8822
http://www.okspain.org/

SRI LANKA

Tourist Office
212/1 Bauddhaloka Mawatha
Colombo 7, Sri Lanka

Ceylon Tourist Board
78 Steuart Place,
Colombo 3, Sri Lanka

Tourist Information Section
Embassy of Sri Lanka
2148 Wyoming Ave. N.W.
Washington, DC 20020
202-483-4025

SUDAN

Travel & Tourist Agency
P.O. Box 769
Khartoum, Sudan

SURINAME

Tourist Board
Grote Combeweg 99
P.O. Box 656
Paramaribo, Suriname
http://www.surinam.net/surinam.html

SWAZILAND

Tourist Office
P.O. Box 451
Mbabane, Swaziland
http://www.travel.co.za/travel.html

SWEDEN

Swedish Tourist Board
Sverigehuset-Kungstradgarden
Box 7473
S-103 92 Stockholm, Sweden
http://www.luth.se/luth/present/sweden/

Swedish Tourist Board
655 Third Ave. #1810
New York, NY 10017
212-949-2333; 800-346-3436

SWITZERLAND

Swiss National Tourist Office
Bellariastrasse 38, P.O. Box 695
Zurich 8027, Switzerland
http://www.SwitzerlandTourism.ch
http://www.swissinfo.ch/swissinfo/
    general.html

Swiss National Tourist Office
608 Fifth Ave.
New York, NY 10020
212-757-5944

SYRIA

Ministry of Tourism
rue Victoria
Damascus, Syria
http://www.al-shahr.com/visitsyria/
    anglais/indexa.html

TAHITI

Tahiti Tourism
300 N. Continental Blvd. #180
El Segundo, CA 90245
310-414-8484
http://www.tahiti-explorer.com

TAIWAN ROC

**Tourism Bureau of the Republic
of China–Taiwan**
9th Fl., 290 Chungshiao E. Rd.
Chung-Hsiao East Rd.
Section 4, Taipei
http://peacock.tnjc.edu.tw/ADD/TOUR/
    main.html
http://www.cybertaiwan.com/

Taiwan Visitors Association
World Trade Center #7953
New York, NY 10048
212-466-0691

TANZANIA

Tourist Corp.
IPS Building, P.O. Box 2485
Dar es Salaam, Tanzania

Tanzania Tourist Office
205 E. 42 St., Room 1300
New York, NY 10017
212-972-9160

THAILAND

Tourism Authority of Thailand
4 Ratchadamnoen Nok Avenue
Bangkok 10100
Thailand
http://www.mahidol.ac.th/Thailand/
    Thailand-main.html

Tourism Authority of Thailand
5 World Trade Center #3443
New York, NY 10048
212-432-0433

TOGO

Office National Togolais du Tourisme
B.P. 1289
Lome, Togo, West Africa

TRINIDAD & TOBAGO

Tourist Development Authority
The Cruise Complex
1-D Wrightson Rd.
Port of Spain, Trinidad
809-623-1932
http://www.tidco.co.tt
http:www.VisitTNT.com

TUNISIA

Tourist Office
1 Av Mohamed V
Tunis, Tunisia
http://www.tourismtunisia.com/

TURKEY

Ministry of Tourism
Ismet Inönü Bul. 5
Bahçelievler, Ankara, Turkey
http://www.turkey.org/turkey

**Turkey-Tourism &
Information Office**
821 United Nations Plaza
New York, NY 10017
212-687-2194

TURKS & CAICOS ISLANDS

Tourist Board
Front St.
Cockburn Town, Grand Turk
809-946-2321
http://www.fortmyers.com/turks/
t-chome.html

UGANDA

Uganda Tourist Board
P.O. Box 7211, Parliament Avenue
Kampala, Uganda

UKRAINE

http://www.gu.kiev.ua

UNITED KINGDOM

British Tourist Authority
551 Fifth Ave., 7th Floor
New York, NY 10176-0799
212-986-2200; 800-462-2748
http://www.visitbritain.com/

U.S. VIRGIN ISLANDS

Division of Tourism St. Croix
P.O. Box 4538
Christiansted, USVI 00822
809-773-0495
http://www.usvi.net

Division of Tourism St. John
P.O. Box 200
Cruz Bay, USVI 00830
809-776-6450

Division of Tourism St. Thomas
P.O. Box 6400
Charlotte Amalie, USVI 00830
809-774-8784

URUGUAY

Tourist Information
541 Lexington Ave.
New York, NY 10012
http://www.turismo.gub.uy/index-e.html

UZBEKISTAN

http://www.cs.bilkent.edu.tr/~pf/travel/
uzbekistan.misc.html

VANUATU

National Tourism Office of Vanuatu
P.O. Box 209, Kumul Highway
Port Vila, Vanuatu

VATICAN CITY

Apostolic Nunciature
Piazza Pio XII 3
Rome, Italy

VENEZUELA

Corp. de Turismo de Venezuela
Av Lecuna parque Central Torre Oeste
 Piso 37
P.O. Box 50.200
Caracas, Venezuela
http://venezuela.mit.edu/tourism/

VIETNAM

Tourist Office
54 Nguyen Du St.
Hanoi, Vietnam
http://www.sino.net/asean/vietnam.html
http://www.GoVietnam.com/vntravel.html

Saigon Tourist Travel Service
800-760-8333

WALES

(see also United Kingdom)

Tourist Board
Brunel House, 2 Fitzalan Rd.
Cardiff CF2 1UY, Wales
http://www.tourism.wales.gov.uk/

WESTERN SAHARA

http://www.charm.net/~wsahara/

WESTERN SAMOA

Tourism Council of the South Pacific
P.O. Box 13119
Suva Fiji
http://public-www.pi.se/~orbit/samoa/
 welcome.html

YUGOSLAVIA

Tourist Association of Yugoslavia
Mose Pijade 8/IV, 11000
Boegrad, Yugoslavia
http://www.yugoslavia.com/

ZAIRE

Department du Tourisme
15 Ave des Clinques
B.P. 12348
Kinshasa-Gombe, Zaire

ZIMBABWE

Tourist Dev. Corp.
P.O. Box 8052
Tourism House, Causeway
Harare, Zimbabwe
http://africantravel.com/stbroz.html

Zimbabwe Tourist Office
1270 Ave. of the Americas #412
New York, NY 10020
212-332-1090

United States

ALABAMA

Bureau of Tourism
Box 4309
401 Adams Ave.
Montgomery, AL 36103-4309
334-242-4169; 800-ALABAMA
http://alaweb.asc.edu/ala-tours/tours.html
http://www.touralabama.org

ALASKA

Division of Tourism
Box 110801
Juneau, AK 99811-0801
907-465-2010

Anchorage Convention & Visitors Bureau
1600 A St. #200
Anchorage, AK 99501-5162
907-276-4118

Juneau Convention & Visitors Bureau
369 S. Franklin St. #201
Juneau, AK 99801
907-586-1737

ARIZONA

Office of Tourism
1100 W. Washington St.
Phoenix, AZ 85007
602-542-TOUR; 800-842-8257
http://www.arizonaguide.com
http://www.state.az.us

ARKANSAS

Department of Parks & Tourism
One Capital Mall
Little Rock, AR 72201
501-682-7777; 800-828-8974,
800-NATURAL
http://www.state.ar.us
http://www.travel.org/arkansas.html

CALIFORNIA

Office of Tourism
801 K St., Suite 1600
Sacramento, CA 95814
916-322-2881; 800-TO-CALIF
http://gocalif.ca.gov/

Anaheim VCB
714-999-8999

Northern California
http://www.northcoast.com/unlimited/
    tourist_information/info/info.html

Lake Tahoe Tourist Information & Lodging
800-824-0328

Los Angeles Visitors Bureau
685 S. Figueroa St.
Los Angeles, CA
213-689-8822; Hotline 213-777-4636
http://www.ci.la.ca.us/index.html
http://www.virtually.com/los_angeles/
    LAsite.html

San Diego Convention & Visitors Bureau
401 B St. #1400
San Diego, CA 92101
619-232-3101
http://www.sandiego.org/

San Francisco Convention & Visitors Bureau
201 Third St. #900
San Francisco, CA 94103-3185
415-391-2000

COLORADO

Colorado Travel & Tourism Board
1625 Broadway, Suite 1700
Denver, CO 80202
800-265-6723
http://www.state.co.us/visit_dir/
    visitormenu.html

Boulder CVB
303-442-2911

Colorado Springs Convention & Visitors Bureau
104 S. Cascade #104
Colorado Springs, CO 80903
800-888-4748
http://www.coloradosprings-travel.com/
 cscvb/

Denver Metro CVB
303-571-9400
http://infodenver.denver.co.us/

CONNECTICUT

Dept. of Economic Development
Division of Tourism
865 Brook St.
Rocky Hill, CT 06067-3405
800-CT-BOUND
http://www.connecticut.com/tourism/

DELAWARE

Delaware Development Office
Tourism Office
Box 1401
99 Kings Highway
Dover, DE 19903
302-739-4271; 800-441-8846
http://www.state.de.us/tourism/intro.htm

DISTRICT OF COLUMBIA

D.C. Committee to Promote Washington
1212 New York Ave. N.W. #600
Washington, DC 20005
202-789-7000; 800-422-8644
http://dcpages.ari.net/dctour.html

FLORIDA

Department of Commerce, Tourism Florida
126 W. VanBuren
Tallahassee, FL 32399-2000
http://fcn.state.fl.us/fcn/centers/tourism/
 tourism.htm
http://infoguide.com/

Daytona Convention & Visitors Bureau
800-854-1234

Everglades National Park
http://florida-keys.fl.us/everglad.htm
http://www.gorp.com/gorp/resource/
 US_National_Park/fl_everg.HTM

Florida Keys & Key West
800-352-5397

Fort Lauderdale CVB
954-765-4466; 1-800-22-SUNNY
http://www.sunny.org

Miami Convention & Visitors Bureau
305-539-3000
http://www.miamiandbeaches.com

Orlando/Orange County Convention & Visitors Bureau
407-363-5800

Kissimmee St. Cloud Convention & Visitors Bureau
407-847-5000; 800-327-9159

Greater Miami Convention & Visitors Bureau
305-539-3063; 800-933-8448
http://www.miamicity.com/index.html

Palm Beach Convention & Visitors Bureau
800-554-PALM
http://www.palmbeachfl.com

Space Coast Office of Tourism
813-464-7200; 800-345-6710

GEORGIA

Department of Industry, Trade & Tourism
Box 1776
285 Peachtree Center Ave., Suite 1000
Atlanta, GA 30303
404-656-3590; 800-847-4842
http://www.state.ga.us

Savannah
http://savga.com/attract/tourist.htm

HAWAII

Visitors Bureau
2270 Kalakaua Ave., Suite 801
Honolulu, HI 96815
808-923-1811; 800-257-2999
http://www.visit.hawaii.org

Hawaii Visitors Bureau Big Island Chapter
250 Keawe St.
Hilo, HI 96720
808-961-5797

Kauai Visitors Bureau
2016 Umi St. #207
Lihue, Kauai, HI 96766
808-245-3971; 800-AH-KAUAI

Maui Visitors Bureau
Box 1738
Kahului, Maui 96732
800-525-MAUI

Destination Lanai
808-565-7600

Destination Hilo
808-935-5294

IDAHO

Travel Council
700 W. State St., Statehouse Mall
Boise, ID 83720-2700
208-334-2470; 800-VISIT-ID
http://www.state.id.us/tourism.html

ILLINOIS

Bureau of Tourism
629 E. Washington St.
Springfield, IL 62701
312-814-4732; 800-223-0121
http://www.state.il.us/tourism/
http://www.enjoyillinois.com/

Chicago Office of Tourism
800-487-2446, 800-2-CONNECT
http://www.ci.chi.il.us/Tourism/

INDIANA

Department of Commerce
Tourism Development Division
1 North Capitol, Suite 700
Indianapolis, IN 46204-2288
800-289-ONIN
http://www.state.in.us/tourism/index.html

IOWA

Department of Economic Development
Division of Tourism
200 E. Grand Ave.
Des Moines, IA 50309
515-242-4705; 800-345-IOWA
http://www.state.ia.us/tourism

KANSAS

Department of Commerce Development
700 S.W. Harrison St. #1300
Topeka, KA 66603-3712
800-2KANSAS
http://www.state.ks.us

KENTUCKY

Department of Travel Development
2200 Capital Plaza Tower, 22nd Floor
500 Mero St.
Frankfort, KY 40601-1974
502-564-4930; 800-225-TRIP
http://www.state.ky.us/tour/tour.htm

Louisville & Jefferson County Convention & Visitors Bureau
800-792-5595
http://www.louisville-visitors.com

LOUISIANA

Office of Tourism
Box 94291
Baton Rouge, LA 70804-9291
504-342-8119;
800-723-6114,
800-33GUMBO
http://www.state.la.us
http://www.louisianatravel.com

New Orleans Metropolitan CVB
504-566-5009; 800-748-8695
http://www.nawlins.com

MAINE

Office of Tourism
139 State House Station 59
Augusta, ME 04333
207-623-0363;
800-449-9492
http://www.visitmaine.com/

MARYLAND

Office of Tourism Development
217 E. Redwood St.,
9th Floor
Baltimore, MD 21202
800-MD-IS-FUN
http://sailor.lib.md.us:80

MASSACHUSETTS

Office of Travel & Tourism
100 Cambridge St.
13th Floor
Boston, MA 02202
617-727-3201; 800-447-MASS
http://www.mass-vacation.com/

MICHIGAN

Department of Commerce
Travel Bureau
Box 30226
333 S. Capitol Ave.
Town Center Bldg., Suite F
Lansing, MI 48909
800-543-2-YES

MINNESOTA

Office of Tourism
121 E. 7th Place, 100 Metro Square
St. Paul, MN 55101-2112
612-296-5029; 800-657-3700 US
http://www.state.mn.us/explore/index.html

MISSISSIPPI

Department of Economic & Community Development
Division of Tourism
520 George St.
P.O. Box 849
Jackson, MS 39205
601-359-3297; 800-927-6378
http://www.mississippi.org
http://www.decd.state.ms.us/TOURISM.
   HTM

MISSOURI

Division of Tourism
Box 1055
Truman State Office Bldg.
Jefferson City, MO 65102
800-877-1234
http://www.ecodev.state.mo.us/tourism/

Branson Convention & Visitors Bureau
800-214-3661

MONTANA

**Department of Commerce, Travel
Promotion Division**
1424 Ninth Ave.
Helena, MT 59620
406-444-2654; 800-847-4868
http://travel.mt.gov

NEBRASKA

**Department of Economic
Development**
Travel & Tourism Division
Box 98913
301 Centennial Mall South #88937
Lincoln, NE 68509
800-228-4307
http://www.ded.state.ne.us/tourism.html

NEVADA

State Tourism Commission
State Capitol Complex
Carson City, NV 89710
800-237-0774
http://www.gorp.com/gorp/location/nv/
    nv.htm

Las Vegas Convention & Visitors Bureau
3150 Paradise Rd.
Las Vegas, NV 89109-9096
702-892-0711
http://www.lasvegas24hours.com

NEW HAMPSHIRE

Office of Vacation Travel
Box 856
Concord, NH 03302-0856
603-271-2343; 800-386-4664
http://www.visitnh.gov

**Mt. Washington Valley Chamber
of Commerce & Visitors Bureau**
800-367-3364
http://www.4seasonresort.com

NEW JERSEY

Division of Travel & Tourism
CN 826
Trenton, NJ 08625-0826
609-292-2470; 800-JERSEY-7

**Atlantic City Convention & Visitors
Bureau**
609-348-7100

NEW MEXICO

**Dept. of Economic Development
& Tourism**
491 Old Santa Fe Trail
Santa Fe, NM 87503
505-827-7400; 800-545-2040
http://www.newmexico.org

Albuquerque CVB
800-284-2282

Sante Fe CVB
800-777-CITY
http://www.nets.com/santafe

**Taos Chamber of Commerce
& Visitors Center**
800-732-TAOS

NEW YORK

State Department of Economic Development
New York State Travel and Information
   Center
One Commerce Plaza
Albany, NY 12245
518-474-4116; 800-CALL-NYS
http://www.state.ny.us/tour.html

New York Convention & Visitors Bureau
Two Columbus Circle
New York, NY 10019
212-484-1200; 800-NYC-VISIT
http://iloveny.state.ny.us/iloveny/nyc.html
http://www.nyo.com/nyoinfo/
http://www.nycvisit.com

NORTH CAROLINA

Travel & Tourism
N.C. Department of Commerce
301 N. Wilmington St.
Raleigh, NC 27601-2825
919-733-4171; 800-VISIT NC
http://www.commerce.state.nc.us/
   commerce/press/travelgu.html

NORTH DAKOTA

Tourism Promotion
Liberty Memorial Building
State Capitol Grounds
604 East Blvd.
Bismark, ND 58505
800-437-2077
http://www.state.nd.us

OHIO

Division of Travel & Tourism
Box 1001
Columbus, OH 43266-0101
614-466-8844; 800-BUCKEYE
http://www.ohiotourism.com/

Akron/Summit Convention & Visitors Bureau
800-245-4254

Cincinnati Convention & Visitors Bureau
513-621-2142; 800-344-3445

Cleveland Convention & Visitors Bureau
216-621-4110; 800-321-1001

Columbus Convention & Visitors Bureau
614-221-6623; 800-354-2657

Dayton/Montgomery County Convention Bureau
800-221-8235

Erie County Visitors & Convention Bureau
419-625-2984

Toledo Convention & Visitors Bureau
419-321-6404

Youngstown/Mahoning County Convention & Visitors Bureau
800-447-8201

OKLAHOMA

Tourism & Recreation Department
500 Will Rogers Building
Oklahoma City, OK 73105-4492
405-521-3981; 800-652-OKLA
http://www.oklaosf.state.ok.us/osfdocs/
   tourhp.html

OREGON

Oregon Tourism Commission
775 Summer St. N.E.
Salem, OR 97310
503-986-0000; 800-547-7842
http://www.traveloregon.com/

PENNSYLVANIA

Travel Council
902 N. Second St.
Harrisburg, PA 17102
717-232-8880; 800-VISIT-PA
http://www.state.pa.us/visit/index2.html

Philadelphia Convention & Visitors Bureau
800-CALL-PHL, 800-321-9563
http://www.libertynet.org/phila-visitor/

Pittsburgh Convention & Visitors Bureau
800-366-0093

RHODE ISLAND

Economic Development Corp.
7 Jackson Way
Providence, RI 02903
401-277-2601; 800-556-2484
http://www.state.ri.us/tour.htm

SOUTH CAROLINA

Department of Parks, Recreation & Tourism
1205 Pendleton St.
Columbia, SC 29201-0071
803-734-0122; 800-868-2492
http://www.sccsi.com/sc/

SOUTH DAKOTA

Economic Development & Tourism
711 E. Wells Ave.
Pierre, SD 57501-3335
605-773-3301; 800-732-5682
http://www.state.sd.us/state/executive/to
  urism/tourism.html

TENNESSEE

Tourist Development
Box 23170
320 Sixth Ave. N., Suite 500
Nashville, TN 37202
615-741-2158
http://www.state.tn.us

TEXAS

Department of Economic Development
Travel & Information Division
Box 12728
Austin, TX 78711-2728
800-452-9292

Texas Department of Transportation
Division of Travel & Information
P.O. Box 5064
Austin, TX 78763
800-452-9292

Dallas Convention & Visitors Bureau
214-746-6677; 800-752-9222

Houston Convention & Visitors Bureau
800-231-7799

San Antonio Convention & Visitors Bureau
210-270-8700; 800-447-3372

UTAH

Travel Council
300 N. State St.
Salt Lake City, UT 84114
801-538-1030; 800-200-1160
http://www.utah.com/

VERMONT

Department of Travel & Tourism
134 State St.
Montpelier, VT 05602
802-828-3236; 800-837-6668
http://www.cit.state.vt.us
http://www.travel-vermont.com/

VIRGINIA

Division of Tourism
1021 E. Cary St., 14th Floor #500
Richmond, VA 23219
804-786-4484; 800-VISIT-VA
http://www.state.va.us/home/visitor.html
http://www.virginia.org

WASHINGTON

Department of Trade & Economic Development
Tourism Development Division
Box 42500
Olympia, WA 98504-2500
800-544-1800
http://www.travel-in-wa.com/

Seattle-King County Convention & Visitors Bureau
206-461-5840
http://www.cyberspace.com/bobk/re.html

Olympic Peninsula
http://www.olympus.net/travel/travel.html

WEST VIRGINIA

Division of Tourism & Parks
Capital Complex, Building 17
Charleston, WV 25305-0312
800-CALL-WVA
http://www.vvweb.com/

WISCONSIN

Department of Tourism
201 W. Washington Ave.
Madison, WI 53702
608-266-2161; 800-432-TRIP
http://tourism.state.wi.us/

Milwaukee Convention & Visitors Bureau
800-231-0903

WYOMING

Tourism and Travel Commission
Interstate 25 at College Drive
Cheyenne, WY 82002
307-777-7777
http://www.state.wy.us:80/state/tourism/
   tourism.html

Cheyenne Area Convention & Visitors Bureau
800-426-5009

Chapter

26 Airports

As far as I am concerned, an airport is a place you should pass through—rapidly—on your way to and from a flight to somewhere else. Alas, it most often does not work out that way. On some trips from my remote home that involve one or two changes of plane, I end up spending more time in the airport than I do in the air.

Here are some savvy tips to help you reduce the time you spend at the airport as well as to protect you from bad things that can happen there, including paying to send your luggage on a fabulous vacation trip to an airport other than the one where you are going.

✓ Arrive at the airport at the right time.

✓ Speed your way across the terminal.

✓ Don't check your bags if possible.

✓ The bad news about lost luggage.

✓ Carry your own.

✓ Tag that bag.

✓ Consider the joys and pains of checking your luggage at the curb.

✓ Stand up for your rights at the island of lost or damaged baggage.

✓ Find out if an airline club is for you.

✓ Get in and out of airport parking lots smartly.

✓ Know the rules at airport security.

✓ What you need to know about X-ray machines and metal detectors.

✓ Save time going through customs.

Arrive at the Airport at the Right Time

When should you arrive at the airport for your flight? My favorite travel experiences include trips where I have dashed across the terminal, through the metal detectors, and arrived breathless at the gate to hear the agent declaring the final boarding call for my flight. "Thanks for waiting for me," I tell the flight attendants as I move to my seat.

Of course, that same dramatic arrival could have just as easily ended up with the following greeting: "I'm sorry, Mr. Sandler, but because you are late we have given your seat to a standby customer. I'll see if we can book you on another flight sometime soon."

Read the fine print on your airline ticket carefully or check with the airline to find out its rules and recommendations on arrival times; there is a difference between the two. The recommended time is supposed to take into account delays in checking in, going through security, and moving from the entrance to the gate. For international flights, you may have to pass through customs or immigration controls before departure. The required time represents the point at which the gate agent is authorized to give away your seat or your reservation to someone ready and waiting.

You might want to call the airline before you head to the airport to see if the flight you are taking is empty or full. An agent in charge of loading a fully booked (or overbooked) flight is going to be looking for any excuse to open a seat for someone standing at the counter; if there are plenty of available seats, there is no one to bump you.

Most domestic airlines recommend arrival at the airport an hour before flight time and require your presence at the gate 10 or 15 minutes before departure; for international flights departing from the United States, the recommended arrival time is generally two hours before departure, with appearance at the gate by 30 minutes before departure.

If you're flying from a European, Asian, or Middle Eastern airport, many airlines recommend—or require—arrival as much as three hours before departure because of extra security screening procedures.

Speed Your Way Across the Terminal

- *Travel light.* Use a suitcase that will fit into an overhead rack or under the seat in front of you. This will speed up your check-in process and shave 20 minutes or more off your arrival. You're also pretty likely to arrive at your destination with your bags.

- *Get your boarding passes before you go to the airport.* Ask your travel agent or the airline to issue you a boarding pass with seat assignment at the time you pick up your tickets. This may not be possible if you make your reservation close to the departure date.

  With your boarding pass in your ticket envelope, you can go directly to the departure gate without having to wait at the check-in counter.

  If you were unable to obtain boarding passes before the beginning of your flight, ask the agent who checks you in to provide them for any remaining flights on the remainder of your trip.

- *Pack your bags with care.* Know the contents of your bags and keep any objects likely to attract the attention of the security screeners in an easily opened location. I'm not in any way recommending you travel with a gun, but if your hair dryer is shaped like one and regularly sets off alarms at the security counter, you might want to keep it at the top of a carry-on bag so that you don't have to unpack an entire suitcase to assuage the guard's curiosity.

  Be prepared to turn on any personal computers, video cameras, or other electronics in your baggage. Security guards may want to see that these devices are real.

Don't Check Your Bags if Possible

Dante did not know about baggage claims at crowded airports; if he did, they might have been one of the regions of hell.

The best way to avoid the hassles of baggage claim, of course, is not to check any bags. Travel as light as you can and use the overhead racks or the space under the seat in front of you to hold your luggage.

If you must check your bags, here are some hints to ease the pain:

- Make sure your bags are well marked with your name and address in several places. After you've done that, stick a few of your business cards or a piece of paper with your name and address inside the outside pockets of the bag.

- Mark your bags in some way to make them stand out from all the others that look so similar. Tie a ribbon to the handle, place a tape mark on the top, or attach some unusual stickers to the top and side.

- If your bags are not there when you arrive, spend the time doing other things: Take care of your rental-car paperwork, make some phone calls, or call your next appointment.

- Odd-shaped luggage, including strollers, skis, golf bags, and other items may not arrive on the luggage carousel and may instead be unloaded elsewhere in the baggage room.

- Before you head out on a trip, spend a few moments writing down a detailed description of your bags and place the information in your wallet or with your tickets. You'll need the information if you must file a report with the lost-luggage department.

The Bad News About Lost Luggage

Your suitcase may contain $20,000 in jewelry (it shouldn't!) but the law says that the most an airline is obligated to pay for lost baggage on a domestic flight is $1,250. And that amount of money is based on the depreciated value of your possessions and not on their replacement value.

On international flights, bags are valued at no more than $9.07 per pound. (If you're wondering where that strange number comes from, think metric: It's $20 per kilogram.) If the bag was not weighed at check-in, the airline will assign a weight of 70 pounds, making the luggage worth up to $635 per bag.

(If your trip includes both a domestic and an international leg, the cheaper international liability applies. That figures, huh?)

If you have flown on more than one airline on the segment of your trip, tracking your misplaced bag is the responsibility of the last airline on your trip.

You are entitled to collect for your loss in cash, but some airlines may want to pay you off in vouchers for future flights. If you receive such an offer, it should be for an amount larger than your claim, and you should assure yourself that there are no unreasonable restrictions on your use of the vouchers.

Carry Your Own

Some airlines, at some times, are very strict about limiting the number and size of carry-on bags. Most airlines will allow only two pieces of carry-on luggage per passenger, and you may be required to place them under your seat rather than in overhead racks.

The rules can vary based on the type of planes. Some have larger overhead racks than others, while some jumbo jets with as many as nine or ten seats in a row may simply not have enough space. And you can expect gate agents to be stricter about the rule when the plane is full.

Here are some savvy ways to maximize your carry-on capacity and be more comfortable while on board:

- If possible, choose flights that are less crowded. Fly off-peak hours and midweek, for example.
- Pick flights on larger planes with more storage space.
- Choose the appropriate seat. If you can, snare an aisle or window seat next to an empty middle seat and stuff your belongings under one or both seats. Avoid the bulkhead row and some exit rows, which do not have underseat storage in front of them.
- Don't use up your limited allowance on small bags. If you travel with a laptop, get a bag large enough to take the computer as well as your other business papers.
- Board early to take possession of whatever space is available.

You can also apply a bit of guile. Carry your coat over your bags if you're one over the limit. In a real pinch, see if you can talk another passenger into lugging your third bag onto the plane.

Tag That Bag

Cover your luggage with address tags; they are your best defense against the vagaries of airline baggage handlers. But list your office address and not your home address. There is no reason to advertise the fact that your home is empty.

Consider the Joys and Pains of Checking Your Luggage at the Curb

One way to shave some time off your check-in at the airport is to give your bags to the curbside check-in counter. If you have your boarding pass, you should be able to proceed directly to the departure gate.

However, there are some important safeguards you should follow before you walk away from your bags:

1. First and foremost, make certain that the person taking your bag is actually a porter for the airline you are flying. Believe it or not, some resourceful thieves have set up stations at airports and made off with a cartload of bags.

2. Check to make sure your flight has not been canceled and is more-or-less on schedule. If there is a problem with your flight, hold on to your bags and join the throngs at the check-in counter. Or, follow one of my other hints and head for the nearest telephone; you may be able to make changes to your flight much more quickly than waiting in line.

3. Check carefully that your bags are marked with proper tags for your destination. (The code to my home on Nantucket Island is ACK; I have seen clerks prepare to send my bags to Akron, Ohio, more times than I can recall.) Make certain that copies of the tags are attached to your boarding passes. Pay special attention to the tags if your trip includes a change of planes. If there is any part of the

tag you don't understand, ask the porter to explain it to you before the bags disappear down the chute to the bowels of the airport.

Stand Up for Your Rights at the Island of Lost or Damaged Baggage

If you find yourself the last person waiting at the carousel, it may be that your bags have gone on a vacation trip by themselves. You should immediately head for the airline's baggage office, which is usually near-by the baggage room.

Similarly, if you find your bags damaged, your best bet is to file a report before you leave the airport.

If you wait until you arrive home or at the hotel and discover something is missing from your bags, most airlines require you to notify them within 24 hours of your arrival.

Fill out the forms immediately, taking care to be as specific as you can about the description of the bags as well as their contents. Remember that the airline will use your form as the initial basis for searching for missing items as well as paying a claim if they cannot be recovered.

Don't surrender your ticket receipt and baggage claim tag without a photocopy or unless the form includes a notation that they have been taken.

If you are in the middle of a trip, make sure the airline has information on how to reach you while you are on the road as well as when you return home.

If you discover a missing item after you return home, or if you want to modify your report on the contents of your luggage, call the airline as soon as possible. Make a note of the name and phone number of whomever you talk with.

The good news is that most misplaced baggage is eventually found, and airlines do a good job of reuniting passengers with their bags. You can increase the odds in your favor by paying close attention when your bags are checked and by clearly marking your bags with your name and address. And help yourself out by packing prescription drugs and other important personal items in your carry-on bag.

Find Out if an Airline Club Is for You

Modern road warriors who find they know the concourses of major airports better than their own backyards may want to consider joining an airline club.

The clubs, which typically cost about $100 to $300 per year plus a one-time sign-up fee, return some of the civility that is missing from air travel and especially airports. You'll find quiet rooms with comfortable chairs, desks with telephones and laptop chargers, television and game rooms, and complimentary or low-price snacks and beverages.

Just as important, most airline clubs offer special-service desks for making and changing reservations, obtaining boarding passes, and other airline functions.

Other features at many clubs: conference rooms available for free or minimal charge for meetings, baggage-storage rooms for travelers who may want to travel into the city or make short day trips from the airport, and exercise and shower rooms.

Should you join a club? The best way to answer is to look closely at your travel schedule. Take the annual fee—let's use $300—and divide it by the number of visits you are likely to make. If you figure you'll pass through a club 30 times in a year, the cost of membership works out to $10 per visit, which is very reasonable for the service provided. If you're likely to use the club only half a dozen times in a year, the cost rises to $50, which may be a bit high for a few free drinks and a comfortable chair.

Other things to consider:

- How many clubs does the airline operate, and in which airports?

- Where in the airport are the clubs? If you are a member of American's club but are flying on Delta, how convenient will it be to traipse across the terminal to American's club? (In some airports, such as Boston's Logan and JFK in New York, airlines are located in separate buildings.)

- Do you have the right to visit another airline's club?

- Are you permitted to bring a guest? How many per visit? If you are traveling with your family, can your children accompany you?

Get In and Out of Airport Parking Lots Smartly

Call the airport's central phone number (or its parking-lot information number) to find out how crowded the lots and garages are. If you are advised that space is tight, plan on arriving early or find another place to leave your car.

Here are some more savvy tips on airport lots:

- Many airports have two or more types of parking, including "long-term" lots that are at some distance from the terminals and more expensive "daily" lots that may be just across the road from the check-in counters. Some airports also have valet-parking services; if you are flying first class or business class, check with your airline to see if they have any special arrangements for their full-fare customers.

- If you're looking forward to making a hasty exit from the airport when you return from your trip, park close to the exit instead of close to the terminal. You may have to lug your bags a bit further, but you may also be able to avoid an annoying traffic jam on the upper level of a garage.

- Hide your parking receipt in your car so that you won't lose it. (Yes, I know someone out there is going to say that leaving the receipt in the car is an aid to a thief. But if you're hiding the receipt out of sight, your car is no more likely to be broken into than any other. And a thief could very easily obtain a parking ticket from the entry machine or work in cahoots with the garage.)

- Make a note of your parking space number on your airline ticket envelope, a document you're likely to keep close at hand on your entire trip.

Know the Rules at Airport Security

Airport-security checkpoints are an unpleasant but necessary element of modern travel. Remind yourself that these folk are there to protect you and do what you can to help the process work smoothly.

Know what is permitted in luggage and know what you have packed. The X-ray operator at the checkpoint is trained to stop any bag carrying devices shaped like guns or knives, or electronics or other containers that can conceal explosives. Beyond that, understand that some items are not considered safe for carriage.

Here's a partial list of items you cannot carry on board a plane:

- *Guns or other weapons*. If you have a legitimate reason for carrying such devices, check with the airline or airport well ahead of your arrival to find out how you can ship them.

    A true story: I was flying back from Geneva, Switzerland, at a time of heightened security, and the metal detector found a small pocket knife (a Swiss Army Knife, as a matter of fact) that I carry in my computer bag to help with emergency repairs. I've carried one for years and rarely give a thought to it when I travel. When it was found, though, I had to undergo a personal search and unpack all of my bags for detailed screening. The knife was put into a sealed envelope and given to the captain of the plane for safe carriage to America. About five minutes into the flight, a flight attendant came to my seat with the knife in an envelope. "With the captain's compliments," she said.

- *Volatile, flammable, or explosive items*. These include many types of aerosol sprays, paints, lighter fluid, adhesives, and other chemicals. You are also barred from carrying fireworks.

- *Loose matches and liquid-fuel lighters*.

- *Compressed gases*, including divers' tanks.

You should also avoid carrying wrapped or sealed packages; the security guards may ask you to unwrap them for examination. Carry wrapping paper separately for gifts.

What You Need to Know About X-Ray Machines and Metal Detectors

The high-tech hardware at the entrances to airport concourses are there for a good reason—to detect guns, knives, and bombs. The machines and the equipment accomplish their roles with less than perfect success, but most travelers agree that they are better than nothing.

Although the makers and operators of the detectors claim they will not harm unprocessed photographic film and magnetically recorded information on floppy disks and inside portable computers and video cameras, ask yourself the following question: Am I carrying irreplaceable information?

- *Protect your film.* According to the experts, the machines will not do damage to standard film (ASA speeds below 400) or to magnetic media. However, this claim is based on the equipment being in like-new condition and being properly operated. And damage from X-rays may be cumulative: If your film is scoped three or four times as you fly around from place to place, the chances of damage increase.

    You may want to purchase a lead-lined box or bag to carry your unprocessed film. You'll probably have to open it to show the contents to the inspectors, but at least it won't be accidentally X-rayed.

- *Protect your PC.* I fly a great deal and almost always travel with a laptop computer and often with a video or still camera. I have never suffered a loss I can blame on the detectors, but I nevertheless almost always ask for an eyeball inspection of my devices rather than putting them on the belt. I put up with the slight delay, ignore the pained expressions of some guards, and pass my computer and film around the machines. (Keep a close eye on your property when you do so—you could end up saving your data and losing your device to a thief.)

- *Watch out for accidental exposure.* Don't rest your film or computer on top of the X-ray machine while you prepare it for hand inspection. The device may not be as fully shielded on top.

    Although X-rays may not damage a hard disk in a computer, the magnetic field that surrounds the power supply for the X-ray tube and the motor that moves the conveyor belt are a real problem.

Save Time Going Through Customs

The excitement of flying to a foreign nation, or of returning home from a visit abroad can quickly turn to annoyance when you find yourself at the end of a line of hundreds of tired travelers waiting to go through passport control.

Other than joining the diplomatic corps, there are a few things you can do to speed your way through the process:

- Fly a national carrier to its home country. For example, Air France to France or British Air to the United Kingdom. Citizens of a country generally choose to fly on an airline from home, and as an American you have a good chance of finding fewer foreigners like yourself waiting to go through the passport booths reserved for visitors. Similarly, when you return you'll likely find fewer people waiting to go through the booths for U.S. citizens.

- Fill out your entry cards carefully and fully on the plane and then head directly for the passport lines. Answer questions simply.

- Don't make small talk or try out your jokes on the passport official. They are looking for people who seem nervous or are trying to distract them. Answer the questions you are asked and don't give the officer a reason to pull you out of the crowd.

Chapter 27

Travel by Car

When you think about it, renting a $20,000 car for $40 or $50 per day is a pretty good deal. The trick is to keep it a good deal; in this chapter I show you how to save money on auto rentals and how to avoid being taken for a ride with unnecessary insurance and other charges.

- ✓ Save money at the auto-rental counter.
- ✓ Save time when you rent a car.
- ✓ Watch out for rental gotchas.
- ✓ Find out if your driving record will keep you from renting a car.
- ✓ Know the truth about insurance coverage for rental cars.
- ✓ Learn the inside tips to getting a taxi at the airport.
- ✓ Know how to avoid being cheated in a taxi.

Save Money at the Auto-Rental Counter

Auto-rental prices seem to go up and down in great wavelike cycles every few years; in recent years the trend has been upward in major metropolitan areas and locations where demand is slight and downward in high-competition areas such as Orlando and Las Vegas.

Here are some tips on how to pay less for a set of rental wheels:

- Think beforehand about what size and type of car you need. A family of four with suitcases will probably not be comfortable in a subcompact, while a couple out for a drive to the country has no real need for a seven-passenger van.

- Join a rental-car company's priority program, even if you don't rent cars very often; members regularly receive special discount offers.

- Save special offers you receive in frequent-flyer club and credit-card statements.

- Read the airline in-flight magazine as you fly to your destination. This is a prime place for advertisements from rental companies; if you see a better rate at another company, stop by their counter when you arrive.

- If you have some flexibility in your travel plans, remember that most rental-car companies offer lower prices for weekend rentals; weekend is typically defined as Friday morning through Monday morning. Weekly rental rates are usually priced at about the same level as five daily charges.

- Car-rental companies charge for 24-hour periods, but typically allow a one-hour grace period before you are charged for another day.

- Some travelers always reserve the lowest-priced special-offer car, figuring correctly that these vehicles are in limited supply. Nearly every rental-car company will upgrade you to the next-higher available class of car if the one you have reserved is not at hand. If you find that the agency actually does have the car you request-ed but didn't really want, you can usually pay to upgrade to a bet-ter one at the counter.

Save Time When You Rent a Car

Joining a rental-car company's priority club can shave a fair amount of time off your wait at the airport. All of your important information—name, address, driver's-license number, and credit card—will already be on file, along with your car-rental preferences.

Even better, members of the club can usually go to a special check-in counter at the airport, or can even skip the check-in completely and go directly to the car lot.

Watch Out for Rental Gotchas

How does a $24.99 rate become a $62.37 bill? It's simple: You didn't read the fine print. There are dozens of ways car companies can raise the bottom line on your rental; it's up to the savvy consumer to remove them from the bill one by one. Here are some tips:

- Read the small print carefully to learn about blackout dates when an advertised price may not be available.

- In some airports, renters are assessed a fee if they use an agency with a lot on the airport grounds.

- Be sure you understand the rental agency's policy on fuel. At most companies you have three options:

  1. Pick up the car with a full tank of gas and return it with whatever fuel is left. When you do this, the rental company will happily fill the tank for you, usually at a rate of as much as 50 cents per gallon more than you'd pay at a nearby station.
  2. Pay for a tank of gas ahead of time. You have no responsibility to refill the tank when you return the car under this plan, but you'll receive no credit for any fuel in the tank, either.
  3. Pick up the car with a full tank of gas and stop off to fill the tank at a service station on your way to the airport when you return. This is almost always the most economical way to rent a car.

- Do not move your rental car until you have walked around it once or twice to check for damage, including dents, scratches, and broken glass. If you find any problems, ask for another car or demand that the agent attach a signed report on the condition of the car to the rental agreement.

Find Out if Your Driving Record Will Keep You from Renting a Car

Ask your travel agent or the rental-car company in advance whether your driving record will be checked. Some companies check for accidents—no matter whose fault, moving violations, and other points against your record. This is especially true in certain major metropolitan areas. You may be denied the chance to rent if they feel you are too much of a risk. There's nothing you can do about your past history, but you may be able to find a company that doesn't check.

Know the Truth About Insurance Coverage for Rental Cars

Do not pay for insurance coverage you don't need. And, do whatever you can to avoid having to pay collision damage waivers (CDW) at the rental counter. The daily rate for such coverage is one of the worst deals in insurance.

CDW coverage can add $6 to $15 per day to your rental costs; at $10 per day this is equivalent to an annual policy costing $3,650!

The coverage is not required, and in some states it is not permitted. CDW is not technically insurance, but instead it is a promise that the rental company will pay for damages to the car; if you decline the waiver, you accept responsibility for any damages up to the full value of the car.

Under CDW, however, the company will not pay for bodily injuries or damages to your personal property. And the fine print may also revoke your coverage if the rental company believes you damaged the car when driving it in a negligent manner, on unpaved roads, or out of the state in which you rented the vehicle. Some companies void their CDW coverage if a driver drinks alcohol or if a nonauthorized driver operates the car.

If you are traveling on business, check with your employer to see if your company has a policy to cover you.

If you own a car, call your insurance agent and find out how well you are covered under your present policy for any rentals. Check with your credit-card company to find out about coverage they may provide for rental cars charged to your account; consider upgrading to "gold" or "platinum" levels to increase your auto coverage if necessary.

If you are traveling outside the United States, double-check with your insurance agent and credit-card issuer to be sure of your coverage. And note that your coverage may not apply to luxury or exotic cars you rent.

The renter may also offer personal accident insurance (PAI) to pay some or all medical costs related to an accident. Again, this may be unnecessary duplication. Your personal or employer medical plan should take care of injuries suffered while on the road.

Personal effects coverage (PEC) or personal effects protection (PEP) is intended to protect your luggage and possessions from theft or damage. Your homeowner's or renter's policy may provide coverage for thefts from a rental vehicle; check with your insurance agent.

If your personal automobile coverage and your credit-card coverage do not protect you adequately in a foreign country, ask your insurance agent about a special rider for international driving. Or, if you plan to be abroad for a few weeks, you may want to contact an insurance agency in the foreign country to see if a short-term policy is available for sale. Obviously, compare the costs of the policies to the rental-car company's rates.

You'll find more details about rental-car insurance in the chapter on auto insurance later in this book.

Learn the Inside Tips to Getting a Taxi at the Airport

Few things are more fun than arriving at the airport after a 10-hour red-eye to find several planeloads of other travelers in line ahead of you at the taxi stand. Even more fun: There are no taxis in sight.

Here are some strategies to get out of the airport quickly:

1. Ask the taxi dispatcher if there is a better place to wait for a cab. It may make sense to walk to another less-crowded terminal.
2. See if there is a "share-a-ride" program at the airport. The dispatcher will assist in bringing together groups of passengers heading to destinations nearby to each other.

Even if there is no official program, there is nothing to prevent you from asking people at the front of the line if they are going near your destination. Offer to split the fare—or even offer to pay the entire fare—and you should be able to move forward quickly.

3. Consider booking a car service or limousine before you leave. Rates for car services are usually close to those of taxis, while airport limos are usually surprisingly affordable most times of the day. You can share the cost with others in your party, and you can skip the taxicab line completely.

    If you didn't book a car service before you left, you can try calling for a vehicle when you land at the airport. The dispatcher may have a car already en route to the terminal with a passenger.

    You may see some drivers of cars or limos hoping to find a passenger to pay the freight on their trip back to the city. At many airports, it is against the rules for a car-service driver to pick up a passenger without a prearranged reservation. That doesn't mean you can't accept a reasonable offer.

Know How to Avoid Being Cheated in a Taxi

You're an out-of-towner, and the taxi driver doesn't seem like the sort of guy you'd like to cultivate as a new best buddy. He seems to know where he's going, right?

Here are some tips to keep from being taken for a ride by a taxi driver:

- Know where you are going. Consult a map before jumping into a cab and have an idea of the best route; ask the driver how he will take you to your destination and don't be afraid to check it out on the map.

- Know the approximate mileage to your destination, or the standard flat rate. If you are getting into a cab at the airport, ask the dispatcher there for the price range for your trip.

- Watch out for scams: Make sure the meter is at zero before you get into the cab and read the posted notices in the cab for information about additional charges such as airport, nighttime, or luggage surcharges.

- If the taxi charges a flat rate, determine the price beforehand and check the quoted rate against a list that should be posted inside the cab.

- Be sure you understand—ahead of time—policies on share-a-ride trips. Except in certain circumstances such as rush-hour crunches, most such programs do not require each passenger to pay the full fare indicated on the meter.

- Obtain a signed receipt, with the driver's name clearly indicated (it should be the same as the name on the license displayed in most cabs). The receipt should indicate pick-up point and destination and the total fare. The receipt can be your evidence if you want to file a complaint with the local regulatory board for taxis.

Chapter

28 Hotels

What's the difference between a $125 standard room and a $75 standard room at the same hotel? If you answered $50, you're a savvy consumer.

Most larger hotels sell the same room for a range of different prices—starting with a "rack rate" that is the full list price and going down from there to discounts based on the time of year or day of the week, special rates for members of associations or attendees at conventions, and rooms that are sold at deep discounts to hotel consolidators. In this chapter, I show you some ways to get those lowest rates.

✓ Get the best hotel rates.

✓ Ask for the best room in the house.

✓ Fight if you are bumped from a reservation.

✓ Get a room at a sold-out hotel.

✓ Check out the room before you check in.

✓ Find the cheapest phone in the hotel.

✓ Pick the best stateroom on a cruise.

✓ Safeguard your possessions when you travel.

Get the Best Hotel Rates

Toll-free phone numbers to a national reservations desk for a chain of hotels are convenient, but the best rates and the largest selection of deals and special options are usually available with a direct call to the front desk.

Here's some savvy advice on booking a room:

- Do your research using toll-free numbers. Ask the reservations clerk for the best available rate, being sure to mention any special discounts you may be eligible for, including AAA, AARP, and hotel clubs.

  If you think the rate is acceptable or nearly so, go ahead and hold the room, making certain you understand the cancellation policies; don't commit to a reservation you cannot get out of.

  Now call directly to the hotel and ask for their best rate. Then ask a second question: Are there are any special deals available?

  In general, local outlets of a hotel chain observe any national special rates but they also often adjust their rates to reflect their local bookings. This won't help you if you're looking to rent the last room available over Labor Day weekend, but if they have a whole lot more rooms than people for a slow Tuesday in March, you can hope for—or ask for—a break.

  Take the better of the two deals, being sure to cancel any duplicate reservations.

- Calling the hotel directly is the best way to make special requests, from choosing a particular room or floor to asking for a rollaway bed or other special furnishings. A national reservation service will almost always tell you that they will pass along your special desires but not guarantee them; if you call the hotel directly, ask for the name of whoever makes a promise to you and keep that information with your confirmation number.

Ask for the Best Room in the House

I live on a resort island, and one of my favorite pastimes involves reading the real-estate listings: One shady real-estate agent sometimes bills a piece of property as having "possible ocean views." What does that mean? I figure it means that if you build a two-story house with a roof walk and stood on that platform with a ladder and a telescope you might be able to see the Atlantic. That is, if the fog has lifted and your neighbors haven't built their own houses in the way.

It's the same sort of thing with hotel rooms. Don't pay a nickel more for a room that says "ocean view" or "mountain view" or "premium" or any other level without knowing exactly what it is you are paying for. Here are some savvy hints:

- Ask the reservations clerk for a definition of terms. You'll get a much clearer picture if you call the hotel directly rather than asking a national service in Omaha about the view out the window in Boston.

- If you are told of a particularly wonderful room, ask for its number and find out if you can request it specifically. Again, this is much more likely to be honored if you call directly to the hotel, and you'll stand more chance at a small, locally managed operation.

- Learn about room "series." In many larger hotels, room classifications are identified by the numbers on the door. All of the "02" rooms, for example, may be alike: 1202, 1002, 902, and so on, may all be larger corner rooms overlooking the lake. The "03" rooms, across the hallway, may be budget rooms with views of the back alleyway. If you've stayed in 1507 and like it, determine if all "07" rooms are the same and then ask for one when you make your reservation or show up at the check-in desk.

- Even if you don't have a particular room in mind, make known your preferences at check-in. Here are mine: I want a quiet room, away from the elevators, vending machines, and the all-night lounge. If I'm on an extended business trip, I'll ask for a room with a desk I can work at. And don't be shy about marching back down to the front desk if you don't like the room you've been given.

Fight if You Are Bumped from a Reservation

When is a guaranteed room not a guarantee of a room?

Although most hotels honor their promise of a room when you have a reservation, it is also true that many travelers find there is no room at the inn when they arrive.

How does this occur? Sometimes hotels make mistakes, renting too many rooms. Sometimes hotels deliberately overbook, expecting (like the airlines) that a certain percentage of those with reservations will fail to show. And sometimes hotels are victimized by guests who refuse to leave at the time they promised when they checked in—in many states, it is a difficult, time-consuming process for a hotel to dislodge a guest who doesn't leave on time.

Here are some tips:

- Make sure you have with you the confirmation number for your reservation; it doesn't hurt to ask for and record the name of the clerk who takes your reservation.

- Call directly to the hotel to confirm your reservation a day or two before you arrive.

- If you show up at the check-in desk and find a problem, stand your ground. Politely but firmly tell the clerk you want to speak to the manager. Don't step aside to let the clerk tend to other customers; make it clear that the only way you'll leave the desk is with a key to an acceptable room.

- Listen carefully to what is said: If there are "no rooms at the rate you were quoted," tell the clerk you will accept a better room—a suite, a concierge-floor room, a luxury room—at your quoted rate.

- Your safest bet is to guarantee any booking with a major credit card. Credit-card companies require hotels using their cards in this way to give their guests priority treatment. You still may not get to stay at the hotel where you have a reservation, but you must be offered a comparable room in a hotel reasonably nearby with the first night's stay free, given free transportation to the new hotel, and afforded other services including forwarding of all phone messages and mail to your new location.

  If you have been bumped from a hotel where you had a guaranteed reservation and don't feel you are being treated properly, go to the lobby phone and call the customer-service department of your credit-card company—the number is on the card—and enlist their assistance.

- If you are still not satisfied with the way you were treated, be sure to take notes on everything that occurred, including the names of front-desk personnel. Contact area tourist boards with your complaint. Send a detailed letter to the customer-service department at the national office for the hotel chain.

Get a Room at a Sold-Out Hotel

There are six major conventions in town, it's spring break, there are two weddings going on . . . and the hotel you want to stay at has the nerve to tell you they are completely sold out?

If you are absolutely determined, here are some ways to not take "no" for an answer:

- Call the hotel directly. Many chains do not release their entire inventory to national services, keeping some rooms for local rental only.

- Let the manager know what you're looking for and leave your name and phone number. And keep calling every few days to see if rooms have become available.

- If you are calling weeks or months in advance, ask about their policies: Is there a date after which reservations cannot be canceled without a penalty? Call again just before and on that date to see if any rooms have opened.

- Find out the guarantee time for reservations. If someone with a reservation must cancel before 6 P.M. to avoid being charged for the room, start calling that afternoon through just after 6 P.M. to try to snare a late cancellation.

Check Out the Room Before You Check In

You wouldn't buy a suit without trying it on, and you wouldn't (or you shouldn't) pay for a meal if you're not satisfied with the quality.

Why, then, would you pay for a hotel room if you find it unacceptable?

If you have any doubts about the quality of a hotel or motel room, ask to see a room of the quality you will be renting before you sign the register. If you have already checked in, don't be shy about going back to the front desk and asking for a new room or your money back.

Find the Cheapest Phone in the Hotel

The most expensive way to place a telephone call in a hotel or motel is to dial it directly from the bedside phone. Hotels typically add sur-charges of 25 to 50 percent over already high standard long-distance charges; in foreign locales the markup can be even more.

Instead, use a telephone credit card to place your long-distance calls at a discounted rate. But first check to see if the hotel charges for 800 and 888 "toll-free" calls; for no good reason other than greed, many hotels charge as much as a dollar for any use of their phones.

The guaranteed cheapest phone in the hotel: the telephone booth in the lobby.

Pick the Best Stateroom on a Cruise

How do you pick the best stateroom on a cruise? Start by laying out your own priorities. If you are the sort of person who uses a hotel or cruise room only to sleep and shower, then you shouldn't spend a pre-mium for the view. Here are some tips:

- To avoid noisy spots, consult the ship's room map. The stern of the ship is often the noisiest because of the sound of engines; the bow can become noisy when a vessel enters port and the bow thrusters, winches, and other equipment are in use.

  If you are in search of quiet, avoid staterooms near lounges, the-aters, kitchens, laundry rooms, elevators, and other equipment.

- If you are worried about seasickness, consider the location of your cabin. On many ships, the up-and-down motion of the vessel is most noticeable at the bow, followed by the stern; the most stable position is amidships. The side-to-side rolling of the ship is more intense higher up (on most ships, nevertheless the higher-priced neighborhood). So, the best spot may be down low in the middle of the ship.

You should also pay attention to the typical weather patterns in your cruising destination; if you head for the Caribbean during hurricane season, don't be surprised by wild seas and winds.

- If you are insistent on getting a good view study the room map and discuss your interests with your travel agent and the cruise company. Some questions to ask: How big are the windows or portholes? Are there stairs, lifeboats, columns, or other parts of the boat in the way?

Safeguard Your Possessions When You Travel

How can you guard against theft of your property from a hotel room?

The best advice: Don't bring with you anything of great value. But if you must bring something theftworthy with you, here are some tips:

- Use the hotel's safe for items such as airline tickets, extra travelers' checks, and other small items. The lock boxes may be large enough to hold a laptop computer or a camera as well.

  Be aware, though, that in most instances the hotel's liability for theft from its safe is rather limited. In this country the liability is only $500 in many states; some hotels may voluntarily accept more liability, perhaps for a charge. Ask for a written copy of the hotel's policies and be sure to obtain a signed receipt for any deposits you make.

- Another danger area: Be sure you understand the hotel's liability for any bags you leave with the bellhop and any property you leave in a car that is parked by a valet or left in the parking garage or lot. You may find that the hotel accepts no liability at all for your property.

  If you are given any assurances about the security of your property or liability, be sure you have it in writing. Check carefully claim checks and receipts to make sure they accurately reflect the items you have left behind and include any promises you have been given.

- Consult your insurance agent to find out how well covered you are under your homeowner's or renter's policies. If you do a lot of traveling and regularly bring with you expensive cameras or computers or even jewelry, inquire about a special rider for your policy to increase your coverage on the road.

SECTION IX

Insurance

Chapter

29 Auto Insurance

An automobile policy is one type of insurance that is easily understood by all drivers, but most of us are a bit fuzzy on the details. Insurance companies do everything they can to contribute to the confusion, too. And they don't really mind if you pay too much and receive too little for your money.

Here are some tips on getting the most for your auto-insurance dollar:

✓ Choose the right agent.

✓ Choose the right car.

✓ Choose the right policy limits.

✓ Seek special discounts.

✓ Don't pay twice for coverage.

✓ Know what to say at the auto-rental counter.

✓ Ride with security: bicycle insurance.

Choose the Right Agent

Look for an agent willing to compare several insurance companies and policies and one who will work with you to get the most for your insur-

351

ance dollar. In some states, insurance rates are set by a government agency, but that does not mean you should not search for a company that offers better service or has a better reputation for paying claims fairly and promptly. Your agent should also be able to provide information on financial ratings on companies; you want a company that is able to stand behind its promises.

Choose the Right Car

Undecided whether to buy an identically priced Isuzu Trooper or a Ford Explorer? Would a $200-per-year savings on auto insurance on the Trooper tip the scales?

Rates vary greatly based on the value of the car, its history of theft, safety in an accident, and the cost of repairs. The savvy consumer will consult with his or her insurance agent to choose among several makes and models before buying a car. You can also write to the Insurance Institute for Highway Safety, 1005 North Glebe Road, Arlington, VA 22201 and ask for the Highway Loss Data Chart.

Choose the Right Policy Limits

Pay attention to the policy terms to customize your insurance to your vehicle and your needs and to save money. Here are some savvy tips:

- Set the collision deductible to a level as high as you feel comfortable with; according to the Insurance Information Institute, changing the deductible from $200 to $500 could cut the cost of collision and comprehensive (fire and theft) coverage by 15 to 30 percent; going to a $1,000 deductible could reduce that cost by 50 percent.

- Drop collision or comprehensive coverage, or both, on older cars. Basically, you are looking for vehicles that are worth less than the total of your annual premium for the coverage plus the deductible.

Seek Special Discounts

One size does not fit all; not in hats, pants, and shoes, and not in auto insurance either. There are significant discounts available to certain classes of drivers or cars, but you have to know when to ask your agent for them. Here are a few to ask about:

- If you put less than the average of about 12,500 miles per year on your car, look into a low-mileage discount, available in some states.
- Make sure your agent has taken advantage of special discounts for things such as automatic seatbelts, air bags, or antilock brakes. Many companies also reduce rates if you have a burglar alarm in the car, or have added other security devices (including etching the VIN on the windshield, an inexpensive way to reduce rates in some states).
- Look into other discounts, including households that insure more than one car with one company, and benefits for good-driving records. Some companies will reduce the high rates for student drivers if they present a good report card.

Don't Pay Twice for Coverage

Eliminate duplicate coverage. Don't pay for an auto insurer's towing coverage if you are also a member of AAA. Don't buy a small life-insurance policy as part of auto coverage if you have a larger life-insurance policy through another insurer. Similarly, ask your insurance agent to see if your health-insurance coverage is comprehensive enough to remove the need for medical insurance as part of an auto policy.

Know What to Say at the Auto-Rental Counter

You've been driving for years without an accident. You're very careful anyway. And you made it to the airport this morning completely without mishap. So why not take a chance and skip the extra insurance coverage on your rental car? After all, you'll be using it for only a few hours.

It's a bad idea to go "bare" on a rental car. To begin with, the average cost of a new car is moving toward $25,000. And it's likely to be a different car from the one you drive, with a different response to the brake and gas pedals and the steering wheel. And then there's the fact that you're an out-of-towner with unfamiliar places to go and pressing things on your mind. Finally, you're likely to be tired after a day of travel.

But wait: I'm not recommending you pay the generally outrageous daily rates for insurance that the rental-car company will offer to tack onto the rate. Except in some unusual situations, you are better off making other arrangements for coverage.

First, the coverage you have under your personal auto policy would extend to renting a car, providing its usage is for pleasure and not business, according to the Insurance Information Institute.

If your employer provides you with a car, your business auto policy should cover its use on a business trip. Check with your insurance agent to find out about its applicability to personal trips.

And if you are traveling on company business, check to see if your employer has any special coverage to protect employees on the road, or any special arrangements with auto-rental companies.

If you don't own a car, look into buying a nonowner auto policy, which costs a few hundred dollars a year. Compare the cost of this specialized policy to the daily rate charged by rental companies.

One of the best added features of some credit cards is an auto policy for any rentals charged to the card. Be sure you understand the type of coverage offered by the card company and pay attention to exclusions. Many of these policies do not cover exotic and luxury cars, and some do not extend coverage outside the United States. If you find a card with a good insurance policy attached, it may be worth a $50 annual fee to use that card for travel.

If you do end up at the counter without a policy of your own, here are a few pointers about the coverage offered by rental companies:

- *Collision damage waiver.* This is actually not insurance, but instead a promise by the rental company that it will not charge you for any damage sustained by the car. It does not provide liability coverage or provide for medical expenses. The CDW may be voided if you are found to have caused an accident by reckless driving, speeding, driving while intoxicated, or other actions including taking a car on unpaved roads.

In some states, including New York and Illinois, insurance for collision damage is already included in the rental price, and rental-car companies are not permitted by law to charge extra for the CDW.

Rates for CDW are typically about $8 to $12 per day. Think of this charge on an annual rate and you'll get an idea of just how bad this coverage is: $10 per day is $3,650 per year, just for collision coverage.

Your credit-card company's auto-rental coverage should kick in here to supplement or stand in place of a policy of your own.

- *Personal accident insurance.* You shouldn't need this coverage if you have a health-insurance policy, or an automobile policy with personal-injury protection.

  PAI usually sells for about $3 per day. Once again, this works out to a very expensive annual rate.

- *Personal effects coverage.* A policy to cover the theft of personal items in the car. Your homeowner's or renter's insurance should include coverage for off-premises theft; you will have to pay any deductible in the policy, though.

  The rental company's coverage, which typically costs about $1 to $2 per day, might make sense if you are traveling with anything of value, or if you will be leaving your vehicle unattended for a period of time. Be sure to read the details of the coverage to see if there is a deductible and to see if anything specific such as cameras, computers, jewelry, and other items are excluded from coverage.

  Better yet, don't leave anything of value in your car.

  In any case, be sure you have copies of receipts and full descriptions of all possessions in your suitcases and other bags. You'll need that information for any claim.

- *Additional liability insurance.* This policy protects you from claims of other drivers. Once again, you would do a lot better carrying a personal umbrella policy that costs a few hundred dollars a year and extends your home, auto, and personal coverage.

  Purchased from an auto-rental agency, this policy typically costs about $8 to $10 per day, the equivalent of as much as $3,650 per year.

Ride with Security: Bicycle Insurance

Bicycles have come a long way since the $25 Schwinn many of us grew up with. Today fancy racing bikes and off-road cycles cost as much as several thousand dollars. And not surprisingly, they have become tempting targets for theft. One industry estimate says that about 9 million bikes are stolen each year.

Your best insurance against theft is a good lock, properly applied. Be sure the bicycle frame and at least one wheel are secured to a metal rack or post; don't run the cable through the wheel alone—a thief with a wrench could choose to leave the relatively inexpensive wheel behind and take the rest of the bicycle. You should also see whether your local police department has a bicycle registry where you can record the bike's serial number and description; this may help in recovery of a stolen bike or help you file a claim with your insurance company. Keep your receipts; a photograph of the bicycle may also help.

Here are some more bicycle tips:

- Bicycles are usually covered under your homeowner's or renter's insurance, although you may have a deductible of several hundred dollars. If you own an expensive bike, discuss with your insurance agent the purchase of a rider to extend and improve on your coverage.

    The rider may also include the cost of repairs in case of an accident.

    Such a policy, also called a floater, generally costs about $9 per $100 of value without any deductible.

- Your homeowner's or renter's policy provides liability coverage in the event of a collision that results in injury to another party. There are no deductibles for liability claims.

30 Homeowner's and Renter's Insurance

As comedian George Carlin has observed, your home is the place you leave your stuff when you go out to buy more stuff. And when you leave your house, you have to worry that someone doesn't break in . . . and take your stuff.

That's one of the reasons homeowners buy insurance. Another reason is to protect themselves against losses caused by catastrophes, from fire to storm damage. And renters, though they're not responsible for the house or apartment itself, still may want to buy some protection for their stuff.

In this chapter, I show you how to conduct a survey of your insurance coverage and then do the same for your home or apartment. Then we look at ways to reduce insurance costs. And finally, we look at insurance policies for an increasingly common high-price and easy-to-steal item: the personal computer.

✓ Protect yourself against insurance insufficiencies.

✓ Perform a survey of your own home or apartment.

✓ Conduct an annual survey of your insurance coverage.

✓ Know how to lower your homeowner's and renter's insurance cost.

✓ Consider your insurance costs when you buy a home.

✓ Improve your home security.

✓ Understand renter's insurance.

✓ Is your PC in good hands?

✓ Buy replacement coverage for your PC.

Protect Yourself Against Insurance Insufficiencies

Before the fire, before the storm, before the burglary, before the electrical power surge: ask yourself these questions.

1. Do I know what I own, and what they would cost to replace?
2. Can I prove it all to the insurance company?
3. Do I have sufficient insurance coverage to pay for a loss?

Perform a Survey of Your Own Home or Apartment

You can save yourself a tremendous amount of trouble and possibly many thousands of dollars by doing the following:

1. Conduct a detailed inventory of your possessions. Make an itemized list of everything of value, with information on price paid and purchase date, if possible; hold on to any receipt to help substantiate claims.

   One modern-day improvement to a written inventory—and one that your insurance company may find to be irrefutable proof—is a video tour of your home or office. Use a camcorder to make a running commentary on every room. Stop in front of a television set, for example, and announce into the microphone the make and model number plus the serial number for the device; if you have a copy of the receipt at hand, read onto the record the information including store, date, price, and any identifying number on the receipt.

   If you don't have a video camera, you can also use a still camera to take room-by-room pictures.

   Store the inventory in a safe-deposit box or away from your home or apartment.

2. Store in a safe place receipts and descriptions of your possessions. Make up a detailed list and assign replacement costs to the items you own. Take your list to the mall and price new furniture, clothing, and electronics; or consult catalogs and newspaper ads for an idea of the cost of items.

Conduct an Annual Survey of Your Insurance Coverage

Sit down with your insurance agent at least annually to review the amount and type of coverage you have in place.

The purpose of homeowner's insurance is to protect from theft, fire, and other perils (not including flood, war, and a few other exclusions). Therefore, the value of the policy should reflect the replacement cost of the house and attached structures but not the land.

Consult the real-estate pages or ask your friends and neighbors for an estimate of construction costs for a home such as yours. Your insurance agent may be able to help, or you can hire a professional appraiser. Be sure to remove from the price the value of the land, which should be there whether or not a house is installed.

For a rough estimate of rebuilding cost, figure the square footage of the house and multiply it by the average building costs in your area. In some parts of the country, construction is as inexpensive as $50 per square foot, while in other regions the rates can cross $100 per square foot. (Colder climes, for example, require sturdier construction, insulation, and larger heating systems.) Additional cost items include basements, fireplaces, decks, and custom-design features.

Make certain that the value of your insurance policy is keeping up with increases in local building costs. Ask your insurance agent or company representative about adding an "inflation-guard clause" to automatically adjust the dwelling limit when you renew your policy to reflect current construction costs in your area.

Few homes are totally destroyed, but why take that chance? Most insurance companies recommend you insure your home for 100 percent of the cost of rebuilding it.

Your mortgage lender will have something to say about the amount of coverage you purchase: They will want you to have coverage at least sufficient to pay off your loan if the house is destroyed.

Keep your insurance agent up to date on any improvements or additions to your house since you last talked about your insurance policy.

Most insurance policies offer replacement-cost coverage for structural damage, and you should seek nothing else; however, some companies will not offer that sort of coverage for very old houses because of changes in construction techniques and because of the great expense of re-creating old wood and plaster elements. They may instead offer a modified replacement-cost policy that will allow for the reconstruction of a similar house using contemporary techniques. It may also be possible that building codes will not permit construction of a noncomplying structure.

Next, consider the coverage you have for personal possessions including furniture, clothing, and appliances. The limit of the policy is usually shown on the Declarations Page under Section I, Coverages, Personal Property.

A standard policy sets coverage at 50 percent of the amount of insurance on the structure to as much as 75 percent. Compare that amount to your estimate of replacement cost of your possessions.

Note that most policies offer only limited coverage for expensive items such as jewelry, furs, works of art, and hobbies and collections; consult your insurance agent to find out about purchasing a special endorsement or floater to add coverage for those items. Check on the value of any such scheduled items in your policy. A scheduled item is one that is specifically named and assigned a value.

Some items, such as paintings and jewelry, may go up in value over time. (They can also go down, of course.) Other valuables, such as fur coats or expensive cameras or electronics, may go down in value. Don't pay for coverage you don't need.

As with insurance for the structure, a replacement-cost policy pays the dollar amount needed to replace a damaged item with one of similar kind and quality without deductions for depreciation. An actual cash-value policy pays the amount needed to replace the item, minus depreciation.

Know How to Lower Your Homeowner's and Renter's Insurance Cost

Homeowner's insurance is an essential coverage. It is required by mortgage lenders to protect their interests; you should make certain your own assets are covered properly, as well.

The quality and cost of this insurance can vary greatly. Here are some ways to get the most coverage for the least cost:

- Shop around. Call more than one insurance agent, or insist that your agent price policies from multiple companies. Ask friends and neighbors about their experience with insurance companies; the most valuable experience would be that of someone who has filed a claim in recent years.

  Ask your agent or the insurance company directly about ways to reduce cost.

- Look into special discount programs.

  Some companies give discounts of as much as 15 percent if you buy your home and auto policies from the same insurer. Some insurers will grant discounts to long-time customers who have held policies for several years.

  Ask if the company gives a discount if none of the residents in the home are smokers on the assumption that this reduces fire risk.

  Some insurers offer discounts of about 10 percent to retired seniors, on the assumption that they are at home more and can guard against fire and other loss.

  Look into group-coverage discounts for members of associations or groups.

- Make certain you are comparing the same coverage and features when you look at various prices.

- Raise the deductible. Deductibles on homeowner policies generally start at $250. By increasing that deductible to $500, the Insurance Information Institute estimates you could save up to 12 percent; going to $1,000 could save as much as 24 percent; and a deductible of $5,000 could reduce insurance rates up to 37 percent.

Consider Your Insurance Costs When You Buy a Home

Newer homes, with modern electrical, heating, and plumbing systems and other improved structural features, can typically command discounts of 8 to 15 percent.

Avoid flood-prone areas to save on potential damage and to avoid the cost of separate flood-insurance coverage. (A standard homeowner's policy does not protect against flood damage.)

Home-insurance rates are lower if your home is near a hydrant or a fire station. The quality of the fire department itself can also affect rates.

Improve Your Home Security

Insurance companies typically grant discounts for burglar alarms (with higher discounts if the alarm is connected to a central station or to the police department), smoke detectors, and beefed-up locks. A large discount may be offered for a fire-sprinkler system, although the cost of such a system may outweigh its value, at least in terms of insurance savings.

Check with your insurance agent for details.

Understand Renter's Insurance

A renter's policy covers your possessions and gives liability protection; the protection of the structure is not covered. A typical policy protects you against losses due to fire or smoke, lightning, vandalism, theft, explosion, windstorm, and water damage from plumbing. The liability portion of the policy offers protection if someone slips and falls in your home or is injured by any of your possessions and then sues.

If you have any particularly valuable possessions, from artwork to jewelry to computers, consult your insurance agent to make sure you have adequate coverage; you may need to add a floater to the policy that "schedules" specific possessions, or expands coverage limits.

In any case, hold onto receipts and other documentation for pricey possessions. A photographic or video inventory can also be valuable.

Students under age 26 attending college may have limited coverage in a college dorm under their parents' homeowner's- or renter's-insurance policy. Again, consult your insurance agent.

In some states, some insurance companies may issue policies for roommates or unmarried couples sharing an apartment.

Here are some ways to get the most coverage for the best price:

- Be sure that you have adequate and appropriate coverage for your possessions, including special floaters for individual items of great value.

- Understand the difference between cash-value and replacement-value coverage.

  Cash-value coverage pays for stolen or destroyed items on the basis of its depreciated value. If you bought a television set five years ago for $300, today it might be worth only $100, and that would be the amount paid by the policy. It would be up to you to make up the difference in buying a new set.

  Replacement-value pays the cost of a new, equivalent item. In the example of the television, the set might sell today for $450.

  Replacement policies will usually cost more, but may make economic sense.

- Set the deductible at a level you feel comfortable with. If you can sustain a $500 loss without serious pain, go for that level rather than a lower one. The lower the deductible, the more the policy will cost you.

- Look for discounts. Some companies reduce rates if your apartment or home has a security system, smoke detectors, or deadbolt locks. Additional discounts may include reductions for older retired renters and for nonsmokers.

Is Your PC in Good Hands?

The PC in the family den is almost as common as the barbecue in the backyard. That's something that is not lost on your average burglar, either: PCs are reasonably portable and easily disposed of for a few hundred dollars.

So, your PC is insured as part of your homeowner's or renter's policy, right? Maybe.

Your first step, perhaps before you even bring a PC home, is to check with your insurance agent to see if there is adequate—or any— coverage under your existing homeowner's or renter's policy. Many policies now include about $5,000 worth of coverage for PCs for personal use, although some carriers have chosen to pointedly exclude computers from personal policies, and others may refuse to offer coverage in some high-risk urban areas.

But:

- If your computer is used as an extension of your business or if you operate a business from your home the PC and peripherals may not be covered.

- If your machine is used for a home-based business, consider purchasing a separate business policy to cover the equipment and to protect against other liability you may incur (such as the FedEx man tripping on your kid's skateboard on the way to delivering a package to your office), or look into a rider to your homeowner's or renter's policy to cover the equipment.

- Understand the difference between policies that guard only against "named perils" such as fire and those that offer "all-risk" protection.

Buy Replacement Coverage for Your PC

If you do have a policy, you should make certain it provides for "replacement-cost" payment rather than "cash value." The cash value of a PC drops precipitously over time even if it is perfectly suitable for playing Space Invaders or writing a novel. A machine you purchased for $2,000 a year ago may only be worth $500 today; it would nevertheless cost you about $1,500 to replace it with today's model.

You'll also need to pay attention to the deductible on your policy, which can end up being more than the value of the PC.

Keep track of receipts for hardware and software purchases and maintain a listing of all equipment including specifications, serial numbers, and purchase prices; it's not a bad idea to send a copy of that list to your insurance agent to keep on file. Even better, use your camera or video camera to take detailed pictures of the setup to help bolster your claim. (Performing a videotaped inventory of your entire home is another good insurance practice.)

31 | Life Insurance

Woody Allen once gave us a memorable definition of purgatory: being locked in a small room with a life-insurance salesman.

One reason why insurance agents are so anxious to sell life insurance is that these policies are good moneymakers for companies and agents. The most profitable are whole-life policies—profitable for those who sell them, that is.

The simplest way to buy coverage is a term policy, which covers a specific period of time. The coverage expires at the end of the period, and the insurance company keeps the change. Rates for term policies start out low for younger clients and go up in price as they become older; it's all based on the actuarial tables that lay out the statistical chances of a person of any particular age surviving to the end of the term.

An interesting variation of term insurance is the "level-premium" policy, which locks in an annual rate for a number of years (typically 10 or 20 years). The rate per year starts out higher than you would pay for a one-year policy but somewhere around the middle of the time period becomes less expensive per year. You can cancel at any time, although you will end up losing money compared to a standard-term policy if you do so before that middle point.

Whole-life policies—in variations that include universal and variable plans—are based on a "permanent" concept rather than on term. In other words, if you have a whole-life policy and you keep it current by paying all premiums, you own something of value. It will pay off the stated amount when you die, and it also builds a cash value while you live.

Whole-life coverage is more expensive than term for two reasons: first, because almost all policyholders (their survivors, actually) eventu-

ally end up collecting benefits. By contrast, most term-insurance policies never pay off benefits because holders either move from company
to company or stop buying coverage as they reach an advanced age. The
second reason is that whole-life policies build up a value, which can be
borrowed against or cashed in by the policyholder. The rate of return on
a life-insurance policy, though, is well below that of other investments.

About that cash value: There's another important "gotcha" to
understand here. The cash value exists only for as long as the policy is
in force; if you die the face value of the policy will go to your beneficiary while the cash value goes back into the paperwork of the insurance company.

Here's an example of whole life at work: Let's say you had a
$250,000 whole-life policy that has built up a $50,000 cash value.
Before your death, you could close out the policy and receive $50,000
to spend on your retirement. Before you jump up and down with
excitement here, consider the fact that you may have spent $100,000 in
premiums over the years to reach that point.

Alternatively, you could borrow the $50,000 in cash value from the
policy and spend it in any way you wanted. Now you'd have a loan to
repay with interest. Let's say you die soon after the loan, though. Your
beneficiaries would then receive only $200,000—the face value minus
the cash value that was given out as a loan.

Here's another "gotcha" that qualifies as a legal form of a shell
game: so-called "vanishing-premium" policies claim that the interest
earned on the cash value of a policy can be used to pay the premiums
in future years. What they are really saying is that their projections say
that the money they hope to earn on their investments should be
enough to pay your premiums at some point down the road. That's a
big "if," and one that is usually based on some pretty optimistic estimates of earnings. I'd recommend against this particular wrinkle; if
you're being pushed, ask to see the insurance company's projections on
interest and dividends and its performance in meeting those goals over
the past ten years or so.

- ✓ Know the reasons to buy life insurance.
- ✓ Know the reasons to *not* buy life insurance.
- ✓ Know how to buy term insurance.

✓ Consider viatical settlements/living benefits in time of need.

✓ Just say no: life insurance on children.

✓ Another bad deal: credit life insurance.

Know the Reasons to Buy Life Insurance

Do buy life insurance:

- To protect a breadwinner's family in case of death before they are able to provide for themselves.
- To pay off the remaining balance on a home mortgage for the surviving spouse.
- To pay off estate taxes.

Know the Reasons to *Not* Buy Life Insurance

Don't buy life insurance:

- As an investment. The best of whole-life policies rarely perform better than the worst of money-market mutual funds. The old financial planner's mantra is still correct: Buy term insurance and invest the rest.
- To guarantee insurability at a later age. You either need life insurance now or you don't.

Know How to Buy Term Insurance

Term life insurance is a fairly straightforward product; look for a highly rated company (AA or better) with the features you want. One way to search for the lowest prices is to use one of several life-insurance dealers. They sell direct, without having to pay commissions to agents.

They will take down your vital information—age, general health condition, including whether or not you are a smoker, and one or two other details—and then produce a list of quotes from companies they represent.

Try these companies:

Policy Previews Insurance Information. (800) 472-5800. Charges $50 for a report on the five least expensive policies from more than 600 companies.

Quotesmith. (800) 431-1147. A free comparison of rates from among more than 100 companies. You can also check their offerings online, at **http://www.insure.com/Quotesmith**

SelectQuote. (800) 343-1985. A free report with the best rates from about 20 companies.

Consider Viatical Settlements/Living Benefits in Time of Need

Depending upon your medical and financial condition and your family obligations, viatical settlements of life insurance-policies are either a godsend or an extremely ghoulish sideline in modern business.

A viatical settlement is a way for an insured person to receive some of the proceeds of a life-insurance policy before dying, when the money goes to his or her estate. (The term "viatical" comes from the Latin *via*, which means road; viatical has come to mean an allowance for travel expenses.) Another term for the same sort of program is a "living benefit," as opposed to the standard "death benefit" that is delivered after the insured person departs the premium-paying population.

Viatical settlements have gained some appreciation from victims of extended terminal diseases, including AIDS. The money received from the buyer of the policy can be used to pay for medical or housing expenses, or for travel or other final wishes.

A viatical settlement is essentially the sale of the benefits of a life-insurance policy to a third party; the new beneficiary then pays the original owner of the policy a portion of the death benefit. Here's where the ghoulish part comes in: The new beneficiary is going to seek a medical estimation of life expectancy. If the owner is given a year to live, the new beneficiary is going to deduct the interest cost of the money for a year and the cost of paying premiums to keep the policy in force (plus an added cushion in case the owner outlives the prediction, which is good news for the owner and bad news for the new beneficiary).

In general, viatical settlements are arranged as they are needed, sometimes between the insured person and the insurance company and at other times between the insured person and a third party.

Some life-insurance policies—both cash value and term—may already include a life benefit, called an "accelerated-death benefit" that will give a terminally ill patient as much as 90 percent of the policy's face value when the policyholder is given a life expectancy of less than a year. Check with your insurer.

You should also consult your financial adviser before entering into a viatical agreement. In certain circumstances, you may be required to pay capital-gains tax on the difference between the payment you receive and the amount you've paid in premiums. You also may owe state tax, although several states, including California and New York, have made these settlements tax-free.

And income of this sort may also affect your eligibility for public-assistance programs based on financial need, such as Medicaid.

The Congress is considering making changes to federal laws to remove tax liability from life benefits.

You should also put your quest for a viatical settlement out to bid. The amount of the payment can vary greatly from one company to another. (Another ghoulish note: Some companies may figure you'll die off sooner than the others.)

Study offers and don't make irrevocable decisions without careful consideration; in some states there is a 15-day cooling-off period before any viatical settlement transaction is complete.

Here are some associations that may help with decision making:

American Council of Life Insurance, 1001 Pennsylvania Ave. N.W., Washington, DC 20004-2599.

National Association of Insurance Commissioners, 444 North Capitol St. N.W., Washington, DC 20001.

National Association of People with AIDS, 1413 K St. N.W., Washington, DC 20005.

National Viatical Association, 7910 Woodmont Ave., Suite 1430, Bethesda, MD 20814.

North American Securities Administrators Association, 555 New Jersey Ave. N.W., Washington, DC 20001.

Viatical Association of America, 1200 19th St. N.W., Suite 300, Washington, DC 20036.

Just Say No: Life Insurance on Children

Short and sweet: purchasing a life-insurance policy on a young child is a sucker's bet or worse. A term-life policy doesn't benefit the child in any way—he or she has to die for the policy to pay off. And a whole-life policy with a cash value is a poor way to invest for college. A better route is an early regular investment plan in mutual funds or stocks.

Remember that the real purpose of life insurance is to provide for living expenses for surviving family members.

On the other hand, there is one important way for the family breadwinners to directly protect their young children: providing an emergency source of funds for college. The cost of college, as well as living expenses for the family, should be factored into your calculation of life-insurance coverage for breadwinners.

Another Bad Deal: Credit Life Insurance

Another bad deal is credit life insurance, which promises to pay off your outstanding balance should you die. The rates are high, and if you're doing things right, you shouldn't have large personal credit obligations. Instead, make certain your term life-insurance policy coverage—which costs much less per thousand—is large enough to pay off any outstanding debts as well as provide for your family in the event of an untimely demise.

32 Medical and Disability Insurance

Although many of us concentrate on life insurance as a way to take care of our loved ones in the event of our death, there are two policies that are probably more important in most lives: medical insurance and disability insurance. Both can be complex, with greatly varying ranges of coverage and prices.

My number-one tip here is to spend the time to understand any policy offered by your employer; set up an appointment with your personnel or benefits office. If you are responsible for obtaining this coverage on your own, interview several insurance agents to find one who can explain policies to your satisfaction and who can put your business out to competitive bid to several quality insurers.

✓ Choose a disability-insurance policy with care.

✓ Don't pay for duplicate medical insurance.

Choose a Disability-Insurance Policy with Care

It's not at the top of most people's insurance Top Ten, but for most of us, one of the most important policies may be disability insurance. Think of it this way: Life insurance pays your family if you die, whereas disability pays your family if you live . . . but are unable to work.

And don't think this is something that you're too young to worry about: According to industry statistics, one out of three people between the ages of 35 and 65 will become disabled for at least three months, and one in ten will become permanently disabled before age 65.

If your employer offers a generous package of benefits, you may have disability coverage already; check with the benefits administrator for details. If not, contact a competent insurance agent.

Here are some tips on shopping for disability coverage:

- Understand the distinction between short-term and long-term disability coverage. A long-term policy will replace your income for your entire life, or until a specified age, such as 65, when you would be presumed to retire from work. A short-term policy may promise to pay for only a few months or years; this is better than nothing, but not much benefit to a young breadwinner with a family.

- Go for as long a term of payments as you feel comfortable paying for, and seek as high a disability payment as possible. Typical policies promise to pay you about 60 to 75 percent of your income; they don't want to pay 100 percent because that doesn't give you much of an incentive to go back to work. In any case, the income from a disability policy is not subject to tax and therefore you should be able to get by on a reduced portion of your previous income.

- Read the fine print about your occupation. The best sort of disability policy promises to pay you for as long as you are unable to engage in your "own" occupation. A much less valuable version would pay you only if you are unable to engage in "any" occupation. You don't want some insurance adjuster assigning you to work at McDonald's after you are forced by accident or illness to leave your occupation as a rocket scientist, right?

- You can adjust the cost of a disability policy by accepting a longer elimination period—the length of time after an accident or illness before you begin to collect. If you choose, for example, a less expensive six-month elimination period, the insurance company is gambling that you'll return to work before that period elapses. From your point of view, you should compare the cost savings in a long elimination period against your ability to do without income during those months.

- Seek a noncancelable or guaranteed renewable policy. The insurance company is bound to keep the policy in force as long as you make payments. A noncancelable policy locks the premium in place for the entire term of the agreement. A guaranteed renewable policy prevents the insurance company from singling you out for a premium increase; the rate can go up only if an entire class of policyholders faces the same boost.

Don't Pay for Duplicate Medical Insurance

If you and your spouse are both employed, you may each have medical coverage that could be extended to each other and to your family. Study the provisions of both plans—it might be worthwhile to meet with the benefits administrator at each of your workplaces—to see which plan offers better coverage at a better price.

In some cases it might make sense to keep each independent policy, while in other cases you might be better off declining one insurance and bringing your family together under the other.

You cannot collect twice for the same medical incident or treatment, so duplicate coverage has no value.

33 More Insurance Tips

✓ Research insurance trends and companies.

✓ Put an umbrella over your insurance coverage.

✓ Use your umbrella policy to save money on other coverage.

✓ Get out from under private mortgage insurance.

✓ Ask for a volume discount.

Research Insurance Trends and Companies

Internet users can keep up to date on the latest in insurance trends and learn about things such as crash tests, financial ratings, and tax-law changes on the Insurance News Network at **http://www.insure.com**

Put an Umbrella over Your Insurance Coverage

If you own any property, drive a car, earn a decent income, or have any prospects of ever having a decent net worth, you should have a good umbrella.

Personal umbrella policies are among the best buys in insurance and should be considered by most people. Umbrellas provide extended coverage—typically $1 million or more—if you must pay damages from a lawsuit or if you incur costs to fight such a suit. They often include coverage for things excluded on standard homeowners' policies, such as libel and slander suits and extension of automobile liability coverage to international driving.

With an umbrella policy, you are protecting yourself against most claims that could take away your assets and even your future earnings. Umbrella policies typically cost only about $150 to $300 for $1 million in coverage and are usually intended to extend your coverage in existing auto or home policies. The issuer of the policy may require you to maintain a particular level of liability coverage on those underlying policies. The cost of an umbrella may rise if you present some particular risks, such as owning a boat or swimming pool, or if you own property used for hunting.

Use Your Umbrella Policy to Save Money on Other Coverage

Here's a savvy way to make good use of an umbrella policy: Take out an umbrella with a high liability level ($1 million or more) and then reduce the liability levels on your auto and homeowner's policies. Umbrella coverage kicks in when you exhaust the liability of other policies, and is generally cheaper per thousand in large quantities than the smaller liabilities of other policies.

Get Out from Under Private Mortgage Insurance

One of the worst deals around is PMI, which some mortgage lenders will require you to buy and others may try to sneak by an unwary consumer. This coverage, which is often priced well above other forms of insurance, protects only the lender and not you.

Try to remove PMI from any mortgage before you go to closing; if the bank insists on its inclusion for any loan below a particular down-payment level, go back to the bank when your payments reach that level and ask that the extra charge be removed from your account.

Ask for a Volume Discount

Here's one reason to consider putting all or most of your insurance eggs in one basket: Many companies offer significant discounts if you bring much of your business to them. Ask your insurance agent.

You may also be able to save money on the cost of an umbrella liability policy, a worthy addition to most coverage, if you have your homeowner's and automobile policies with the same company.

SECTION X

Going to School

34 Paying for an Education

Become a savvy consumer of education. Perhaps you haven't thought of a college education for your children in that way, but in most cases once again the power resides on your side of the table. Except for the most exclusive of schools, a college needs you more than you need it. They need to fill their dormitories and their classrooms and their quotas or goals; you can do them a favor by enrolling your child.

This is not to say that you're going to win an acceptance to Harvard with a C- average and no money (although stranger things have happened), but if you come up with a good match for your child's academic credentials and interests you may find an admissions officer asking you this question: How can we help you?

✓ Ease the college bite with advance planning.

✓ Look for alternate sources of loans.

✓ Search for financial aid on the Net.

✓ Structure your income and assets for maximum financial aid.

✓ Negotiate for a better offer.

✓ A way for Grandma and Grandpa to help without paying gift tax.

✓ Buy a tuition gift certificate.

✓ Know the pluses and minuses of custodial accounts for children.

✓ Learn how to reduce your college-loan payment after the bills come in.

✓ Reduce the cost of college before registration.

✓ Save on musical instruments for youngsters.

Ease the College Bite with Advance Planning

Getting a head start on college financing gives you more time to search for money and may bring you a higher scholarship or loan. Here are some tips:

- Apply early for Federal Student Aid. This probably won't increase the amount of aid you receive, but it might tip the scales between a grant and need. For example, a child might be deemed worthy of $15,000 in aid. Early in the process, a college might disburse that as $10,000 in a cash grant and $5,000 in the form of a loan; later on, the larder may be less well stocked, and the offer might be $5,000 in a grant and $10,000 as a loan.

- Similarly, work with your child to search for scholarships from organizations and corporations early in his or her high-school years. Learn the requirements and the qualifications of successful applications well ahead of the deadlines.

Look for Alternate Sources of Loans

Consider taking out a home-equity loan to help pay some or all of the cost of college. The interest on these loans—up to $100,000—is considered part of your tax-deductible mortgage, reducing the cost of the loan by your tax-bracket percentage. As with any other use of a home-equity loan, though, don't forget that you are putting the roof over your head at risk; don't borrow more than you can comfortably repay.

Another source of lower-cost borrowing is the cash value of any whole-life insurance policy you may own. Be aware that any outstanding loan balance will be deducted from the payout should you die.

Search for Financial Aid on the Net

If you're smart enough to use the Internet, perhaps you should be smart enough to qualify (or help your kids qualify) for extra scholarship money online.

Here are some resources:

- *FinAid*, the Financial Aid Information Page, sponsored by the National Association of Student Financial Aid Administrators. Here you'll find links to aid programs and other information. You'll find it at **http://www.finaid.com**

- *FastWEB* includes a searchable database of scholarships from around the country. Fill in the onscreen form and click on the enter button for a report on offerings that match a student's experience, school record, and interest. FastWEB is at **http://www.fastweb.com**

- *The Student Guide to Financial Aid*, produced by the U.S. Department of Education, offers information about the financial-aid process, how to apply for college, and other useful tips. Find it at **http://www.ed.gov**

Structure Your Income and Assets for Maximum Financial Aid

Federal guidelines for college financial aid are based on two elements: a percentage of income above a rather low family living allowance, and a percentage of your total liquid assets (shares in the stock market, mutual funds, bonds, savings accounts, and other such investments).

Your principal home and all of your designated retirement investments are not included in your assets.

Your child is also expected to contribute 50 percent of all income (after a $1,750 after-tax exemption) toward college expenses.

Before you sit down to calculate how much your lifestyle will be affected by your child's acceptance to college, you should consider some of the ways you can restructure your assets and income to maximize your chances for aid. Be sure to consult your accountant for advice on your specific situation. Here are some general suggestions:

- Pay off consumer debt including credit cards, car loans, and personal loans. The financial-aid formula does not take into account your personal debt, but it does weigh your assets against your eligibility for aid. Therefore, it makes sense to use savings to reduce your debt (and your monthly overhead). You are almost certainly paying more for a credit-card balance, for example, than you are earning on investments.

- If you don't have savings available for eliminating consumer debt, consider taking out a home-equity loan for the purpose. The interest rate on this secured loan is sure to be less than you'll get from other lenders, and the interest is tax deductible. Just be careful not to put your home at risk with a loan beyond your ability to pay it off.

- Look for ways to shift income out of the "base year" for your aid application. The base year is the year before your child begins college. If you are due a bonus or other income in that base year, see if your employer is willing to pay it the year before, or to defer it into the year after the base year.

  If the income is shifted into the second or later years of your child's education, the college could reduce financial aid in later years, but this doesn't always happen. The money has already been allocated, and the school has a vested interest in keeping your child on its books. In any case, you've already received the benefit of the lower base year.

  Consult your accountant to see if there are other ways to reduce your income during the college years. If you own your own business, you may be able to defer earnings past graduation.

  Pay attention to withholding in the year before your base year so that you do not have to contend with a large tax refund, which counts as income in the year following.

- Hold off on realizing capital gains in investments in base years, or balance gains with losses to avoid boosting your income. The financial-aid formula demands you spend more of income than assets.

- Reduce or eliminate voluntary contributions to retirement plans in your base year. Although the IRS allows you to exclude those contributions from taxable income, the federal financial-aid formula does not exclude them from its calculations and you will therefore be expected to pay more toward college from your income.

   You may be able to increase your retirement contributions in the years leading up to the base year and the college years, giving you the tax benefits in earlier years (and adding four years or more to the compounding effect). Consult your accountant for details specific to your situation.

Negotiate for a Better Offer

Your child wants to go to Beantown and has been accepted at Boston University with an offer of $10,000 per year in guaranteed loans; that's not quite as good as the $7,500 grant and $5,000 loan offered by Syracuse University, though. How should you choose?

Before you accept a second-best offer, think like a savvy consumer. Call the admissions officer at Boston University and say: "We'd love to accept your offer, but we've received a better deal from Syracuse. Can you match the offer?"

Two points here: First, many admissions officers have flexibility to improve on offers if they need to, and second, relatively few consumers of college education ever ask them to do so.

Your chances of getting more money from a college are greater early in the admissions cycle before all of the available scholarship and loan funds have been committed.

A Way for Grandma and Grandpa to Help Without Paying Gift Tax

Here's a way for Grandma and Grandpa to help pay for some or all of their grandkid's college education without incurring a gift-tax liability:

Give the money directly to the college to pay tuition or room and board for the student; there is no tax on the contribution.

Buy a Tuition Gift Certificate

One way to fund a portion of college-tuition bills is to make a gift of shares of stock or mutual funds to your child.

You are permitted to give up to $10,000 per year to your child without incurring a "gift tax" on your largesse. Your child will have to pay taxes on the gift, but this will likely be at the minimum tax bracket of about 15 percent instead of at your rate.

Another advantage of holding on to your money until the last moment in this way is that it enhances your child's eligibility for financial aid because the investment is considered your savings rather than your child's; the student is expected to contribute at least 35 percent of savings to college while parents are obligated to fork over only 5.65 percent.

Note that if you make a gift of mutual funds you will be liable for tax on any annual capital gains distribution in the year you transfer the shares.

Know the Pluses and Minuses of Custodial Accounts for Children

Many parents set up "custodial" accounts for their children as a way to save on taxes as they prepare for college bills. Most of these accounts use the Uniform Gifts to Minors Act, usually referred to by its unpleasant abbreviation UGMA.

Under that law and IRS rules, children under the age of 14 can earn $650 per year in tax-free interest, with the next $650 taxable at the child's tax bracket, which is presumably lower than Mom's or Dad's. Remaining interest goes against the guardian's tax rate. After age 14, the liability is entirely the child's.

So far, so good, but there are two significant "gotchas" with UGMA savings.

First, once the child reaches the age of 18 (or 21 in some states), the child is no longer a minor and takes over legal control of the account. That means he or she could decide to buy a Harley or a ski chalet or take the money to Las Vegas instead of using the funds for a college education.

Second, you may not want to build up too much money in an UGMA account if you plan to apply for financial aid. Under current aid guidelines, the student is expected to use at least 35 percent of savings to pay for college, while parents are called upon to commit only up to 5.65 percent of their savings. The decision comes down to deciding whether to pay extra in taxes while you save versus receiving more free aid or a low-rate loan once your child is ready for college. Consult your accountant for advice on your particular situation.

Learn How to Reduce Your College-Loan Payment After the Bills Come In

Many loans underwritten by the Student Loan Marketing Association (also known by its friendly nickname of Sallie Mae) come under a program called the Sallie Mae Great Rewards program. Intended to improve the repayment rate on student loans, the deal is this: If you make your payments on schedule during the first 48 months of the loan, the already low interest rate on the remainder will be reduced by 2 percent.

Ask if your Sallie Mae loan includes this feature; see if it can be added if possible. And then take advantage of the offer. There aren't many better financial deals around.

Reduce the Cost of College Before Registration

Here's a way to reduce the cost of college and reduce the pressure of early years at school: See if your child's high school offers advanced-placement courses that are eligible to earn college credits. (You'll have to find out if the college they will attend will accept the credits, too.)

Every credit earned before going off to school is one that won't have to be purchased at full college prices.

Save on Musical Instruments for Youngsters

Before you sign up your child for a rental program from a music shop, look into buying a used or new instrument. You can always resell the instrument at the end of the school year to another incoming student, saving both families some money.

There is a large market in used musical instruments that are rented to students. These are not the finest quality units, but they are usually just fine for learning.

The best time to shop is in June, after schools have returned many of their units.

Ask for a reasonable warranty on the instrument and check to see that there is a good supply of replacement parts, such as mouthpieces, specific to the particular instrument.

Another source for used instruments is the pawnshop, where you will sometimes find better quality instruments than at a store renting to students. Be sure you know the fair price for the instrument before you try to make a deal.

Business Products

35 Purchasing Office Supplies and Equipment

There are few retail environments more competitive than office supplies and equipment; the savvy consumer can do quite well with some careful shopping.

In years past, business managers would stroll to a downtown office-supply store and buy pencils, notebooks, and mechanical adding machines off the shelves. You can still do that (although high-tech calculators and computers have completely supplanted adding machines), but that is probably not the savvy way to shop. There is nothing wrong with these stores, and indeed they can offer personalized service and support that is missing almost everywhere else. And in certain circumstances, such as treating yourself to an ergonomically correct chair, the extra cost may be worth a visit to a specialist.

But if you are looking for the lowest price on commodities, check out the office-supply superstores such as Office Depot or Staples, the warehouse membership clubs such as Sam's Club, Price-Costco, or BJ's. Then look into catalog mail-order companies such as Viking or Global. Finally, there is a developing marketplace in shopping over the Internet. Any of these large-volume, large-selection superstores should be able to offer significant discounts from retail shopping.

For my small office, I have not had to set foot in an office-supply store in years; my friendly UPS guy carries the load right to the door of my supply closet.

Here are some specific suggestions on major office purchases; the same advice applies to items you buy for your home office.

✓ Don't sit still for a bad chair.

✓ Buy the right desk for your task.

✓ Buy the right copier for home and small offices.

✓ Save money on copier and laser-printer toner and parts.

✓ Cut the chatter with a high-speed fax machine.

✓ Consider fax paper life and cost.

Don't Sit Still for a Bad Chair

We all know what we want in a chair: a comfortable place to sit and work. Unfortunately, for many of us, that's easier to describe than find.

The basic advice here is: Don't scrimp on quality. An uncomfortable chair will cost you in productivity, number of hours at work, and could even result in health problems.

Here is some advice from the experts on choosing a work chair:

• This is not a purchase that can be made on the basis of a picture in a catalog or specifications on a brochure. You've got to test it out.

• Buy from an outlet that has a liberal policy on returns and exchanges. Some catalog stores will send chairs in this way; be sure they will refund shipping costs in both directions if the chair proves to be inappropriate.

• Look for a good warranty and repair policy.

• Start by making sure the chair can be adjusted so that your feet rest firmly against the ground while your thighs are level on the seat. The chair should easily adjust in height to accommodate different users.

• There should be a firm support in the lumbar area in the small of your back. An even better feature is an adjustable lumbar support.

- The seat cushion should be rounded at the front to reduce pressure on the knees and hips. Even better is an adjustment that allows you to set the angle of the cushion; for most people the best position for the cushion is a slight downward slope so that the hips are elevated above the knees.

- Armrests, if included, should be padded and adjustable in height and should angle from front to back. They should be adjustable so that they can sit above the computer keyboard at desk surface; they should not force you to sit further back from the desk than is comfortable.

- The casters on the bottom of the chair should be selected with the floor surface in mind; soft rubber casters work better and do less damage on wooden and other hard floors, while hard casters are appropriate for carpeted surfaces.

Buy the Right Desk for Your Task

The next step in outfitting an office suite is to choose an appropriate working surface and short-term storage module, also known as a desk. Here are some pointers:

- Select the dealer on more than just price. Do they offer a decent warranty? Can they obtain replacement parts or accessories? Don't overlook used furniture dealers, either; many businesses lease equipment, and some good bargains are available in buying furniture turned back at the end of a lease.

- Choose the proper desk height for the task. A desk that is used for formal purposes and for handwritten work is usually set with a top surface 29 to 30 inches above the floor. A drawing table is sometimes a few inches higher, with an adjustable tilt. And a desk meant to be used with a computer is usually a few inches lower, or comes with an extendable keyboard drawer that sits a few inches below the desktop.

- Make certain that any keyboard drawer is wide and deep enough to accommodate the sort of keyboard you use; you should bring the keyboard, or at least its measurements with you to a furniture store. Pay attention, too, to a comfortable position for the computer mouse. The keyboard shelf should either be wide enough to allow it to sit alongside the keyboard, or there should be an extension tray for the mouse. The worst setup is one that places the mouse above and behind the keyboard on the desk surface; that is a prescription for arm, neck, and shoulder pain.

- A well-designed desk includes provisions for routing the half dozen or so wires that go to and from the computer. Some desks have holes in the top and back sides for the wires, while others include channels to hold cables.

- Consider the quality of construction of the desk. Better-quality furniture uses hardwood and is assembled with interlocking wooden surfaces; cheaper furniture uses plywood or particle board and is held together with staples. If it has drawers, this is a good place to look. Check the quality of the sliders and the hardware and see if they move in and out smoothly; if they are balky or misaligned with nothing in them, they will become only worse when they are full.

- The quality of steel desks is usually related to the thickness (the gauge) of steel used. Look for solid joints and roper alignments of sides and drawers.

Buy the Right Copier for Home and Small Offices

The so-called "paperless revolution" has bypassed most of the business world, and the photocopier has become an essential part of all offices. It is also increasingly used in home offices. Here are some buying tips:

- Start by determining the level of usage for the machine. Copiers are primarily mechanical devices, subject to wear and tear and paper jams and other problems.

    If you are basing your usage level on the previous machine in your home or office, be sure to increase it by a fairly substantial margin. The new machine is almost certain to have heavier use.

    Copier manufacturers rate their machines based on expected use. Leave room for growth in your business.

- The next consideration is speed, and here there are two numbers: time to first copy, and throughput of multiple copies. Most machines save power and protect mechanical parts by cycling down when they are not in use; in some homes and offices, the machine is turned off between uses. Either way, the copier will take from a few seconds to as much as a minute to warm up before making that first copy. Once everything is up to temperature, though, additional copies will cycle through much faster.

  Unless you are expecting to do a lot of major copying jobs, I wouldn't spend a lot of money to obtain a particularly speedy machine. Take your monthly newsletter job to a neighborhood speedy printer or office-supply store for those big jobs; they will be quicker and probably cost less in quantity than using your smaller machine.

- Similarly, think twice before you buy an expensive and sometimes balky feeder or document sorter unless you have regular need for copies of a large document. So, too, for other special features such as built-in staplers, two-sided printing, and capacity for unusual-sized paper.

- A good feature is an enlargement/reduction lens. This allows you to shrink oversize documents to standard paper sizes, or blow up sections of a document for display.

- But the most important feature of a copier is the service contract and/or warranty.

  A typical office copier is designed to have its major parts repaired or replaced by a technician. A basic office machine requires monthly checkups or service calls.

  Home units, which receive much lighter use, are designed differently: the major parts, including the drum and toner cartridge, are replaced with new equipment on a regular cycle. This makes copies more expensive than those done on a business machine, but usually results in a more trouble-free system.

  Devote your time to studying the maintenance and warranty policies of the dealer and manufacturer. Here's where it may make sense to pay a bit more to get better service.

  You should also make sure that you have a period of time to try out the machine before the sale is final. If the machine and the service you receive on it is not satisfactory during the trial period, why should you believe it will be to your liking once the machine is paid for or under long-term contract?

Save Money on Copier and Laser-Printer Toner and Parts

One unfortunate but common mistake for copier buyers is to concentrate on the machine and overlook the cost and convenience factor involved in keeping it supplied with toner and parts.

Copier and laser-printer toners are similar but not identical from manufacturer to manufacturer, and even between models from the same maker. In some machines, the toner helps lubricate the moving parts, while other systems require different temperatures to fuse the toner to the paper.

This does not mean you cannot find alternate and less expensive sources for toner. In fact, most copier and laser-printer makers purchase their supplies from outside companies. Just be sure that the product is certified for your make and model.

If you have any doubts about the reliability or compatibility of a supplier, try a sample unit before you make a large purchase. Be sure to compare toner cartridges or bottles of identical capacity or weight; if a third party sells replacement toner in smaller or larger containers be sure to figure that into your cost calculations.

In addition to new compatible cartridges, look into sources of recycled toner cartridges for copiers and laser printers. Manufacturers reuse the plastic case and some of the internal parts from used original cartridges and refill them with toner. Properly done, a recharged cartridge will work fine and do no harm to the machine. But beware of garage operations that do shoddy work or reuse a particular cartridge too many times. Buy from a reputable source and start out with orders of small quantities to test their quality.

Cut the Chatter with a High-Speed Fax Machine

You can save as much as 50 percent in telephone costs by buying a machine capable of transmitting and receiving at 14,400 bps (sometimes listed as 14.4 Kbps) instead of the more common 9,600 bps. But the savings will come only if you make a connection with another machine capable of 14.4 communications. And, you won't be able to link up at that speed if your phone line is weak.

The faster 14.4 machines are usually more advanced in other ways, including compression and error checking, than are older 9,600 devices.

Given a choice between a similar 9,600 or a 14,400 machine at the same price, go for the faster machine. If there is a price differential, consider how often you use the machine for sending; if you transmit dozens of faxes each week, the faster speed may be worth $25 or more per year over the life of the machine. (If you use the machine mostly to receive incoming calls, you needn't spend extra for higher speed unless you want to be kind to the people who send you faxes.)

Consider Fax Paper Life and Cost

The common thermal paper used by many fax machines will fade over time, especially if the pages are exposed to strong light or heat. If you receive faxed documents that you want to store in a file, you can purchase a machine that uses an ink jet to print on plain paper instead of on the lower-cost thermal-printing systems that require special fax paper. The ink-jet plain-paper machines are more expensive to purchase and slightly more expensive to use because you must replace ink cartridges and paper as needed.

A more expensive form of plain-paper fax machine is one that uses a laser-printer mechanism; the quality of faxes will be high, but the per-page cost of such a machine can easily be as much as 10 to 20 cents.

The alternate means to obtain faxes that can be filed is to use a photocopying machine to make copies.

36 Computers in the Home and Office

Personal computers have penetrated into nearly every business and into more than 40 percent of American households. Along the way they have changed the way we work, shop, do homework, and entertain ourselves. In 1997, more than ten million new PCs will be sold in this country. A large portion of the growth is being fueled by the burgeoning Internet, which has now entered into more than 35 percent of homes.

These are amazing numbers when you consider that the vast majority of owners of PCs are completely in the dark about how their machines work and what to do when something goes wrong—as it almost certainly will.

In this chapter we explore some repair and maintenance strategies, including ways to deal with hardware- and software-support desks. I also clue you into a way to save money by using software upgrades.

And then I explain some savvy strategies for choosing an Internet Service Provider. Finally, we guard against unwanted electrical and viral invasions of your machine.

✓ Know what to do when your computer won't compute.

✓ Learn how to get proper telephone support when you can't fix it yourself.

✓ Think carefully before you buy an extended PC warranty.

✓ Save money by using software upgrades.

✓ Choose an Internet Service Provider wisely.

✓ Take advantage of free E-mail service.

✓ Protect yourself against an unwanted power play.

✓ Post an electronic security guard for your computer.

Know What to Do When Your Computer Won't Compute

One of the real terrors of working in our computerized world is that sinking feeling when your computer suddenly won't start, or your printer won't print, or your modem won't do whatever it is that a modem does. All of a sudden, you realize two things: how dependent you have become on these modern contrivances and how utterly clueless you are about how they work and what to do when they won't compute.

The fact is that as computers have become more capable, they have also become infinitely more complex. There are so many combinations of hardware, software, and operating systems that it is all but impossible to automatically configure and install systems, no matter what Microsoft, Intel, and Apple may claim. You can come close, but the problems that are left unsolved are often the most difficult to solve.

The good news is that the computer industry has been pretty good about offering free telephone support for purchasers of hardware and software. Some companies will answer any question any time, while others have begun to put into place limits that are typically one year or 90 days. After the deadline passes, users can still purchase telephone consulting.

Before you call the store that sold you the computer, the mail-order company that shipped it, or the software maker, there are two important steps you can take by yourself.

1. When all else fails, read the manual. (And if the machine and software is working on some level, consult the extensive online help screens.) I say this with some authority and a sense of irony, as the author of a best-selling book called *Fix Your Own PC*.

This is not to say that instruction manuals are perfect, or even close. In fact, they are almost uniformly awful; if they were any good, there wouldn't be tens of millions of dollars in sales of computer titles at bookstores. It is also sometimes true, however, that the answer to your problem lies somewhere in the manual. Start there, and then be prepared to move on to more specialized searches for the truth.

2. Ask yourself what has changed since the last time your system was working properly. Did you add a new piece of software or hardware? Have you made changes to the operating system (Mac, DOS, Windows)?

   If you can identify a change, try undoing it to see if this fixes your problem. Be sure to keep close notes on anything you do so that you can undo your undo if need be. If you have a PC with Windows 95, here is a good reason to invest in a sophisticated "uninstaller" program. This software allows you to remove a program and restore all previous settings with the click of a button. The removal does not have to be permanent, either; most of these programs can put removed programs and settings into a temporary storage directory and put them back into place later.

Learn How to Get Proper Telephone Support When You Can't Fix It Yourself

Some telephone-support lines are so heavily used that callers can expect to routinely wait as much as an hour to get through. One company proudly introduced a "help line DJ" who attempted to entertain those waiting on line, including reports on expected waits for different types of problems.

In recent years, though, computer companies have used new technologies to deliver information in various automated ways: recorded tips available by telephone, "fax vaults" of information that can be requested by phone for transmission to your fax machine, and Internet Web sites crammed with information offered by the company and users.

Here are some savvy ways to obtain worthwhile support for computer problems:

- *Help diagnose the problem*. If the problem is intermittent, keep a pad by the keyboard and make notes anytime it recurs. Record details on error messages and program behavior. What were you asking the program to do when it misbehaved? What had you done beforehand in the same session? Were there any other pieces of software open or running when the problem occurred?

- *Be prepared to discuss recent changes to the system*. A good technical-support specialist will focus in on this question right away. What have you done to the computer—new hardware, new software, new settings to programs or the operating system—since the last time it worked.

- *Details, details*. Keep an up-to-date log of all your hardware and settings. Start with the basics—manufacturer, serial number, processor type and speed, amount and type of RAM, hard-drive maker and size, sound card, CD-ROM, and other internal devices such as modems. Now go into the your PC's setup screen (check your instruction manual for information on how to display it). Record all of the information you find there, including hard-drive type and settings.

   If you are using Microsoft's Windows 95 on a PC, print out the Device Manager report on your system, which includes a great deal of technical information you can use to help solve a problem or reconstruct your settings after a meltdown. (Go to Settings, then Control Panel, then System, and finally choose Print.)

   Move on to your software: Keep a list of all programs you use, including version numbers and serial numbers.

- *Look for an automated helper*. Before you join the line for a human helper, look for collections of FAQs (Frequently Asked Questions) and other sections of solutions to common problems on the manufacturer's Web page or from a faxback service. If your problem is related to installation or a hardware conflict, you may find that you are not alone.

   When you call into a technical-support line, you may be asked if you want to listen to a series of prerecorded problems and solutions based on common calls; go ahead and listen. You may find the solution, and in any case it won't add to your waiting time. In fact, some support lines are set up so that they move callers to a priority queue if they've already spent the time trying to solve a problem through automated responses.

- *Send an E-mail or fax to the support department.* It may take a few days before you get a response, but you won't have to spend the time and money on a phone call.

- *Post a question.* Go to an Internet newsgroup for an unofficial response from a fellow user, or use a manufacturer's own bulletin board system to see if they have a forum for their users.

- *Master the phone system.* Make notes when you use an automated technical-support system. If it requires a complicated set of button pushes to navigate from the opening greeting to the waiting line for a real human being, write down the sequence. The next time you call in, you can push 1-4-1-#-8-3 (or whatever the secret electronic pathway) and save a few moments of wait.

- *Take down names and numbers.* Find out the name of the person who is helping you and ask if there is a way to get back to them directly for follow-up calls. Ask also if there is a case number assigned to your call. Your goal is to avoid having to start at square one with each call you make.

- *Make them take down yours, too.* It's also valuable to give your name and phone number to the technician in case you get cut off.

- *Oh, them changes.* Keep your own notes on changes you have made to your system on the basis of suggestions by the technician. He or she may say, "Try changing the IRQ to 12," and if that doesn't work move on to something else. You're going to want to reset your system to its previous state unless you're looking forward to making a bad situation a whole lot worse.

- *Go up the ladder.* If you don't have confidence in the background or capability of the person who is supposed to help you, gently ask if there is someone else at the company who can help. If that doesn't work, ask a bit more firmly for a supervisor. If you're still at a dead end, or if the technician doesn't move you up the line, it's time to raise your sights. Call back to the company—this may be at a different phone number from the help desk—and ask to speak with customer service, or ask for the vice president of sales, or ask for the president of the company. It doesn't much matter whom you end up with: Your goal is to reach an executive on the sales side. Don't be unpleasant, but be firm about your needs and the fact that you don't feel you are receiving the help you should get. I have had entire computer systems replaced overnight when I made an end-run around the technician.

Think Carefully Before You Buy an Extended PC Warranty

If you buy your computer from an electronics retailer and some mail-order companies you are almost certain to be asked and perhaps pushed toward buying an extended warranty.

"This is an expensive piece of electronics with all sorts of things that can go wrong," the salesperson may say. "You don't want to be changing your own hard drive, do you?"

My usual response: "I thought you told me this was a good product?" And then I decline the offer. Here's why:

- First, you should include in your purchase decision an appraisal of the warranty offered by the maker. Major makers offer three to five years of coverage on the major hardware elements; that service may be offered at your home or office (on-site service is usually available only for the first year and may not be available in all parts of the country), or may require you to bring your machine in to a service depot or ship it to a central facility.

  Don't buy a machine whose maker will not stand behind it. If you have a choice between a machine with a short warranty and a machine that costs a bit more but offers a longer warranty, spend a bit more on the machine and skip the extended warranty pushed by the salesperson.

  Read the section on warranties in Chapter 2, Your Rights As a Buyer.

- Consider using a credit card that offers warranty extensions for certain products. The card may cover computers, or may cover computer components such as modems, hard disks, keyboards, monitors, and other peripherals.

- Understand that modern computer hardware is generally very reliable, and that failures—if they occur—tend to happen in the early days of use or at the end of the machine's life several years down the road.

- Consider how long you really expect to use the machine. The pace of change for PCs is so intense that a two-year-old machine is practically an antique.

- And finally, don't be unnecessarily terrified of making repairs to a computer. Almost every job, from installing memory to changing a hard drive to swapping a power supply requires nothing more than a screwdriver, half an hour, and a bit of attention to detail. Invest in a good hardware upgrade and repair book—I've written a few— and save yourself hundreds of dollars on fixing your own PC.

Save Money by Using Software Upgrades

A careful shopper may be able to save hundreds of dollars by buying outdated closeout software from some mail-order companies. Be sure that whatever version you buy is appropriate for your hardware and operating system; for example, if you are running Windows 95 on a PC you do not want to buy software for DOS or Windows 3.1.

Then, here is an even better deal: You may be able to immediately upgrade your outdated software to the current version of the program through special offers made by the maker of the software or by mail-order companies. Be sure that the total cost of the original software and the upgrade is less than the price for a fresh copy of the latest version.

Choose an Internet Service Provider Wisely

Okay, you're not the last person on earth to hook up to the Internet. But the end, give or take a few billion users, is in sight.

Here are some important tips to help you make an intelligent decision when going onto the Net.

First of all, it is important to understand the difference between an online service and an Internet Service Provider (ISP).

Online service providers actually predate the Internet; they were born as subscription-based libraries of information, games, and services. Even further back, some of these companies were born as computer timeshare operations, where corporate America could rent time and space on huge mainframe computers as they were needed.

Major online companies include America Online, CompuServe, and the Microsoft Network. Subscribers pay a monthly or hourly fee to explore the world created by the provider, participate in electronic "chat rooms," and send electronic mail.

In more recent times it has been impossible not to be aware of the spectacular growth of the Internet, which is at its heart an electronic superhighway that connects thousands of computers around the world. Major corporations, publishers and broadcasters, colleges and universities, government agencies, and millions of individuals have opened up roadside attractions along the electronic superhighway to hawk wares, entertain, and provide information to any and all comers.

The direct route to the net is to sign up with an Internet Service Provider, a company that accepts local telephone calls from computer modems and channels them onto a high-speed trunk line that connects to the Internet itself. When you use an ISP, your front page is usually one of the major "browsers" such as Netscape Navigator or Microsoft Internet Explorer.

The online services took a little while to see the writing on the wall, but eventually nearly all of them realized that most of the excitement was on the Internet and not in their proprietary offerings. And so, we now have a hybrid creature: the online service as an enhanced gateway to the Net. If you sign on to America Online or CompuServe, for example, you'll see that service's front page and you'll still have access to dozens of databases, chat rooms, and services available only to subscribers. But increasingly, many of the online service's subscribers are using their electronic connection to move directly onto the Internet, in most cases using a gateway from within America Online or CompuServe for that purpose.

The gateway services make it a bit easier to log onto the Internet, and in theory there are all sorts of extra services available—technical support, parental guidance monitors, and more.

But here come the problems: The online services have grown tremendously, and with that growth have come problems: difficulty in finding an available telephone connection and slow response once you do log on.

Sooner or later, serious users of the Internet should ask themselves whether they need to use an electronic handholder or whether they want to go directly onto the superhighway without having to board a tourist bus to get there.

Your options in looking for an ISP range from local mom-and-pop storefronts to midsized regional services to gigantic national providers related to carriers such as AT&T, Sprint, and MCI.

On the one hand, it is relatively easy to change from one ISP to another. However, you can open yourself up to a huge headache if you become a heavy user of E-mail if you change your electronic address.

Here are some hints on how to find the best ISP for you:

- Ask for local references. Talk to users in your area. Ask the following questions: Is the service reliable? Is it always possible to sign on, or are there times when you can count on a busy signal? What speed of modem connection is actually delivered? How good is the technical support?

- Ask for a free trial period. See what quality of technical assistance they provide in setting up your account. Try out the service during the times when you expect to use it most.

- Obtain a full list of access telephone numbers. Be sure that there are several in your local dialing area; your home phone bill can quickly jump into triple digits if you have to call long distance even within your state.

- Find out if the ISP has a toll-free phone number that you can use to check on your mail or log onto the Internet while you are traveling. Compare the per-minute price to the charge your long-distance carrier would charge for a credit-card call to your local area.

- Ask about the ratio of users to modems; don't expect one modem for each subscriber, but if the ratio is 10:1 or higher, your chances of making a connection go down, especially at busy times. (The busiest time of the day for most services is the afternoon and early evening, when students merge with the business world.)

- Call the service's technical-support line at a time when you are likely to be using the Internet. If you can't get through, or if you are put on hold for an unacceptable amount of time, you should consider taking your business elsewhere. An even better test is to come up with a technical question of your own about configuring your machine to use the Internet; see if the support person understands your question and gives you an answer you can understand.

Take Advantage of Free E-Mail Service

Nothing in life is truly free, but here's a way to get an electronic mail service without paying for it. It's called Juno, and it is an advertiser-supported service that allows you to send and receive text messages to anyone in the world with access to the Internet or online services such as AOL that give their users a gateway to the Internet.

It works like this: You'll dial into the Juno service from your computer (using one of 400 local phone numbers—if you live in a remote corner of the United States you will have to pay long-distance charges) and reach a screen with your messages listed. In the process you'll see some advertisements—no better or worse than putting up with commercials when you watch a movie or the ballgame on television.

You cannot use Juno to access the World Wide Web, or to send and receive computer files; it is just a messaging service. But it works fine for that purpose. One more limitation: As we go to press, the software is available only for Windows users, and not for DOS or Macintosh systems.

There are three ways to obtain a free account with Juno. One is to order a copy of the software from Juno, paying a shipping and handling fee ($8.82 as we go to press). Or you can obtain a free copy of the software by borrowing the program on disk from a friend or colleague using the service, or by using an Internet-capable computer and going to **http://www.juno.com**

Protect Yourself Against an Unwanted Power Play

Think of a surge suppressor as a fuel filter for your computer and other expensive electronic devices; it's also very inexpensive insurance against a not-uncommon threat.

We tend to take for granted the electrical power coming from wall outlets in our homes and offices. But in fact, in most localities the voltage regularly rises and falls within a range of 10 to 20 volts due to loads and atmospheric conditions. Nearly every modern computer and electronic device can adjust for power fluctuations within that range.

But what happens if lightning strikes a power line, or a transformer in the distribution system fails? In that situation, a momentary spike or surge of power of several hundred or several thousand volts can move down the line and into anything plugged into a house or office current. The device does not even have to be turned on, by the way.

And the threat is not limited to electrical lines, but also includes telephone cable and in certain circumstances network cabling within an office.

A true story: I used to live in a rural area of upstate New York where all of the power and telephone lines were mounted on poles. One August afternoon we sat in the relative safety of the rec room watching a violent thunderstorm roll through the valley. Suddenly there was a flash of light a few hundred feet away and an almost immediate clap of thunder and, strangely, a strangled chirp from the telephone. Something drew me to my office in the den, and there I encountered a chilling sight: the blown-apart pieces of my computer modem and a cloud of brown smoke. The electrical spike had traveled down the phone line and into the house, meeting and destroying an unprotected modem and continuing from there into my computer where it also destroyed a serial communications card. Luckily it stopped there, just short of melting down my PC itself.

I used the first dollars from the insurance settlement to purchase a surge protector that also protects incoming telephone lines.

Here's how to buy a surge protector:

- First, don't scrimp to save a few dollars. Look for a solidly constructed device with adequate specifications. And you might also look for a protector with a guarantee or insurance policy that promises to pay for losses if the suppressor does not protect your equipment properly.

- Look for a device that meets the UL 1449 standard. This is the starting point for an adequate suppressor; you should also see a voltage listing for the 1449 standard, indicating the average voltage the unit will allow through before shutting down or sacrificing itself to protect your more expensive computer or big-screen television. A rating of 330 volts (also expressed as .33 kV) is acceptable; avoid cheaper units that allow more power to leak through.

- The cheapest units will have to be replaced after sustaining a surge; one step better are devices with a replaceable fuse. The most sophisticated suppressors have resettable circuit breakers.

- Be sure to match the amperage capacity of the suppressor to the devices that will be plugged into it. Don't overload a suppressor or the circuit into which it is plugged. (Laser printers, photocopiers, and large monitors and color televisions are the biggest power draws in most homes and offices; in most cases they should be plugged into separate circuits.)

Surge protectors will not guard against the loss of data on your system if they shut the PC down because of overvoltage or undervoltage. If you are concerned about loss of your business plan, the Great American Novel, or other data, consider purchase of an Uninterruptible Power Supply, which is an electronic switching device coupled with a large rechargeable battery; a UPS kicks in if power fails or drops below an acceptable level in a brownout. Buy a UPS with sufficient power to allow you to make an orderly shutdown of your system; basic systems are not intended to allow you to operate your system for an extended period of time.

Post an Electronic Security Guard for Your Computer

Sadly, some of the best technical minds around the world devote their energies to finding ways to use computers to cause trouble. They have created a world of programs called viruses that can attach themselves to other pieces of software and travel from disk to disk or over the Internet and take over your computer; in the benign version they may produce a message on your screen and then go away, while the most nasty of the viruses can take over your operating system and erase or corrupt the files stored on your hard drive.

Another threat comes from commerce over the Internet. There are creeps lurking on the wires who are hoping to steal your account name and password. They may be after your access to the Internet, or they may want to try to purchase products using your credit-card information.

Here are some ways to protect yourself against high-tech breaking and entering on your personal computer system. (If you have a problem at work, notify your network administrator or MIS professional.)

- Be very careful with your passwords. The best procedure is to not write down your passwords, or at the least to not write them down in a location anywhere near your computer. Some users maintain a log of passwords that is kept in a locked safe. Don't store them in a file in the computer; if the PC is stolen, so will be your secrets.

- Choose your passwords carefully and change them every few months. Don't be so obvious as to use your name, nickname, telephone number, or other words that a clever thief or saboteur could guess. On my system, I use a word and number combination that means nothing to anyone but me, and I change it every few months. Example: the name of an old friend and the middle two digits of your social-security number. These are both easy to remember, but unlikely to be guessed.

- Assign passwords to partitions on a computer, or to highly sensitive documents (most word processors permit you to protect files in this manner). This is an especially important protection for laptop and portable computers that are liable to be stolen or lost.

- Purchase and use a virus-protection package, keeping it updated with new virus descriptions, which are usually available monthly or quarterly. Be especially careful to scan any floppy disk you introduce into your system before you take any programs from the disk; under no circumstances should you boot your PC from an untested floppy disk.

  You should also scan any files downloaded from the Internet or from an online service such as America Online or CompuServe before they are run for the first time.

SECTION XII

fraud

37 Guarding Against Rip-offs Old and New

Fraud is the dark underbelly of commerce, a whole industry of people who are constantly looking for ways to steal your money without a gun. Savvy consumers learn how to spot someone trying to rob them of their hard-earned and well-saved money.

Tip Number One: If it sounds too good to be true, it almost certainly is.

Tip Number Two: Be wary if someone is putting a tremendous amount of pressure on you to make a decision. If you act in haste, you may end up with a great deal of time to regret in leisure.

Here are some tips to spot phone and online swindles and some suggestions about avoiding phony charities and other fraudulent appeals.

- ✓ Know the tip-offs to phone fraud.
- ✓ Know your rights as a consumer when a telemarketer calls.
- ✓ Check out the companies that try to sell to you.
- ✓ Know what to do with unordered merchandise.
- ✓ Byte back at online scams.
- ✓ File online fraud complaints online.
- ✓ Research online merchants with the online Better Business Bureau.
- ✓ Beware of an old favorite: pyramid schemes.
- ✓ Defend against automatic debit scams.

✓ Guard against phony charities.

✓ Know how to research a charity.

✓ Don't dial that number! Know about reverse-charge phone numbers.

✓ Block those numbers!

✓ Learn to recognize when an 800 phone number is not free.

✓ Watch out for unsolicited collect calls.

✓ Still more: recognize offshore telephone scammers.

✓ Call in the Feds for help on telecommunications scams.

✓ Guard against advance-fee loan scams.

✓ If you don't know much about art, buy what you like.

✓ Consider nothing sacred: Avoid Yellow Pages fraud.

Know the Tip-offs to Phone Fraud

Here are some tip-offs to crooked telemarketers, especially those that prey on older persons:

- They pressure you to act "now" before the offer expires. While it is not unusual for a special offer to be valid for only a particular period of time, it is not standard business practice to push for a decision immediately.

- They offer a "free" gift or vacation, but demand a handling or shipping charge. Be especially wary if you are unable to obtain details of the prize before having to pay the charge.

- There is a request for your bank-account number. There are few good reasons for such an inquiry. Other tip-offs include an offer to send a courier right away to pick up cash or a check.

- They give you a promise that there is no reason to check out the offer with an accountant, the Better Business Bureau, a friend or family member, a lawyer, or the police. If anyone told me that, I'd either walk away from a deal quickly or call everyone on that list plus a few others.

- They claim that the offer is "no risk." There's a risk to just about every transaction, especially to offers that claim total safety.

Know Your Rights As a Consumer When a Telemarketer Calls

Here are your rights as a consumer, as defined by Federal Trade Commission regulations and other laws:

- A telemarketer cannot call you outside the hours of 8 A.M. and 9 P.M. unless you have given the caller permission to do so.
- A company cannot call you again if you have directly asked them to stop calling. Keep records of any such request.
- If the telemarketer is using a prize as a come-on, he or she must tell you that no purchase or payment is necessary to enter or win.
- Telemarketers must not misrepresent any information, including facts about their goods or services, the risk or liquidity of an investment, or the nature of a prize.
- You must be advised of any restrictions on obtaining goods and services, and if a sale is final or nonrefundable.
- It is illegal for a telemarketer to withdraw money from your checking account without your express, verifiable authorization.

As always, there are some exceptions. If you place the call to a marketer of products or services—other than financial services or investment companies—you give up some of your rights.

Check Out the Companies That Try to Sell to You

Before you spend your hard-earned money, spend a bit of time checking out the company.

If you are approached by a door-to-door salesperson with an unusual pitch, call your local police department to see if there are any current complaints. Check, too, with the Better Business Bureau.

You can also call organizations, including:

- The National Fraud Information Center at (800) 876-7060; the NFIC also maintains a page on the Internet at **http://www.fraud.org**
- Call For Action, Inc., in Washington, DC, at (202) 537-0585.

Know What to Do with Unordered Merchandise

When you receive something you did not order, request, or allow to be sent to you on consignment, you can consider it a free gift.

You have no legal obligation to do anything, but some experts advise you to write the seller a letter stating that you never ordered the item and, therefore, have a legal right to keep it for free. According to the Federal Trade Commission, such a letter will help you establish that you never ordered the merchandise and may discourage the seller from sending you repeated bills or dunning notices. You may want to send your letter by certified mail and keep the return receipt and a copy of the letter. This will help you to establish later, if necessary, that you did not order the merchandise.

All that said, you should be careful to avoid unintentionally giving a marketer permission to send you something . . . and a bill. Read the fine print carefully when participating in a sweepstakes or ordering "trial" or "free" merchandise. You may be joining a "club," with regular purchasing or notification obligations.

Another example of this sort of marketing is a "negative option" plan such as those offered by many book and record clubs. Under this perfectly legal but somewhat annoying scheme, you will be sent merchandise unless you instruct the seller to stop.

If you receive bills or dunning notices for unordered merchandise, write a letter to the company stating that you never ordered the item and you therefore have a legal right to keep the merchandise for free. If you choose, you can offer to return the merchandise provided the seller pays for postage and handling. Give the seller a specific and reasonable amount of time in which to pick up the merchandise or arrange to have it returned at no expense to you. Inform the seller that after the specified time period has passed, you reserve the right to keep the merchandise or to dispose of it as you wish.

Free samples that are clearly and plainly marked as such, and merchandise mailed by charitable organizations asking for contributions may be sent legally without an order from you. In either case, you may keep such shipments as free gifts.

Byte Back at Online Scams

New media, old scams: That's the verdict from law-enforcement agencies about a spate of online and Internet fraud schemes. Con artists have moved on from printed, door-to-door, mail, and telephone rip-offs to electronic fraud that in some cases can be the most difficult to trace and police.

In general, remember what most victims of fraud generally forget: If an offer sounds too good to be true, it almost always is.

Among the schemes are ploys to obtain your credit-card number or checking-account information to bill you for misrepresented items or merchandise you didn't request. Watch out, too, for fraudulent "business opportunity" pitches including work-at-home plans or investment schemes, especially ones for exotic markets such as ostrich farming or wireless-communications licenses.

Make sure your children and inexperienced family members using your computer know not to provide personal information, passwords, or credit-card numbers to anyone they meet online.

Watch out, too, for "infomercials" that can creep into what otherwise seem to be noncommercial Web pages or chat rooms. If someone makes a claim about a product or an investment, ask yourself: What is that person's self-interest?

If you have questions about whether an investment salesperson is licensed or an offered security is registered, contact the Office of Consumer Affairs of the Securities and Exchange Commission at (202) 942-7040.

Watch out for high-tech versions of the old pyramid-marketing scheme. These deals promise to pay participants based on income brought in by future members. It may take the form of a fantastic investment opportunity that pays well above market rates, or a sales organization that relies on "associates" to sell to others in the chain.

File Online Fraud Complaints Online

The Securities and Exchange Commission has established an online Enforcement Complaint Center, which can accept electronic reports of possible securities fraud.

Connect to: **http://www.sec.gov/enforce/comctr.htm**

Research Online Merchants with the Online Better Business Bureau

The Council of Better Business Bureaus has announced an online "seal-of-approval" system to help cyber-shoppers identify legitimate vendors.

In order to display a **BBB** seal on its site, a company must be in business more than six months, have no unanswered complaints at the BBB, provide the BBB with substantial information regarding company ownership, management, and previous business records; provide a street address and phone number (which will be verified by a visit from an official of the BBB); agree to handle complaints online; and agree to binding arbitration by the BBB if a customer dispute can't be resolved by the company's existing customer-service program.

You will also be able to click on the seal within a vendor's site and link to a report on the company at the BBB's Web site.

You can find out more about the BBB program and member companies at: **http://www.bbbonline.org/**

Beware of an Old Favorite: Pyramid Scheme

One of the oldest scams, the pyramid scheme, is alive and well and expanding. It has nearly toppled Eastern European governments, spread onto the Internet, and generally recast itself into a thousand variations of the same old song.

Pyramid schemes, also known as multilevel, downline, network, or matrix marketing, typically promise that if you sign up as a distributor, you will receive commissions from your own sale of goods or services as well as from sales by other people you recruit to join the distributors.

Why is pyramiding prohibited by most states and in many federal regulations? Because plans that pay commissions for recruiting new distributors inevitably collapse when no new distributors can be recruited. And when a plan collapses, most people with the possible exception of those at the top of the pyramid lose their investment.

In 1996, federal, state, and local law-enforcement agencies conducted a one-day sweep of the Internet and turned up about 500 pyramid schemes aimed at consumers or investors.

Defend Against Automatic Debit Scams

Don't give out your checking-account number over the telephone or in writing unless you understand why you are being asked for the information and agree to its use.

An illegitimate telemarketing operation can use the bank-account data to generate a "demand draft," which is processed like a check to withdraw money from your account; your signature is not required. According to federal law, a business must have your permission to do so, but you may end up giving that permission without realizing it. Or it may be a case of out-and-out fraud, and the company may be gone before you receive your bank statement.

The law requires the telemarketer to have your express permission to debit your account in writing, in a tape recording that includes your permission, or by means of a written confirmation that is sent to you before your account is debited. It is the tape recording that may cause problems for some; an artful telemarketer may be able to work the legalities into part of his spiel and obtain your permission without your realizing exactly what you have agreed to. Be wary if a telemarketer mentions (as he or she must) that the phone call is being tape recorded.

If you believe you have been a victim of fraud, contact your bank immediately and inform an officer that you did not authorize the debit and that you want to prevent further debiting. You also should contact your state's attorney general.

Guard Against Phony Charities

Giving to a charity is a noble thing, but less than noble is the fact that perhaps as much as 10 percent of the $143 billion Americans gave to charities in 1995 may have been lost to fraud. Beyond that, many tens of billions of dollars were spent not on the causes behind a charity but instead on the machinery of fund-raising.

Here's a basic tip on giving to charities: Unless you know the organization and understand how much of your money goes directly to its activities, you should treat any appeal for a contribution as you would any other consumer or business purchase.

Here are some important tips:

- Ask if the caller or visitor is a paid fund-raiser and what percentage of your donation the fund-raising group will keep. If you don't like, or don't trust, the answer you are given you might want to make other use of your money.

    Realize that any appeal that includes a "free" gift for your contribution is using your own money to buy something that will be given back to you.

- If the caller refuses to give specifics, including information about the charity he or she claims to represent, report the call to your state's attorney general and the local police.

    If the solicitor names a charity but you have doubts about the pitch, contact the charity directly and ask if the solicitation is legitimate.

- Don't make a major contribution on the basis of an oral presentation. Ask for something in writing, including a discussion of the purpose of the charity and how your money will be used. Seek proof of a group's tax situation.

- Understand the difference between "tax exempt" and "tax deductible."

    Tax exempt means the organization doesn't have to pay taxes, which is fine for them but doesn't necessarily do anything for you.

    Tax deductible means the organization has passed muster with the Internal Revenue Service, and you can deduct contributions on your federal income-tax return. If you plan to declare your contribution on your tax form, ask for a receipt with the amount of contribution and a statement that the donation is tax deductible.

Watch out for meaningless information such as the fact that an organization has a "Tax I.D. Number." All organizations have such a number on file with the IRS; it has nothing to do with a group's nonprofit status.

- Hang up or close the door on any high-pressure appeal. If your money is good today, it'll be good tomorrow. A tip-off to a fly-by-night solicitation is an offer to send a courier to pick up your money right away.

  Hang up or close the door and then call the police if you are threatened in any way.

Know How to Research a Charity

To find out information about a charity asking for a contribution, do some research on the group. In most states, charities are required to register with the state's attorney general or another agency. Ask the fund-raiser for information on his or her file with the state.

Ask how much of money raised goes to overhead for fund-raising. Some charities give more than half of the money they receive back to companies who collect the funds; you may want to make contributions to agencies that can use all of your dollars for the cause you want to support.

Here are some national organizations you can contact to find out about charitable groups:

> American Institute of Philanthropy, 4579 Laclede Avenue, Suite 136, St. Louis, MO 63108-2103, or call (314) 454-3040.

> National Charities Information Bureau, 19 Union Square West, 6th Floor, New York, NY 10003-3395, or call (212) 929-6300.

> Philanthropic Advisory Service Council of Better Business Bureaus, 4200 Wilson Boulevard, Suite 800, Arlington, VA 22203-1838, or call (703) 276-0100.

You can also check with the National Fraud Information Center (NFIC), a project of the National Consumers League. Call (800) 876-7060.

Don't Dial That Number! Know About Reverse-Charge Phone Numbers

Dialer beware: There is a burgeoning market in sneaky charges to your phone bill. Some are more obvious than others; presumably by now every phone user knows that they're going to be charged—a lot—for the pleasure of dialing a 900 number to some overhyped undertalented singer's "psychic hotline."

But did you also know that there are several other types of phone numbers that apply per-minute charges to incoming calls. They are:

- 550-XXXX. Group conversation lines (also called chat lines).
- 554-XXXX. Adult information services.
- 920-XXXX. General business applications and information services.
- 940-XXXX. Adult programs (prerecorded).
- 976-XXXX. General-information programs (prerecorded).

Block Those Numbers!

Here are some important hints for savvy phone consumers. First, here's what your phone company is supposed to do for you:

- Most companies are required to offer Selective Blocking Service, or some other similar program, to allow residential and business customers to bar dialing of extra-charge numbers.

  You may find comprehensive blocking for 550, 554, 920, 940, 976, and 1-900 services as well as partial blocking to 550, 554, 940, and 1-900 numbers.

  Call your phone company to find out your options.

Here's what the FTC requires 900-number services to provide callers:

- Disclosure about the cost of the per-minute or flat-fee cost for calls in any advertisement, plus any other fees that might be applied. If the length of the program is known in advance, the ad also must state the total cost of the complete program. This information is not supposed to be hidden in tiny print, either; FTC regulations decree that the cost of the call must be laid out in type at least half the size of the telephone number.

- An introductory message when a call is first answered that reiterates the cost for a call and gives the caller a three-second chance to hang up before the billing is imposed.

- The message must also warn that callers under the age of 18 must seek parental permission before going forward.

- The cost of any other 900 number to which the caller may be transferred. (This is intended to plug a particularly sneaky practice that can stack charge upon charge without the caller's awareness.)

- Procedures to resolve disputes on billing. Billing statements must include a local or toll-free number consumers can call with questions about pay-per-call charges.

  There are, however, a few exceptions to the FTC's rule. First, the rule applies only to calls that are charged to your phone bill. If the call is billed to your credit card, you have fewer protections, although you can still dispute charges under the Fair Credit Billing Act.

  And, you give up most of your rights if you enter into a contractual agreement with an information service. If you are asked to sign a contract read it carefully; be wary of any service that asks you to agree to a contract that is read to you over the phone.

- If you find an error on your phone bill, consult the instructions supplied with the statement. In most cases, your local or long-distance telephone company will handle a dispute on behalf of services that use it as a billing service; in some cases, though, you may be referred to the 900-number company or a third party.

  In any case, you must file your dispute within 60 days after the statement containing the error was sent. The company must acknowledge your notice in writing within 40 days or resolve the dispute by that time.

Within two billing cycles, but no longer than 90 days, the company must correct the billing error and notify you of the correction, or inform you in writing of its reasons for not correcting the error.

The company cannot charge you for investigating a dispute, and the company cannot make an attempt to collect the outstanding balance until it has responded to your letter.

- Be aware that some telemarketers target children. Among industries doing this are "hint" lines for video games.

  Under FTC rules, companies cannot advertise or direct pay-per-call services to children under 12 unless they are educational services dedicated to areas of school study. If the ad is directed to consumers under the age of 18, it must state that parental permission is required to make the call.

- Watch out for sweepstakes tied to calling 900 numbers. This amounts to a lottery, with the cost of your call being the price of admission.

  The FTC requires ads for sweepstakes to state the odds of winning (or how odds will be calculated). And the ad or phone message must inform you of an alternate, free way to enter the sweepstakes.

Learn to Recognize When an 800 Phone Number Is Not Free

We have all been well-trained to think of 800 (and the newer round of 888 numbers) as being free to the caller, and most of them are. However, a small group of businesses—some legitimate and others less so—have found ways to charge for calls placed to "toll-free" numbers.

Companies offering audio entertainment or information services may charge for calls to 800, 888, and other toll-free numbers if they ask you to pay with a credit card or make billing arrangements with you before they provide the service. If you don't use a credit card, FTC regulations say companies must also provide you with a security device, such as a personal identification number (PIN), to prevent other people from using your phone to charge calls to these services.

Also, if you dial an 800 or other toll-free number, the company is prohibited from automatically connecting you to a 900-number service and from calling you back collect. However, the law allows a company to promote a 900-number service during the 800-number call, as long as you would have to hang up and dial the 900 number to reach the service.

Examine your phone bill each month for any charges that list an 800 or 888 number.

Watch Out for Unsolicited Collect Calls

Every time federal watchdogs outlaw a shady practice by telephone-scam artists, they seem to find a new way to cheat unwary consumers out of their money.

One especially sneaky action is placing collect return calls to people who dial "free" 800 numbers.

Under recent Federal Communications Commission regulations, pay-per-call services cannot make collect calls to you if the charge would be more than, or in addition to, the regular long-distance charge for the call. And in any case, you cannot be charged for the call unless you have clearly indicated that you accept the charge

Still More: Recognize Offshore Telephone Scammers

Okay, so you've schooled yourself not to dial 900 long distance or 976 numbers.

But watch out: the phone scammers have other ways of picking your pocket. Here are some hints:

- Watch out for sneaky offshore operators. Some of them lure callers into placing international calls to countries that allow businesses to soak callers with expensive pay-per-call charges without having to abide by U.S. Federal Trade Commission or Federal Communications Commission rules.

  Among principal offenders here are "sex lines" that promise live conversations or computer downloads to callers.

You may be tipped off to the fact that you are calling an international destination by the fact that you have to dial "011" before the area code. But there are some locations near to the United States, including the Caribbean Basin, where you can dial directly with what seems like a domestic area code. For example, the area code 809 serves the Dominican Republic and other Caribbean islands. If you dial this area code, you'll be charged international long-distance rates.

Some callers might even mistakenly believe that 809 is part of the 800 toll-free system, an assumption that some scam artists do not attempt to clear up.

- Realize that, for the most part, each nation can set its own telephone rate, without a limit to the per-minute charge. Companies operating in some countries receive back from their local phone utility a portion of the international long-distance charge; the more often you call, and the longer you stay on the line, the more they profit.

  Here are some numbers to put on your danger list:

  - 246 (Barbados)
  - 284 (British Virgin Islands)
  - 345 (Cayman Islands)
  - 447 (Grenada)
  - 664 (Montserrat)
  - 758 (St. Lucia)
  - 784 (St. Vincent/Grenadines)
  - 809 (Dominican Republic and other Caribbean Islands)
  - 868 (Trinidad and Tobago)
  - 869 (St. Kitts and Nevis)
  - 876 (Jamaica)

  Watch out for these come-ons:

  - An "urgent" message left on your answering or facsimile machine or an E-mail, asking you to call an unfamiliar number. The message may sound like an ordinary business issue, or may claim that you have won a prize. In some particularly odious instances, the message may state, or imply, that a family member has been injured or hospitalized.

♦ Watch out for ads for information or entertainment services that try to mislead by trumpeting that the number is "not a 900 number." That may be true, but the international rates that do apply are likely to be much higher.

Call in the Feds for Help on Telecommunications Scams

The Federal Communications Commission's National Call Center answers consumer questions on communications law and policy. Call (888) 225-5322.

Guard Against Advance-Fee Loan Scams

There are few guarantees in life, especially when it comes to consumer and small-business loans.

Watch out for come-ons for "advance-fee" or "guaranteed" loans, which are often a scam and in all cases are against the law. These ads claim they can guarantee a loan if you pay an advance fee, typically a few hundred dollars but sometimes much more.

One tip-off: delivery of come-ons and paperwork by private courier systems, which allows the company to avoid facing fraud charges by the U.S. Postal Service.

So-called guaranteed loans are not the same as the ubiquitous "preapproved credit offers" from credit-card companies, mortgage brokers, and other financial institutions. There are no up-front fees attached to those offers and, anyway, the fact that you are preapproved does not mean that you will actually receive the credit if the lender doesn't like the information you provide on an application form for the "preapproved" loan.

Here are some important hints for borrowers:

• Never give your credit-card account number, bank-account information, or social-security number over the telephone unless there is a reason to do so and you are familiar with the company.

- Relatively few lenders ask for an application fee for a loan, although you may be asked to pay for some specific services such as a credit report or appraisal. Be sure the fees are reasonable.

If You Don't Know Much About Art, Buy What You Like

If you don't know much about art but you know what you like, buy what you like . . . but don't try to make an investment-grade purchase without independent, professional advice.

The art world is filled with counterfeits and unauthorized reproduction. If you are considering purchase of a print, ask for specific information about the piece, including the edition size, the year of publication, the name of the printer or publisher, and the print medium (such as lithograph, etching, silkscreen, or woodcut). Some states (including Arkansas, California, Georgia, Hawaii, Illinois, Maryland, Michigan, Minnesota, New York, Oregon, South Carolina, and Wisconsin) have disclosure laws that require the dealer to give you such information.

Then consult an art appraiser or museum curator of your choice—not someone recommended by the seller. Make any deal conditioned on the appraisal of the piece, with the promise of a full refund if the work is judged to be misrepresented.

You should be highly skeptical of any "certificates of authenticity" or any other claims made by sellers; on the other hand, you should also stay away from any dealer who refuses to put any claims in writing. These give you a legal standing if you later need to go to the courts to try to get your money back.

Consider Nothing Sacred: Avoid Yellow Pages Fraud

Be sure you know what you are buying if you sign up for an ad or special listing in the Yellow Pages.

The term Yellow Pages and the "walking-fingers" logo are not protected by federal copyright or trademark registration, and there can be many versions of the same book in your area. You'll want to know exactly who is behind the book and how well they distribute the publication.

And law-enforcement agencies report the existence of a not-uncommon scheme in which businesses receive an invoice for their listing in the Yellow Pages that may appear to be a renewal of an existing ad but actually represents an unsolicited new entry in another telephone directory.

If the letter is actually a solicitation, it should bear warning language mandated by the U.S. Postal Service, stating: "This is not a bill. This is a solicitation. You are under no obligation to pay the amount stated above unless you accept this offer." Even if it doesn't include the warning, be sure you know whom you are dealing with when you pay a bill.

Lifestyles

Chapter

38 Helping Hands

What do lawyers, nursing homes, and child care have in common? To my way of thinking, they are all necessary evils of our modern society.

Not that all lawyers, nursing-home providers, or child-care providers are evil. In fact, most are well-meaning folk, offering services that are important in our increasingly complex lives. Women want to work outside the home but need someone to watch the children. Our parents are living longer lives, and there is no one at home to take care of them if they are infirm. And lawyers . . . well, they're there to help untangle us from the webs we weave around ourselves.

✓ How do you choose a good lawyer?

✓ What is legal assistance going to cost you?

✓ How do you pursue a legal malpractice case against your attorney?

✓ How do you choose the proper retirement home for an elderly or infirm family member?

✓ How do you pay for a nursing home or other specialized care?

✓ How do you choose the right child care?

How Do You Choose a Good Lawyer?

Two questions there, actually. First you need to find a group of appropriate lawyers for the particular assignment you have in mind, and then you want to find the good one among them. (I have resisted the urge to let loose with a spate of lawyer jokes . . . although I've got a ton of them. Okay, you've convinced me. Q: What's the difference between a dead skunk and a dead lawyer in the middle of the road? A: Skid marks. In front of the skunk.) Now back to the real question of the moment.

It doesn't make sense to spend $1,000 to collect a $100 bad debt, and it is equally foolish to pay any money at all to an attorney who has no expertise and experience on the sort of legal issue you seek to solve. Don't hire a real-estate attorney for a criminal defense, or the other way around.

For most personal and business matters, it makes sense to begin your search for an attorney by asking for references from others who have had similar cases or situations. Ask among your friends, business acquaintances, and members of any civic groups to which you may belong.

Another source of information—worth whatever you think—is a Lawyer Referral Service offered by many state bar associations. Some plans even include a free or reduced-rate consultation. Some states also offer special programs for senior citizens as well as low-income legal-assistance programs; check with the bar association for information.

You can do some of your own basic research by consulting the Martindale-Hubbell Law Directory, available at most public libraries or through state bar associations. You'll find biographical information about many lawyers and information about the areas of specialization for law firms.

Once you have found an attorney (or better, two or three) you think is appropriate, the best first step is to schedule a preliminary consultation. Most lawyers will give you a free or low-cost short audience to discuss your case and their experience and projected charges. Prepare a simple summary of the nature of the case and the sort of backup material you have for your position. Ask about fees, about whether the attorney himself or herself will be doing the work or whether a clerk or assistant will be involved, and gauge your level of comfort and confidence with the attorney; it's very easy to change lawyers before work is begun and much more difficult afterwards.

What Is Legal Assistance Going to Cost You?

Most likely, more than you expect or want to pay. But you can help yourself a great deal by understanding the ways in which legal fees are calculated and by taking an active stance to protect your own interests.

Ask for a full disclosure of fees and expenses before work is begun. Get it in writing if possible—ask for a letter spelling out the arrangement. Or, make careful, dated notes on what you are told. You might even want to incorporate what you have been told into a letter and send it to the attorney to engage his or her services.

A legal fee is usually based on the following elements:

- Time and labor. The more unusual the case or the difficulty involved in researching it or presenting it, the more hours will accrue. Most law firms in a particular area and of a particular size will charge about the same for similar cases; a small one-person storefront office may have a lower hourly rate than one that has to pay for five floors in a downtown skyscraper. The more complex or specialized cases are usually given to the most experienced or well-connected attorneys, and they generally charge higher hourly rates than others.

- The likelihood that the acceptance of your case will cause conflicts of interest by your attorney. If the lawyer is going to have to turn down work from another client because he or she is representing you, this may result in a higher fee. Be sure to inquire about such a situation.

- The amount of damages you are likely to collect; a law firm is much more interested in a bigger case than in a small one because they are likely to be able to bill more hours or collect a higher contingency fee.

The client is also responsible for most expenses including telephone calls, postage, court fees, and research costs. Some law firms are more insistent in this area than others; a high-tone Boston firm that represented me once charged for every last staple, photocopy, and telephone call. When the lawyer called to update me on the progress, I used to cringe when he'd ask about the weather or my latest travel book; all

I could think about was $3 a minute . . . a nickel a second . . . for the call and his time. Good attorney, but I kept social niceties to a minimum.

One way to save on your legal bill is to do as much organizing of documentation and notes as you can; I prepared a folder of correspondence, contracts, and a written timeline of events and conversations. Lay it all out to give your representative as much information up front as possible. (Have a quick conversation with your attorney, though, about how to present your notes in a way that they are considered confidential for the purposes of the case; otherwise your notes could be subpoenaed.)

Next, keep a close eye on bills as they are presented and don't be shy about asking for detailed explanations of any items. Where appropriate, request copies of letters and documents prepared on your behalf. (You may be billed for photocopying and postage, but at least you'll have some way to gauge the material work performed on your behalf.)

There are four common types of fee arrangements; in some situations there may be a combination of arrangements.

1. *Specific job.* For common legal tasks such as drawing up a will, settling a real-estate transaction, or some simple divorce cases, a lawyer may have a set fee. Be sure to obtain a written statement of the charges; you'll also be responsible for court costs and documented expenses.

2. *Hourly rate.* In some ways this is the simplest arrangement; you'll be quoted an hourly rate for all work performed on your behalf. Don't be surprised to find that every 60-second phone call or five-minute consultation with a colleague in the coffee shop will appear on the bill. Be sure you know the hourly rate and ask for an estimate of the number of hours the lawyer expects to bill.

3. *Retainer.* This amounts to a down payment toward future fees; bills are deducted from the remaining balance of the retainer. Jobs can be billed against the retainer at an hourly rate or a specific job basis. In some instances, a law firm may bill at a lower hourly rate to clients who maintain a retainer with them.

4. *Contingent fee.* Here the attorney collects a fee only if a case is settled or successfully argued in court; the fee comes from a percentage of any award. Contingent arrangements are often used in accident and negligence cases. In general, the willingness of a lawyer to take on a case with a contingent fee means he or she believes you

have a good chance of winning; it also puts the pressure on the lawyer to do everything reasonably possible to collect a fee. On the other hand, a lawyer in a contingency-fee case may be more willing to accept an out-of-court settlement at a lower amount because that is certain money. The client is also usually responsible for payment of expenses and court fees whether the case is won or lost.

How Do You Pursue a Legal Malpractice Case Against Your Attorney?

To win a malpractice suit you'll have to prove that your attorney made a significant mistake or handled the case in a way that other reasonable lawyers would find improper or incompetent. There's obviously a lot of room for subjective judgment, made all the more difficult by the fact that you'll be stirring up an internal battle among some already prickly characters.

The really bad news is that you are asking a lawyer to sue another member of the club, someone he or she may meet again in another professional or social situation. You'll have to find an attorney either of such high standing in the profession that he or she can afford to take on one of his or her own, or one who is so far outside the mainstream that issues of status do not matter.

The basic elements of a malpractice claim must include four elements:

1. *A duty to perform.* You must establish that you had a contract or other arrangement with the attorney establishing that he or she must act properly.
2. *A breach of that duty.* The attorney must have done something to breach the agreement, was negligent, or made a significant mistake on the case.
3. *A causation.* The breach must have caused you damages. The real difficulty here lies in the fact that you'll basically have to prove malpractice by your attorney and the validity of your original lawsuit; if an attorney makes a mistake on a case you weren't likely to win in court, there is no causation.

4. *Damages*. You'll have to establish the value of any losses you suffered as the result of the attorney's actions or lack of actions.

Short of filing a malpractice suit, contact your state's bar association to see if there is an arbitration process; the bar association and the
state judicial system will also have a formal process to file complaints
that could result in disciplinary action against attorneys.

How Do You Choose the Proper Retirement Home for an Elderly or Infirm Family Member?

A nursing home can provide full-time medical and nursing care, meals,
and a social environment for the aged or ill person unable to fully care
for him or herself. That's the good news; the bad news is that nursing
homes can be expensive, can rob a person of individual freedoms, and
can, for some, offer an environment unacceptably different from how
they have gotten by all of their lives.

Actually, let's back up for a moment and consider whether a nursing home is necessary. Here are some of the options available to older
persons and those with health problems:

Obtain specialized services in your own home.

It may be possible to stay in your own home (or move to a smaller condominium) and contract for in-home health services or live-in
nursing assistance.

- *Advantages*. The most obvious advantage is the comfort and security of home. Many health services can be performed in the home,
  and most insurance plans will pay some or all of the cost. In addition, the older resident can hire assistance for housecleaning and
  cooking.

  In addition, the value of the property and the estate can continue to appreciate, and the homeowner can also take advantage of
  home-equity loans and reverse mortgages to pay expenses in
  retirement.

- *Disadvantages.* Some health-care options may be more expensive when delivered to the home; be sure to check with your insurance carrier to determine the level of coverage offered. The retiree will still be responsible for home maintenance, taxes, and other living expenses.

Move to a shared home.

An option for many seniors is a shared home, either organized among friends and acquaintances or put together with the assistance of a house-sharing matchmaker service.

- *Advantages.* Living expenses should be significantly less than those of a single-family home, and the residents share in one another's company.
- *Disadvantages.* Depending on the housing arrangement, there may not be medical or nursing services available. The retiree may have to pay taxes on profits from the sale of his or her own home and may lose home-equity and reverse-mortgage opportunities.

Enter a planned retirement community.

From luxury condominiums on sun-drenched Arizona or Florida golf courses to retirement communities in big cities with their own shopping centers, medical facilities, and entertainment, retirement communities can offer an attractive alternative.

- *Advantages.* Home maintenance and some medical and house-keeping services may be available within the community. The community may provide its own security services.
- *Disadvantages.* Purchase of a new home may be more costly than proceeds of the sale of a previous home. Some retirees may miss the mix of residents found in an unplanned community.

Move to a retirement center.

Some complexes may offer an opportunity to mix a private apartment with shared services including a communal dining hall or meals delivered to apartments, basic medical services, and a social center.

- *Advantages.* For some, the best of both worlds—their own home without the hassles of cooking, housekeeping, and maintenance.

- *Disadvantages.* The retiree may have to pay taxes on profits from the sale of his or her own home and may lose home-equity and reverse-mortgage opportunities. There is also the possibility of rent and maintenance-charge increases; be sure to investigate the financial stability of the center and consult an attorney if there are any elements of the lease that are unclear.

Choose an assisted living center.

This type of retirement center includes a higher level of support, including assistance with grooming and dressing, housekeeping, laundry, and all meals.

- *Advantages and disadvantages.* Similar to those of a retirement center.

Enter a specialized care unit.

Retirees dealing with a specific disease or condition, such as Alzheimer's disease or cancer, may want to move to an environment where knowledgeable specialists can assist them.

- *Advantages.* The housing is specifically designed to accommodate the needs of residents, and caregivers are trained to offer appropriate assistance.

- *Disadvantages.* The arrangement may be unattractive to a spouse or roommate, and in some cases they are not allowed to stay at the center at all. Other disadvantages include taxes and loss of home-equity opportunities related to the sale of a former home. Be sure to investigate the medical facilities as well as the financial underpinnings of the center.

Move to a nursing home.

For some, a nursing home with full-time nursing and medical facilities is the only available option short of hospitalization.

- *Advantages and disadvantages.* Similar to those of a specialized care unit, although patients with certain ailments may find cost and quality of life differences at one or the other option.

How Do You Pay for a Nursing Home or Other Specialized Care?

In general, an individual is expected to pay for a nursing home and most specialized residential care out of personal funds and assets until they run out; many states, though, exclude some holdings, such as the residence of a spouse, from assets that must be contributed.

Children and other family members, other than the spouse, are not generally required to pay for care in most states.

One other option is to purchase a nursing-home insurance policy before institutionalization. Unfortunately, this sort of policy includes a built-in Catch 22: it is expensive at a time when the covered person is unlikely to need payments and impossible to obtain once there is a recognized health problem for the policyholder.

Then there are two government programs: Medicare, which provides a limited amount of coverage in certain circumstances, and Medicaid, which is intended to care for the poor, or those who become impoverished as the result of medical and other costs.

Medicare will cover nursing-home care, but only for up to 20 days, and only after a three-day or more hospital stay for the same illness or condition that requires nursing-home care. And beyond that, the nursing home must offer a bed that is certified for reimbursement by Medicare. An additional 80 days in the nursing home may be covered with a co-payment.

Medicaid rules are mostly set by the states, with varying regulations on how much and what type of assets have to be contributed before the plan will pay benefits. In general, recipients must be at least 65 years of age, or be blind or disabled, need the type of care available in a nursing home, and meet income and asset tests.

How Do You Choose the Right Child Care?

Let's leave aside cost for the moment. I know that's difficult for many people to do, because the cost of child care usually comes right off the top of any income that the mother or father will be able to earn. But the fact is that the most important consideration about child care should be the quality of the environment and supervision provided.

Traditional child-care options include state-certified commercial operations, informal placements with a relative, or small centers operated in homes. Spend the time to personally visit any place where your child may be enrolled; go during the day when the center is in full operation and see for yourself what is going on. Then seek recommendations from current and former clients of the service. Feel free to call state or county social-services agencies to ask if there are any outstanding complaints—or compliments—they may be able to pass along.

In addition, here are some alternatives to traditional child care to consider:

- *A child-care cooperative.* Find three or four families willing to alternate watching each others' children on a rotating basis. This situation lends itself well to part-time jobs. Be sure to find out as much as you can about the background of others in the group and visit the homes where the children will stay.

- *Job sharing.* Two parents in the same family or in two different families can share one job, alternating care for the children. Again, look into the background and home situation of any outside partners.

- *Work-based child care.* This is an increasingly popular benefit at some larger employers, offering a certified child-care facility at the workplace. The parent is nearby in case of an emergency and can visit during lunch.

- *Telecommuting.* Many communications-era jobs can be performed at home full time or for most of the time. If you have a skill, ask an employer whether he or she would be willing to allow you to set up an office in your home with a computer and telephone line. You can then hire a babysitter to watch your child while you work in the den, or some similar arrangement.

Index